Instructional Alternatives
for
Exceptional Children

Editor:
  Evelyn N. Deno
      Professor,
      Department of Special Education
      University of Minnesota
              and
      Associate Director,
      Leadership Training Institute,
      Special Education
      National Center for the Improvement of Educational Systems

Papers prepared for the Exceptional Children Branch of the National Center for the Improvement of Educational Systems by the Leadership Training Institute for Special Education under the Education Professions Development Act.

Copies may be ordered from The Council for Exceptional Children, 1411 S. Jefferson Davis Highway, Arlington, Virginia 22202. Single copy $3.85; discounts on quantity orders shipped to one address: 2-9 copies (10%); 10 or more copies (20%). Orders totaling less than $25.00 must be accompanied by remittance.

The project presented or reported herein was performed pursuant to Grant OEG-0-9-336-005(725) from the National Center for the Improvement of Educational Systems, U.S. Office of Education, Department of Health, Education and Welfare. The points of view expressed are those of the contributing authors and do not necessarily reflect the position or policy of the U.S. Office of Education and no official endorsement by the U.S. Office of Education should be inferred.

Preface

The contributors to this monograph have performed a greater service than merely documenting their experiences in the training of educational personnel to work with exceptional children in regular classrooms. They have developed training models that are powerful reinforcements for the concepts and strategies that have motivated the National Center for the Improvement of Educational Systems since its inception. With these models, the combination of efforts to respond to diverse educational needs by providing skilled, professional services in a manner that is characterized by humanism and explicit dignity for the child have been moved from theory to practice.

Out of this concern for the exceptional child and the search for better ways to educate him, may come important changes in the quality of education for all children, and especially for those from low-income and minority groups who have been handicapped by circumstances over which they have had little control. The underlying elements of the models described here are crucial to the success of any movement toward educational reform. For example, teachers of children with learning or behavioral problems must sensitize themselves to the learning needs and abilities, personal interests and motivations, and many other differences that contribute to the individuality of such children. Teachers of youngsters from minority and low-income families may find that the same sensitization is the essential key to working with these groups. What needs most to be understood and accepted is that a child who is "different" is not "inferior." We must learn to extend the acceptance of the range of human variability.

Teachers of exceptional children have pioneered in broadening the spectrum of acceptable pupil behavior and performance. Educators familiar with the limits of this range generally agree that children should not be boxed into such categories as "discipline problem," "slow learner," or "physically impaired," but should be allowed to develop as individuals. This humanistic approach becomes especially relevant in an era that is increasingly symbolized by a kind of pluralism in which differences are respected and encouraged, rather than scorned and suppressed. To educate youngsters as individuals means to provide more options in the classroom, more specialized skills and confidence for teachers, more diversified curriculum materials and teaching aides than are available in most traditional educational programs, and greater administrator flexibility. It mandates school people to come to terms with technology, and to accept it as a resource to individualize learning experiences rather than as a threatening process of mechanization. For understandable cause, teachers of exceptional children have had more experience with mechanical equipment and, thus, have been able to discern its advantages. Approximately 40% of our children with learning and behavioral problems, however, are in regular teachers' classrooms where they receive no special services.

Individualized instruction requires support services and staffing patterns that are built around personnel whose professionalism stems from a base of competence and performance, rather than paper criteria. It requires teachers trained to (a) identify, through careful observation and testing, the child with a learning problem; (b) diagnose accurately the type of handicap; and (c) develop from the range of behavioral objectives and teaching techniques an individual program to help a child overcome or at least remediate his disability. Training in the use of this identification-diagnosis-prescription model is essential for the development of individualized programs for all children, just as it is for the handicapped.

New training designs should not serve teachers alone, however. Only if they embrace administrators and the full range of professional personnel in the schools can they guarantee the establishment of a climate that is marked by basic humanism and provides each child with an identifiable, individualized path to learning experiences. Such an approach thrives only if there is openness in the school and the system, an openness that allows teachers to discern, feel, and become part of this kind of fundamental attitudinal and behavioral change.

The contributors to this monograph have performed a service that reaches beyond the personnel dealing with exceptional children. In dealing with a strategy that is designed to break the tainted link between "average" and exceptional children, they are also breaking the connection between low-economic status and academic failure. Destroying these linkages is a necessary step in any successful movement toward educational reform.

This monograph reflects the concerns and work of the Leadership Training Institute/Special Education, which is directed by Dr. Maynard C. Reynolds and Dr. Evelyn N. Deno. Dr. Reynolds has been the mentor and conscience of the National Center for the Improvement of Educational Systems in the area of Special Education and I extend my deep appreciation and gratitude for his extraordinarily dedicated service. A pioneer in the field, his contributions to our collective efforts have at all times surpassed our high expectations. Within the Center, and a key agent to the profession throughout the country, Dr. Malcolm Davis, Chief of the Exceptional Children Branch, has performed an important task with integrity and distinction. I am pleased to be associated with all of them.

William L. Smith
Associate Commissioner
National Center for the
Improvement of Educational Systems

Table of Contents

	Page
Foreword	ix
Introduction	xi

Section I: Programs to Train New Kinds of Instructional Management Mediators 1

The Stratistician Model 3
    Judy Ann Buffmire

A Learning Problems Approach to Teacher Education 11
    Philip H. Mann & Rose Marie McClung

An Introduction to a Regular Classroom Approach to Special Education 22
    Wayne L. Fox, Ann N. Egner, Phyllis E. Paolucci, Phyllis F. Perelman, & Hugh S. McKenzie

The Diagnostic/Prescriptive Teacher 47
    Robert W. Prouty & Florence M. McGarry

The Inservice Experience Plan: Changing the Bath Without Losing the Baby 58
    Stan F. Shaw & Wilma Shaw

Section II: Resource Teacher Programs 67

Improved Learning Conditions for Handicapped Children in Regular Classrooms 70
    Norris G. Haring

Precision Teaching in Regular Junior-High-School Classrooms 83
    Norris G. Haring & Don Miller

The Harrison School Center: A Public School- University Cooperative Resource Program 93
    Richard A. Johnson & Rita M. Grismer

The Seward-University Project: A Cooperative Effort
to Improve School Services and University Training .. 104
Stanley Deno & Jerry Gross

**Section III: Training Programs Accompanying Structural
Change Efforts** 123

A Building Administrator's Perspective of
Individualized Instruction 124
Robert J. Lindsey

The Houston Plan: A Proactive Integrated Systems
Plan for Education 132
Charles Meisgeier

The Madison School Plan: A Functional Model for
Merging the Regular and Special Classrooms 144
Frank D. Taylor & Michael M. Soloway

The Fail-Save Program: A Special Education Service
Continuum 156
Glen VanEtten & Gary Adamson

Section IV: Commentaries 167

Where Do We Go From Here? 167
Evelyn N. Deno

Reflections on a Set of Innovations 179
Maynard C. Reynolds

Contributors to the Monograph 187

Foreword

There is an increasingly powerful movement in American education, of which recent court decisions are only one indicator, to hold the public schools of the nation responsible for providing quality education for all children, regardless of exceptionality. Consequently, for many exceptional children, the responsibility will be interpreted as education within the regular classroom. The public schools must become institutions that accept and foster human differences rather than delimiting or eliminating them. Schools and the personnel who staff them must act as facilitators to enable children to become whatever they are capable of becoming, not only without regard for race, sex, or economic status, but without regard for *any* exceptionality.

As a result of this national movement, more and more local and state education agencies are wrestling with the problems that are associated with the movement of exceptional children into the regular classrooms, and with the provision of better instructional services for those exceptional children who are already in the regular classroom. In the process, the question of retraining experienced educational personnel has become a major concern of both administrators and classroom teachers because in order for teachers to help children self-actualize and to prevent them from failing, the teachers must have the necessary skills. Regular teachers tend to be apprehensive about the prospect of having several "handicapped" children introduced into their already crowded classrooms. Their anxiety about their ability to deal effectively with such children is understandable. Administrators, too, are concerned about the ability of regular classroom teachers to "handle" such children and, consequently, they have started thinking about inservice training programs to provide the teachers with the necessary skills. There is little question that appropriate inservice training can play a major role in assisting teachers to provide quality education for exceptional children within the regular classroom. EPDA (Education Professions Development Act) funded projects, some of which are described in this monograph, attest to the success of various training programs.

As the public schools attempt to incorporate ever-increasing numbers of children with special needs into the regular classroom, teacher-training institutions must respond to the changing conditions of the schools and to their demands for teachers with broader and more varied skills. In a period in which teacher turnover may diminish markedly, colleges and universities must re-examine their inservice offerings and begin to provide more appropriate training for those teachers already on the firing line. At the same time, however, the skills needed to work effectively with all children must be incorporated into preservice training programs as well, for as long as teacher supply exceeds the demand, the schools are in the favorable position of being very selective in their choice of teachers and they may begin to demand, from the training institutions, the kinds of skills they require of their teachers.

Educational personnel need never contribute to the academic failure of children or to the problems associated with failure. If, in their undergraduate preparation programs, teachers were trained with the skills necessary to diagnose the educational needs of children and to prepare and implement individual educational programs based upon proper educational diagnoses, the need for much of the special-class placement and academic plateauing of children for great lengths of time could be avoided. There is no reason why teachers cannot have the tools and the confidence to respond effectively to a wider range of human variability, including learning styles, in the regular classroom.

Unfortunately, too many of the nation's regular preservice and inservice training programs are still unresponsive to the urgency of providing adequate training in this area. The training programs described in this monograph, and many other similar programs which are often supported by Federal funds, tend to be developed outside the university's regular offerings instead of being an integral part of ongoing teachers' preparation programs. When the need is so great and so obvious, any training program that has demonstrated its effectiveness in responding to children with exceptional educational needs must be incorporated in part or in whole into regular teacher preparation programs at both preservice and inservice levels.

The cost of Federally supported add-on training programs and the costs of retraining teachers to acquire the skills necessary to respond to children with exceptional educational needs introduce the obvious questions: Why not do the job right with regular training programs? Why not train teachers properly the first time around?

Malcolm D. Davis
Chief
Exceptional Children Branch
NCIES

Introduction

The theme of this monograph is how the interface between regular and special education services can be improved. The programs described herein develop alternatives to segregated special education services, a high priority need that was described in problem definition terms in the 1971 publication, *Exceptional Children in Regular Classrooms*.[1] The latter volume consisted of papers that had been solicited from both regular and special educators who, for some time, had been expressing concern about the adequacy of educational opportunities for children commonly identified as the consumers of special education services. The contributors indicated the practices that seemed most questionable to them and suggested ways of directing Education Professions Development Act (EPDA) Special Education funds to achieve the greatest long-term benefit for the children needing special educational consideration.

The Education Professions Development Act (EPDA) supports training programs for personnel employed in educational systems at all levels, preschool through college, and continuing or inservice education that is directed to the improvement of educational opportunities for all children. EPDA programs are addressed to areas of particular national concern, including the training of particular types of personnel. The programs are Rural-Urban Education, Bilingual Education, Early Childhood Education, Career Opportunities, Educational Leadership, Pupil Personnel Services, Recruitment, Teacher Development for Desegregating Schools, Media Specialists, Triple T, Protocol Material, and Special Education. In contrast to the program emphasis of the Bureau of Education for the Handicapped (USOE), which supports training programs for special educators, the EPDA Special Education program promotes training for regular education personnel to help them acquire the competencies needed in the effective instruction of handicapped children in mainstream classroom settings.

Programs funded through EPDA are administered by the National Center for the Improvement of Educational Systems (NCIES), formerly known as the Bureau of Educational Personnel Development,[2] in the U.S. Office of Education. The Special Education Lead-

---

[1] Maynard C. Reynolds & Malcolm D. Davis. *Exceptional Children in Regular Classrooms.* Minneapolis, Minn.: LTI/Special Education, 1971. Distributed by Department of Audio Visual Extension, University of Minnesota, Minneapolis, Minn. 55455.

[2] Since the change in name is comparatively recent, some authors still use the old title.

ership Training Institute provides technical or program development assistance to EPDA special education projects.

To carry out its technical assistance function, the Special Education LTI disseminates information on promising programs, training-related materials, and other relevant activities through conferences for project personnel and other concerned persons, direct consultation services to projects, and publications. The latter, so far, have been of two types: descriptions of promising programs in the areas with which the EPDA Special Education program is concerned, and "think-pieces" on the relevant issues within these areas. An example of the latter is *Exceptional Children in Regular Classrooms*, published by the EPDA Special Education LTI in 1971.

In the papers making up that monograph, certain common areas of concern were stressed by author after author. The impact of this reiteration gave the impression of a compelling need to direct attention and resources to problems such as the following:[3]

1. The regular and special education systems have developed separately and the prevailing approaches to personnel training, teacher certification, program funding, and service delivery not only have perpetuated the separateness but widened the gap between the two. As more and more children have been accepted into special education programs, and evidence has accumulated that the traffic is virtually a one-way flow, inquiry into what portion of special education's growth is healthy—for both the children and society—appears to be justified. The special education system should not have to assume responsibility for all the children the regular system chooses to reject. The question of who needs or who should receive special education service can be answered only by studying the two service systems; and there must be a better articulation of the services rendered by both systems if the study indicates the need to continue the two.

2. The traditional, categorical ways of defining the children to whom the special education system is responsible for the provision of services are of limited value in making educational management decisions. There are needed first, the development of ways of assessing learning needs in terms that are more directly relevant to the essential educational management decisions than are provided by the traditional categorical criteria, and second, the development of more realistic treatment modes. The traditional medical model on which the categorical approach to special education is based is seriously inadequate on two counts: (a) The criteria used to define the medical syndrome of a categorical disability contribute too little

---

[3] Since all the arguments cannot be reproduced here, readers are encouraged to consult the original papers in *Exceptional Children in Regular Classrooms*.

to the prediction of the kind of instruction a child with that disability may need. (b) The medical-model focus on "cure" or "restoration to normalcy" is not a suitable posture for habilitating a child whose basic disabilities may be incurable but who may need support to adapt appropriately to learning experiences and life conditions.

3. Outcomes of intervention must be evaluated in ways that relate more directly to the public's purposes in supporting formal education. The public is increasingly reluctant to provide tax dollars to pay for education that does not educate.

4. The much-vaunted team approach to the diagnosis and treatment[4] of handicapped children seldom produces the consistent, effective intervention anticipated for it. The result of high specialization in any profession is fragmentation, which is of little value to the ultimate consumer until it is synthesized at the service level. Professionals and parents lack the framework of common language for the discussion of intervention goals, implementation, and adequacy of outcomes.

5. Much of a child's learning takes place outside of school, consequently, parents and peers are the inevitable partners of professionals in the education of the child. Nevertheless, teachers probably exercise the most influence over the child's learning conditions, next to the parents and peers. Specialists should deal realistically with these facts by sharing their knowledge with these primary instruction agents to make them more effective in the teaching roles they are going to perform anyway. This position is dictated as much by logic and the lack of a clear relation between training level of intervenor and success in helping children learn as it is by the short supply of certain kinds of specialists and the funds to employ them.

It is worthy of note that since the publication of *Exceptional Children in Regular Classrooms,* the problems identified in the papers therein have been supported by policy positions adopted by the membership of the Council for Exceptional Children (CEC, 1972).

The advocacy of the maintenance and service of "deviant" children within as normal an approximation of an ordinary childhood milieu as is beneficial for the needy child (the normalization principle) does not rest on data-based proof that such children are likely to show better academic achievement when instructed in the regular classroom; it rests, rather, on two related lines of argument: (a) Evidence has shown that children who were defined as mentally handicapped by conventional criteria and educated in special classes did not achieve better than comparable children who were educated

---

[4] The term "treatment," as used in these papers, is broadly defined as any type of deliberate intervention undertaken to improve a child's functioning.

in regular classes.[5] (b) Recent court decisions support the ethical position that a citizen's right to ordinary social participation should not be abridged by his assignment to facilities that purport to provide treatment or improved opportunity if, in fact, more appropriate treatment is not provided by the assignment.[6]

The preceding propositions are reflected in recent EPDA Special Education program efforts. Projects funded under this program, as well as others supported through BEH or a variety of funding combinations, have begun to explore some of the components of these complicated issues. In many such projects the search was started for ways to provide better control of a child's in- and out-of-school learning opportunities: better individual case-management procedures that more effectively tailor learning conditions to individual child growth and learning needs. Overwhelming evidence has accumulated on the degree to which a child with problems needs some mechanism (person or process) to help him cope with institutions that frustrate his growth because of stereotyped expectations and rigid operating regulations.

The evidence accumulated along the way of these searches led some projects to propose and train for work in the schools a kind of person who could promote better utilization of people, curricula, and materials resources for the assessed needs of an individual child. Most of the programs described here report efforts to package functions and develop a functionary who will bridge some of the conceptual and service gaps identified in the earlier monograph. Their efforts have been focused on three steps: establishing what course of action seems best for the individual; helping adults to acquire the necessary understanding and skills to contribute effectively to the plan of action; and continuously evaluating whether the plan as implemented achieved the desired results. Some administrators saw possibilities for system-wide improvement through the broad application of the principles that are basic to these personnel training programs and they moved to repackage whole delivery systems. In some of the trials reported here, the unit reorganized is a whole school building (Aurora, Illinois) and, in some, an entire school district (Houston, Texas). In at least three such attempts (Minnesota, Vermont, and Texas), long-range, special education program planning at the state education agency level strongly supports system organization on a broad scale.

---

[5] For a summary analysis of research in this area see B. H. Bruninks & J. E. Rynders. Alternatives to special classes for educable mentally retarded. *Focus on Exceptional Children,* 1971, 3, 1-12.

[6] A projected EPDA Special Education monograph by Dr. Weintraub will probe some of the ramifications of the latter position.

The final section of this monograph provides some suggestions for further action that are implicit in the project results.

The papers have been ordered so that the first section deals with college-training programs for the preparation of a type of noncategorical special advocator who can function primarily as a consultant to regular-class teachers and service planning mediators; the second, with programs that focus on resource teacher models; and the third, with descriptions of attempts to restructure whole systems, whether a school building, school district, district-wide special education service continuum, or strategies in continuing education geared to general systems change. All of the programs have so many overlapping characteristics that division into sections and sequence of papers within the sections are admittedly a very rough effort to ease the reader's task in searching for a subject of particular interest. The papers, by general type rather than title, are as follows:

Section I: Programs training service strategists
Stratistician Model	Judy Ann Buffmire
Learning Problems Model	Philip Mann & Rose Marie McClung
Consulting Teacher Model	Wayne L. Fox et al. (Hugh McKenzie)
Diagnostic Prescriptive Teacher Model	Robert Prouty & Florence McGarry
Classroom Specialist Model	Stan & Wilma Shaw

Section II: Resource Systems
Precision Teaching Resource Model (Elementary)	Norris Haring
Precision Teaching Resource Model (Secondary)	Norris Haring & Don Miller
Resource System for EMR	**Richard Johnson & Rita Grismer**
General Special Education Resource Teacher Model	Stanley Deno & Jerry Gross

Section III: Structural Change Approaches
Structural Reform in an Elementary School	Robert Lindsey
Structural Reform in a Total School District	Charles Meisgeier
Preparing Handicapped Children for Regular Class Participation	Frank Taylor
Clarifying Sub-System Service Responsibilities	Glen VanEtten & Gary Adamson

Section IV : Commentaries
Evelyn N. Deno
Maynard C. Reynolds

Readers interested in other programs with the same or different emphases are encouraged to write the Special Education LTI, the Exceptional Child Branch of the National Center for the Improvement of Educational Systems, or the Bureau of Education for the Handicapped, for further information. Anyone interested in learning more about the programs described herein may write directly to the authors of the papers. Addresses are listed in the section entitled "Contributors to the Monograph."

Mrs. Sylvia W. Rosen was the technical editor.

Evelyn N. Deno
January 1973

Section I
Programs to Train
New Kinds of Instructional Management Mediators

The assumption of the programs described in this section is that a "new" or different kind of professional is needed to work mainly with regular teachers to help them develop and carry out more effective instructional programs within their regular classrooms for educationally deviant children.

Because many of the professionals involved with the education of exceptional children have been inclined to perceive and formulate problems in terms of the treatment management possibilities or preferences that are typical of their disciplines, the instructional management mediator conceptualized in these programs would be trained to be able to bridge the communication gap among the professionals. The training of the mediator, which would focus on (a) some of the assessment skills presumed to be possessed by psychologists and (b) some of the curriculum and instructional methods know-how possessed by specialists in basic educational skill areas, would enable him to mediate differences in outlook and language among different school specialists. In the process, he would become a strong force for the achievement of better interactions between the regular and special education services and, ultimately, of total system modification. The mediator would operate as a first line of defense against an excessive reliance upon the transfer of children with learning problems to special education settings.

All the programs in this section focus on the training of personnel to facilitate the development and implementation of individually tailored educational prescriptions. Although there is considerable overlap in the functions the trainees are expected to perform, the programs differ ideologically on how the functions can be performed most effectively. Competency development has a different emphasis in each. Most are eclectic in their approaches and seem to be heavily swayed by what works in making procedural choices. However, consistent application of behavior analysis principles is evident in all aspects of the Vermont program, strong humanistic leanings coupled with acceptance of responsibility to be accountable for outcomes comes through in the George Washington program, and the Miami program leans heavily on a learning process approach. Needless to say, each program demonstrates a strong commitment to the testing of their working assumptions.

Evidence must still be accumulated, and both BEH and EPDA-Special Education are seeking it, on which of the various approaches to the relief of learning problems are most likely to result in the most improvement of children's classroom learning. That is why there are included in this monograph programs that train individuals for similar roles but within frameworks of different orientation.

*The Rocky Mountain Regional Resource
Center's Stratistician Model*

The Regional Resource Centers, funded by the Bureau of Education for the Handicapped, are located in six sections of the country: Eugene, Oregon; New York City; Coralville, Iowa; Las Cruces, New Mexico; Harrisburg, Pennsylvania; and Salt Lake City, Utah.

Most of these centers have determined their program emphases through the assessment of priority needs in their geographic areas. The Stratistician Model was developed at the Rocky Mountain Center as a result of the conditions in the region served by the Center. The strategy facilitates the development of special education service, helps to prevent unessential labeling, and avoids the segregation of service for handicapped children. Several of the RRCs have initiated programs that are directed to similar ends. Because it is one of the most highly developed, the Stratistician Model is included in this collection.

The Stratistician Model

Judy Ann Buffmire, Director
Rocky Mountain Regional Resource Center
University of Utah

Some persons cannot pronounce stratistician (strat-is-tish'un); others cannot spell it; and none knows for certain what it is! The term, derived from strategist and diagnostician, denotes a person who can diagnose educational problems and plan strategies to facilitate their solutions. Simple enough, it seems, but—: What behaviors indicate that a person can diagnose problems? Plan strategies? Function where? For whom? Is the idea of a stratistician relevant to the needs of handicapped children?

The current literature indicates that many people are engaged in conceptualizing educational models that can provide better service for handicapped children, and, where possible, in the mainstream of education (Lilly, 1971; Reynolds & Balow, 1972). The evolving stratistician model is one example of the concept. A stratistician is a trained special educator who functions as a teacher's resource on request and who collects data on the problems of handicapped children in the classroom and on effective facilitation strategies. The model was field tested during the 1971-72 school year with positive

---

The preparation of this paper was supported by Grant No. OEG-0-70-4178(608), Project No. 542930, from the Department of Health, Education and Welfare, United States Office of Education, Bureau of Education for the Handicapped, Division of Research, Washington, D.C. 20202.

results. Because the main factor in the successful trial was the flexibility and problem-solving capabilities of the individual stratisticians involved, as well as their ability to read the environment and promote change in unique situations, a stratistician still must be considered a model in the process of definition.

The decision to explore the use of a special educator as a resource for teachers was made by the Rocky Mountain Regional Resource Center (RMRRC)[1] after many meetings with administrators from the Utah State Board of Education, both special and regular education divisions; local district leaders; and University of Utah staff members. Data available at that time indicated that 42%[2] of the expected population of exceptional children in Utah were not receiving special services. The state laws that make education compulsory and mandatory place the responsibility for the education of all children in Utah on the local school boards.[3] Thus, it was assumed that if the 42% of the unidentified handicapped children had to be in school and were not receiving special educational services, then they were, for the most part, in regular classrooms. In addition, it was found that although the delivery of special services in Utah has been above the national average (Martin, 1972), many identified exceptional children in sparsely populated areas had never been removed from regular classrooms because there simply was no place for them to go.

A number of factors were considered during the decision-making process: available funds, personnel and building limitations, and the swing toward the use of resource rooms for exceptional children in place of self-contained classrooms. One fact appeared to predominate, however. The top priority, special education need in Utah was the identification of better ways to help teachers deal with handicapped children in their regular classrooms. Thus the decision was made to explore a teacher resource model on the basis of two main assumptions:

1. All children can learn regardless of their handicaps.
2. All teachers can perform more effectively.

During the first year in the field, RMRRC focussed on ways of (a) identifying the learning problems of handicapped children in the classroom, and (b) developing a resource system that would help teachers to solve the problems. The two goals could be achieved only

---

[1] The RMRRC is one of six Regional Centers in the United States funded by the Bureau of Education for the Handicapped.
[2] Special Education Report Prepared for the Utah State Board of Education: 1969-70 School Year, 1970, p. 9. A more recent state identification project has indicated that the percentage unserved may be considerably higher.
[3] Utah Code Annotated 1953, Secs. 53-18-1 through 53-18-10.

through access to the classroom, regular as well as special, and the person who could have such access was conceptualized as the stratistician.

The stratistician provides an active interface between regular and special education by establishing a continuum of educational services for the handicapped child. At the same time he is a data collector, an identifier of problems faced by teachers and handicapped children in the classrooms, and a developer of resources to solve the problems. He also collects data for the development of inservice and preservice training packages. Withal, the prime target of the stratistician is the classroom teacher.

Special educators with classroom experience and the MA degree or its equivalent were chosen as the first stratisticians. Beyond these general requirements, individual backgrounds varied. Two stratisticians were trained school psychologists; two have learning-disability training; one specialized in teaching the trainable mentally retarded and one, the educable mentally retarded. Each stratistician appears to have an open nonjudgmental attitude in interactions with other persons, an attribute that has proven to be a high-priority competency for adults working with other adults. Identification of the behaviors that constitute this attribute is currently being undertaken by RMRRC staff members.

The further training of these already skilled people was conducted by RMRRC staff members and consultants during the summer of 1971. Training consisted of the development of communication and interacting skills, observation techniques, acceptance strategies, screening/diagnosis, planning, behavior modification, evaluation, and strategies of dealing with problem behaviors that had been listed most often by teachers.[4] The teachers at each school were

---

[4] To assess classroom problems as perceived by teachers and to determine teachers' attitudes toward handicapped children and willingness to utilize a resource person, a questionnaire was developed prior to the placement of stratisticians in schools. Replies were received from 6% of the state's teachers and 59% of the teachers in the target schools, a total of 365 responses. In addition, a stratified sample of elementary teachers across the state was polled. The ten behaviors that the sample of teachers perceived as the most serious classroom problems were the following:

1. Inattention	6. Carelessness in work
2. Tattling	7. Attracting attention
3. Quarrelsomeness	8. Laziness
4. Cruelty, bullying	9. Restlessness
5. Interrupting	10. Disorderliness in class

The responses as a whole indicated that teachers felt that they would be willing to accept two to three "mildly retarded students" in their classrooms and to work with a resource person (stratistician) to facilitate their work with the handicapped children.

Further information on this study is available as Working Paper No. 4, RMRRC. Similar information from administrators is being tabulated.

oriented during the annual two-day institutes held prior to the beginning of school, and several meetings were held with district administrators and principals. Once the school year began, none of the stratisticians lacked requests for services.

In accord with the research design, stratisticians were placed in elementary schools that varied in the availability of special educational resources. These placements were selected to determine first, in which situations stratisticians were utilized most, and second, the kinds of problems encountered in schools with few resources as compared to those in schools with many available resources. One stratistician was placed in a Title I school with a transient student body; this school had an established resource room, a self-contained classroom, and extensive psychological, speech, and other support services. One school was on an isolated military base with a highly mobile school population that represented a cross-section of cultural attitudes, values, and status; no special classes were offered in the school and support services consisted of occasional visits by a speech therapist and a district psychologist. Another school was initiating a resource room and had an established self-contained classroom; the support services available there were moderate. The fourth stratistician was placed in a traditional school with one self-contained class and limited support services. The fifth went into a progressive school with model support services. Each of the five was in the assigned school fulltime, four days a week. The sixth stratistician operated as an itinerant; his home base was an SEIMC in a multi-district rural region.

Each Friday throughout the school year all stratisticians met at the RMRRC to share problems, answers, inservice training, and coordination of Center activities and field needs. Throughout the year, RMRRC staff pivoted around the stratisticians, providing extensive resources to facilitate their effectiveness when needed. Workshops, resource information, and consultation were also provided to the participating districts on request. The Center staff includes a psychologist, an evaluation director, an inservice training director, a media-curriculum specialist, a publication specialist, and staff consultants in the areas of mental retardation, learning disability, and emotional disturbance. A district liaison consultant is also on the staff. Arrangements were made to bring children to the demonstration district schools for intensive intervention work if all other resources had been explored and found insufficient. This service was never needed during the initial year, however.

Results

It was both an exciting and a frustrating year. Teachers and principals were most positive in their acceptance and use of the stratisticians. The stratisticians' activities included the following areas:

1. Modeling of behavior.
2. Class screening on specific areas.
3. Observation of a single student or of a whole class.
4. Planning (with teachers, administrators, aides, committees, pupil personnel, tutors, university personnel, graduate students, RMRRC personnel, district supervisors, etc.) in classroom management, program development, use of specific curriculum, etc.
5. Evaluation of programs, systems, methods, curriculum, etc.
6. Diagnosis (formal and informal).
7. Instructional skills (individual inservice).
8. Interaction skills, methods and techniques (role playing, reflective listening, congruent sending, "I" messages, etc.) with children, teachers, administrators, agencies, parents.
9. Evaluation of interventions and recycling with feedback to teachers, children, parents, other school personnel.
10. Data collecting, recording, systematizing, and reporting for RMRRC research programs.
11. Go-between for resrouce room and regular-room activities.

Further data refinement is needed to determine if teacher interventions with handicapped children improve with on-the-spot help; what interventions are most successful; what variables influence the success of interventions; any transfer effect to other children; what are emerging inservice training priorities; what preservice changes are indicated; and what needed resources are or are not available.

During the trial year, extensive intervention assistance was given to 162 children; 1,036 short-term contacts plus many uncounted one-time-only contacts were also made. Teacher contacts, both formal and informal (a formal contact is a written request; an informal contact is a conversation in the hall, faculty room, etc.) were so numerous that an accurate count is not available, but 146 teachers were involved in the program. Each stratistician met at least once with every teacher in his school. Obtained data indicated that each stratistician made an average of 9 teacher contacts and 8 children contacts per day. The 146 teachers had a total of approximately 3,700 students; the ripple effect could have touched each of them. The purpose of the initial field year was not to provide service but to collect data and explore the use of a resource person to teachers.

From the descriptive data on the children referred, it was found that the largest cluster of referrals were for the 6-9-year-old age range. As might be expected, 9-year olds were referred most often. There was some indication that the time of year may influence referrals; for example, many more 6-year olds were referred late in the school year rather than earlier. Class-size data indicated that referrals were highest from classes with 25 to 29 students, followed by classes with 20 to 24 students. However, the finding may be an artifact of average class size as, in the participating schools, most classes ranged from 25 to 29 students.

The referring teachers were predominantly female and the referred children, predominantly male. Such proportions are expected because of the ratio of female to male teachers in elementary school and the commonly accepted idea that the boys in our culture have a higher ratio of problems.[5]

Very few of the referrals—less than 8%—involved children with previously identified problems. This result seemed to indicate that the statisticians were reaching the part of the population of handicapped children in the regular classrooms who had not heretofore been served.

The specific educational problems referred most often were clusters of behaviors that included "restless," "not attending," "disruptive," and "aggressive." Thus, for the teachers, psychosocial problems appeared to be the primary area of concern. "Disruptive" behaviors, which were reported with high frequency by the teachers, were classed as "not attending" by the statisticians. If further work substantiates the importance of this psychosocial area, it would be a direct indication of inservice and preservice training needs. "Not achieving to expectancy" was also a high frequency referral. When the teachers were questioned about the meaning of the term, however, they often were unable to define it. The statisticians found that the teachers needed informal training in classroom diagnosis and task analysis, which indicates the great need for diagnostic and prescriptive skills in any interventionist.

As the year went on, referrals increased in frequency for the behavior categories of "distractable," "short attention span," and "lack of motivation." Although conclusions cannot be drawn from these limited data on why the problems increased with time, it may be hypothesized that as frustrations and repeated failures accumulate, handicapped children lose interest and motivation. Increased teacher skills in individualizing instruction, and the participation of a resource person to help identify and encourage the use of new skills, might ameliorate the problem, a possibility suggesting that statisticians could function in schools as trainers of teachers in these areas.

---

[5] In Germany, where most first-grade teachers are men, the handicapped readers are mainly girls.

The interventions most often suggested by statisticians and adopted by teachers included behavior modification techniques and tutors. The use of resource aides, task analysis, and modality change increased throughout the year.

As this paper is being written, the statisticians and other RMMRC staff members are assessing the first-year efforts in the field, writing school profiles and year-end reports; identifying variables and data collection methods to develop communication-skills training packages to use in the schools next year; and trying to determine more effective methods of measuring their impact upon teachers, handicapped children, and districts as a whole. Further refinement is underway on methods of screening and assessing individual students, observation techniques, and planning and consulting with administrators, teachers, aides, and other persons.

It appears that the evolution of the stratistician role will be greatly determined by the ecological components of a school, that is, the socio-economic level, ethnic makeup of the student body, community and parent concern, school philosophy, and organizational factors. Research on these and other as yet unidentified ecological variables will become a major thrust of RMMRC operations. A second research thrust will be the effect of affective variables on the education of handicapped children in the school.

This year's data also indicate that there may be a need for a multi- rather than a uni-stratistician model to meet the varying needs of urban and rural schools. The inherent problems of an itinerant position were not answered during our trial. The identification of differences and similarities in the competencies of the stratistician, the learning-disability teacher, school psychologist, counselor, curriculum specialist, teacher of the mentally retarded, and other specialists must be made before broad utilization of the new interventionist can be justified.

Acceptance of the stratistician model was positive; many districts have asked for help to develop a similar model or train such personnel. Districts that had stratisticians last year are eager to continue with them next year. Student and parent response has been enthusiastic.

Some of the stratistician's functions can now be described. What does he do? He serves as a resource to teachers of handicapped children. It appears that he can help teachers help children. He is also an effective collector of data on the needs of the teachers who deal with handicapped children, and he is effective in finding and developing strategies to meet their needs. But—stratisticians? Despite the pronouncing and spelling difficulties of the term, they served teachers and handicapped children and districts are requesting more of them.

References

Lilly, S. M. A training based model for special education. *Exceptional Children,* Summer 1971, 745.

Martin, E. W. Individualism and behaviorism as future trends in educating handicapped children. *Exceptional Children,* March 1972, 317.

Reynolds, M. C. & Balow, B. Categories and variables in special education. *Exceptional Children,* January 1972, 358.

Special education report prepared for the Utah State Board of Education: 1969-70 school year. November 1970.

University of Miami: A Learning Problems Approach

The learning process approach to problem analysis that is used in this program is reminiscent of the ideas that Kirk, Frostig, Myklebust, and other persons have advanced for the education of learning disabled children. However, the University of Miami program is not restricted to the so-called learning-disabled children. A basic assumption of the program is that the same information processing functions are present in all children and, consequently, can be used as the basis of effective instruction.

A Learning Problems Approach to Teacher Education

Philip H. Mann
*Special Education Coordinator and
Director, Programs in Learning Disabilities
University of Miami*

and

Rose Marie McClung
*Associate Director, Programs in Learning Disabilities
University of Miami*

For some time, special educators have been cognizant of regular-classroom teachers' general lack of the necessary insights, skills, or incentives to work with children who manifest a variety of learning problems. Few of the teachers understand or know how to use the available alternatives for teaching children. They look for materials to show them *what* to teach instead of looking at the children to find out *how* to teach. When the teachers fail, consequently, the children are labeled lazy, emotionally disturbed, clumsy, stupid, or mentally retarded.

The program described here was designed to train experienced, regular-classroom teachers to work with learning-disabled children through a learning problems approach. For one academic year plus one summer session, the teachers participate in the program concurrently with experienced special education teachers and students who are already involved in degree or non-degree programs in the area of learning disabilities. The regular-classroom teachers are trained at the graduate level. One of the unique features of the program is that although **regular and special education teachers concentrate on the same core of studies in learning disabilities and graduate with**

The program has been supported by funds from both the Bureau of Education for the Handicapped and the Education Professions Development Act.

many common competencies, for each group the major emphasis is on its anticipated role. Thus, regular-classroom teachers are trained to teach children with learning disabilities in the public-school regular classes while the special education teachers and students are trained to be special educators. The opportunity for the two groups to share experiences has been one of the most signficant and innovative aspects of the program.

The learning problems approach to educating children implies that the settings for handicapped students will be based on their needs rather than on the number of allocated units that must be filled. Primarily, however, the approach is used to determine through task analysis what it is that children need to know to succeed in the schools as they are now constituted. By delineating the critical skills necessary for success in the academic areas of reading, writing, spelling, and arithmetic, the teacher trained in the use of this approach can then identify children's deficits in the language areas that prevent them from being successful in the given tasks.

This analytical approach to meeting the needs of handicapped children lends itself to implementation in many different educational settings. Traditional as well as open schools can readily adapt the diagnostic-teaching techniques as long as the basic philosophy of the school incorporates the principle of meeting individual needs or, more specifically, of individualizing instruction. Any school, no matter how modern its physical facilities, that concerns itself primarily with the "learners" and omits the atypical child from the mainstream of education, is a lesser educational institution than a one-room, red-brick schoolhouse in which the teacher develops appropriate educational programs for all students, including the learning handicapped. A building does not facilitate learning; people do. Therefore, a program that is child centered should turn out trainees that are not lock-stepped into one way of structuring the environment.

The Theoretical Framework of the Program

The instructional basis of the program is the learning design (Fig. 1) that shows the important parameters of children's learning patterns. The design is a framework that the teachers are taught to use to identify the strengths and weaknesses in children's learning processes. After the identification is made, specific educational strategies can be developed for each child.

In the application of the strategies, the teachers use the principle of "plateau," that is, no child remains in the same place in the skill area of concern for extended periods of time without justifiable explanation. For the child, success must be the mode rather than the exception. The teachers learn to apply the principle by adjusting the

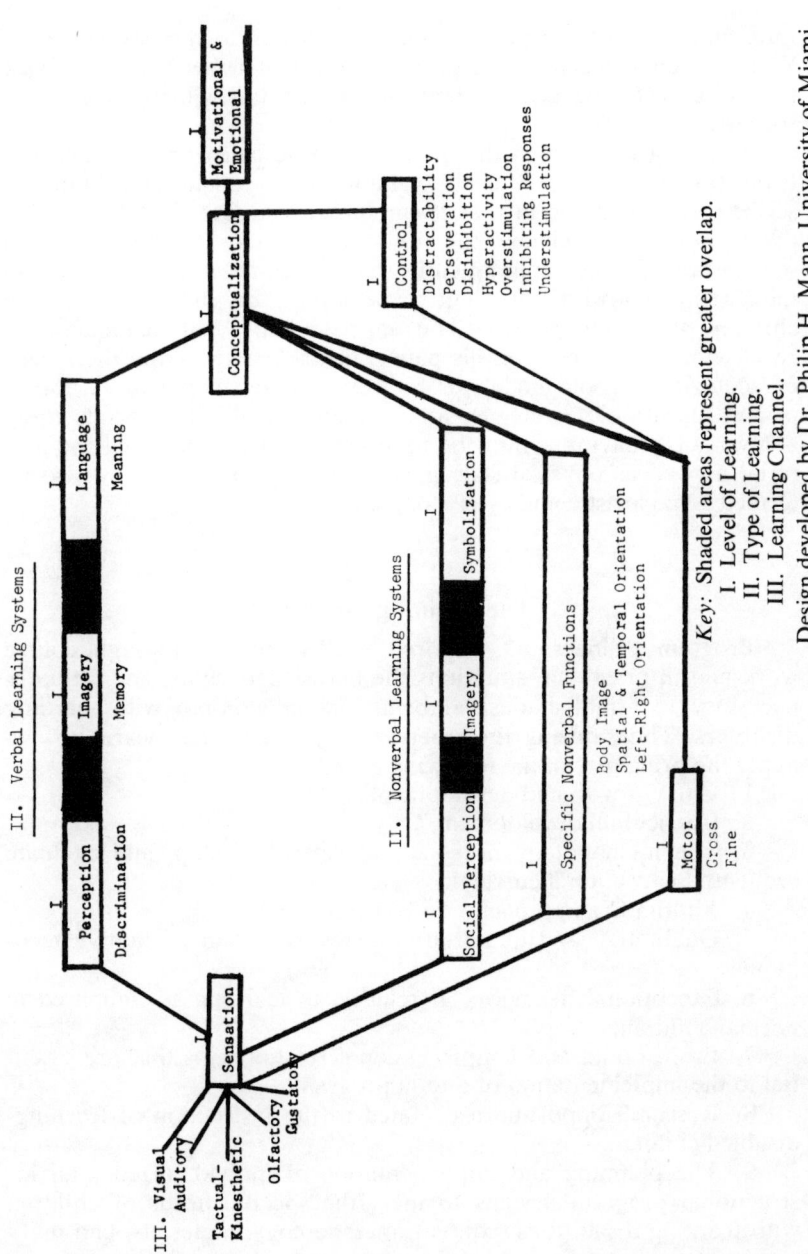

Figure 1. Design of Correlates for Diagnosis and Amelioration of Learning Problems in Children

rate, amount, and sequence of input according to the child's needs. When the child reaches a point of failure, the teacher takes him back to his last accurate achievement and leaves him with the feeling of success.

Teaching children in this manner can be called eclectic because it pulls together the best of all available resources. It can also be described as humanistic in that it emphasizes success. It is humane in that it attempts to change the life style of children who have been school failures and, consequently, have become failure-avoiding in their attitude toward learning; the emphasis on success makes the children strive for success. The approach does not dehumanize a child with "red marks" on his paper; instead, it gives him the means of acquiring a good model for himself. The development of appropriate educational strategies for individual children depends upon analysis of behavior within the total environment, including the material as well as physical setting; as such, the approach may also be termed behavioristic and even atomistic.

The Training Program

Program trainees are required to demonstrate through course work and in practicum situations the knowledge, skills, and attitudes necessary to establish desired behaviors in children with learning disorders. Thus, during their period of training, they learn how to apply the principles in the following areas:

1. Child growth and development.
2. Curriculum development.
3. The methodology necessary to select, develop, and evaluate sequential educational curricula.
4. Multimedia approaches to learning.
5. Qualitative and quantitative assessment and evaluative techniques.
6. Exceptional behaviors in relation to learning as compared to normal children.
7. Professional and nonprofessional relationships that are essential to the implementation of a total program.
8. Research opportunities related to the instruction of learning-disabled children.
9. The planning and implementation of individualized total instructional program designs to meet the specific needs of children with learning disabilities (content, methodology, materials, and management).
10. The behavioral management of children with specific learning disabilities in relation to learning.

In the application of the principles, the trainees are expected to understand the needs of children with learning disabilities in the following behavioral areas:
1. To perform physically at a level that will facilitate learning.
2. To function adequately at the sensory level.
3. To recognize, organize, and integrate data from various modalities for meaningful learning at both verbal and nonverbal levels.
4. To assimilate levels of sensation, perception, imagery, and language for efficient conceptualization.
5. To maintain an emotional and motivational level for effective environmental coping.
6. To develop skills to the degree that performance in general education programs can be realized and maintained.

At the conclusion of their training, the teachers return to different educational settings to serve children with learning difficulties. These settings are,

1. public-school, regular, resource classes for learning-impaired children;
2. public and private residential school classes for children with learning disabilities;
3. diagnostic centers for children with learning disorders;
4. clinics for the learning-disabled child; and
5. public-school, regular classes that include children with mild to moderate learning disabilities.

The program emphasis is on the latter setting.

Some trainees have also become instructors at the junior-college level or in colleges and universities that do not require doctorates for employment.

The flexibility of the program is demonstrated by the concurrent training of regular-class teachers and special education teachers and students. The latter graduate as resource teachers who may work in different settings with regular and special education teachers to meet the learning needs of children. The regular-class teachers become generalists, "transition teachers" or "developmental primary teachers," who can meet the needs of children with mild to moderate learning disorders in the regular classroom. The program does not train such teachers to be school psychologists; they are trained in the dynamics of educational diagnosis and remediation so that they know what to do when children fail to learn with traditional educational approaches.

Trained to be more knowledgeable in the intricacies of learning, these regular-class teachers also have the competencies needed to work with children in transition between the self-contained special classroom and the regular classroom, and to become trainers of other teachers. Through inservice and other inter- and intra-grade level programs, they are able to share the knowledge and skills they have gained through past experiences. Indeed, one of the concommitant advantages of the training program is that school personnel, in general, tend to show a greater degree of acceptance for a regular-classroom teacher who has been trained and returns to the same position and for the new ideas that she is willing to share with them, in this case a learning problems approach to education.

Since the trainees gain an understanding of the role of allied disciplines (medicine, social work, and psychology) in the process of educating children with learning disabilities, they are able to become members of diagnostic teams. So, with their understanding of the community and its resources, they can assume more effective roles in the liaison between school and community.

Practicum Experience

The MA-level practicum includes a variety of observational and directed field placements. Its purpose is to reinforce the theory and understanding developed in course work and to provide supervised experiences.

The trainees begin the observation of children when they start their course work. They are assigned to public and private institutions that serve children with handicapping conditions, under the direction of a faculty member, or they are given assistant responsibilities in special projects. The practicum requires a minimum of 10 hours a week. To insure a variety of experiences, the trainees are rotated through three facilities with a three-month stay in each. Examples of such facilities are the Cerebral Palsy Association, Crippled Children's Society, Vocational Rehabilitation Center, Migrant Child Program, public-school classes for the handicapped, and regular classes at all grade levels. All the trainees are rotated through the University of Miami Mailman Center for Child Development. Here they are able to interact with students and staff from other disciplines in the diagnosis and development of appropriate recommendations for the handicapped children under study.

In the practicum, emphasis is on the understanding of individual children and their educational needs in relation to adaptive teaching materials. Parent conferences and administrative arrangements for the education of the children are explored and tried in real situations. In addition to the supervision of the faculty member, the trainees are also supervised by staff members of the facilities in which they are working.

Beyond the course-work requirements for practice, all graduate students who have had an undergraduate internship experience are required to take *Field Placement in Special Education,* an experience in serving handicapped children that is in line with the student's professional goals. The minimum placement is for six weeks, five full days a week, with at least 180 clock hours spent in the setting under the direction of a staff member of the University of Miami's program in Special Education. Included in this field experience are opportunities for the student to work with master teachers in both regular and special classes, participate as an aide, and assume full teaching responsibilities with learning-impaired children. Many additional observations of children with handicapping conditions are made within the context of regular and special classes.

Evaluation

The program itself is under constant evaluation by all the graduate students and the staff at the semi-monthly seminar meetings, but the most meaningful evaluations of the program are those concerned with the success of its graduates.Trainees also are under constant evaluation; (a) their course-by-course proficiency is analyzed; (b) they are counseled individually and periodically by members of the Special Education faculty; and (c) a series of independent and objective reports and ratings are obtained from the participating practica schools or educational agencies.

The follow-up of students formerly enrolled in the program focuses on a semi-annual report during the first year, and then annual reports for the first five years. These reports objectively indicate the effectiveness with which the student has been able to use his/her training in the development of daily educational programs for learning-handicapped children. The data obtained from these reports serve to guide the future development of the program. Additional feedback on the former trainees are also obtained from their supervisors.

At the present time, comprehensive and well-designed studies are being instituted to examine the effect of the program on past participants, the children they serve, and others. A competent research person has been added to the staff to direct the multivariate analysis.

The Multiplier Effect

The former trainees of the program have been most successful in those educational facilities and school systems in which officials, principals, and teachers strongly advocate a child-centered, individualized approach to educating children. Through dialog at University-school-community conferences and written evaluations of the program, school administrators, teachers, ancillary educational personnel, community leaders, and parents have expressed their support for the learning problems approach. The evaluations have noted that the teachers trained in the program have both the confidence and the technology to meet the needs of children from diverse socio-economic and ethnic backgrounds in a variety of settings. The school officials are impressed with the willingness of the teachers to accept the children that are often labeled "high risk" or handicapped, and to provide the appropriate educational strategies that are necessary to keep them in the mainstream of education.

That the program has had an impact on local school systems can be seen from the following programs that involve former or current trainees:

1. Inservice training programs in a learning problems approach have been set up and carried out for the first time.

2. Three of the six approved Title III programs in the county have been staffed by former trainees of the Pilot Program in Learning Disabilities funded by BEPD.

3. There is a greater awareness within the school system, as indicated by an increase of regular teachers taking courses offered through special education, of the need for training in how to meet the needs of the handicapped child.

4. There has been an increase in requests by principals for additional units within their schools to meet the needs of children with learning disorders.

5. Selected MA-level students in the program have been utilized by the local schools as consultants to screen children in the primary grades for the purpose of early identification of learning disabilities.

During the summer of 1971, the Florida School Desegregation Center at the University of Miami sponsored two-week workshops in the learning problems approach to education for 60 teachers from all over the state. As a result, model classrooms have been set up in many areas and a second series of workshops was conducted by the project staff during the summer of 1972.

The learning problems approach training program has had a significant impact on the ongoing program within the School of Education at the University of Miami. For the first time, a course in special education has been made available to all undergraduates at the freshman level both in and out of the School of Education. A junior-year course in the area of the handicapped is now a one-out-of-four restricted elective for all undergraduate elementary education majors. In the future, every educational program at the University of Miami will provide the students with information on handicapped children and on instructional techniques for use with them. Although general enrollment in education at the University has declined, it is anticipated that regular teachers will continue to take courses in the learning problems approach to education long after the present financial support of the program has been terminated.

The impact of the program at the state level is evident in the participation of the project staff in the development of guidelines for the certification of teachers in the area of learning disabilities. The University of Miami Program in learning disabilities is one of the first of such approved programs in the state of Florida.

Implementation of New Programs

One of the most difficult tasks of a new program at the university level is to establish new courses to implement training; the difficulty is compounded if other departments feel that their current course offerings already cover the projected material. The training of regular teachers by special education staff, for example, implies that other disciplines are not meeting the needs of the atypical learner in the mainstream of education. Thus, to facilitate better understanding of our project within the School of Education, an advisory panel was formed of four professors, representing the divisions of Reading, Early Childhood Education, and Elementary and Secondary Education, to participate in all conferences and special meetings pursuant to the grant.

In a local school system, the consent of local school officials and the principals and staffs of schools must be obtained before any change can be effectuated in the classrooms. The hierarchy of social forces in the system must be acknowledged before an isolated teacher can become a change agent. However, by involving principals, psychologists, and ancillary educational personnel in the training of the teachers through particpation in university conferences, field experiences, and practica within the schools, the administrators become more receptive to a program's philosophy and goals.

Special emphasis should also be placed on involving the community at every level of training. A community advisory committee of parents, university, public school, and other public and private agencies is essential to provide continuous reaction to the content and progress of the program. In addition, minority groups should be represented on committees evaluating student experiences and the relevancy of training to minority needs.

General Applications of the Program

The learning problems approach to teacher education is applicable to diverse educational settings and many types of teacher-training programs. The philosophy of the program is predicated upon the accountability of teacher training to the changing needs of the community served by the institutions of higher learning. The need to accelerate the modernization of teacher training at the university level and the communication of such changes to the educator on the job through inservice training permeates every aspect of the program. The interface of special and regular education in a common core of competencies and the move toward a competency-based program for teacher education are part of the ongoing development of the program.

For educational renewal to become a viable response to the needs of society, the personnel involved in the extension programs and those participating in the needs assessment of local areas must have the expertise to develop comprehensive educational programs and to upgrade the skills of the classroom teacher. The training in this program, which is child centered, humanistic, individualized, and task oriented, is designed to meet such needs. Teachers trained in the program are skilled at needs assessment and in the application of the methodology necessary to select, develop, and evaluate sequential educational curricula. The training gives the regular-classroom teacher, who is often material bound, the knowledge and skills to implement individualized instructional programs for children. The teachers learn to evaluate children's educational needs not only in terms of the classroom setting but in terms of the cultural, geographic, and socio-economic composition of the community as well.

The teachers trained in the program also become educational change agents through inservice training in their schools and the facilitation of better communication among educational personnel on why children are either being dehumanized or succeeding within the educational milieu. Since other teachers are more receptive to new ideas that are used by teachers like themselves, our trained teachers realize that their success as change agents depends on proving that the needs of the atypical learner can be met within the mainstream of education.

The demand for new teachers in the field has slowed down. Institutions of higher learning and school systems are now faced with the responsibility of adding improved educational technology to the repertoire of the existing teachers. The learning problems approach is such a technology and it is designed to help education become more responsive to the continuous changes in our society.

Bibliography

Mann, P. H. Learning disabilities: A critical need for trained teachers. *The Journal of Learning Disabilities,* 2:2, 1969.

Smith, W. L. Ending the isolation of the handicapped. *American Education,* 7:9, 1971.

Proceedings of the Special Study Institute, "Innovative non-categorical and interrelated projects in the education of the handicapped." Sponsored by the Bureau of Education of the Handicapped, Bureau for Educational Personnel Development, U.S. Office of Education, Project Number 19-1800, PL 91-230.

Film, "Think About What"—23 minutes, color.
    Copies of the film may be obtained from the office of:
        Dr. Philip H. Mann
        Coordinator of Special Education
        School of Education
        University of Miami
        Coral Gables, Fla. 33124

University of Vermont: Consulting Teacher Program

This training program was designed to fit a state-wide, special education, program development plan. It is remarkable for the degree of collaboration it represents among such essential institutions as the state education agency, local education agencies, and the state's one university. Because, previously, the University had no substantial categorical program of preparation for special education personnel, and public-school special education programs were meager, it was possible for the state to build on what had been learned from the successes and failures of traditional approaches without having to undo entrenched systems.

Also remarkable are the program's strong commitment to evaluation of the services undertaken and the extent to which funds from all sources have been coordinated to support the essential components of the long-range, program development effort.

An Introduction to a Regular Classroom Approach to Special Education

Wayne L. Fox, Ann N. Egner, Phyllis E. Paolucci,
Phyllis F. Perelman, and Hugh S. McKenzie
Special Education Program
University of Vermont

and

Jean S. Garvin
Director, Division of Special Educational
and Pupil Personnel Services
Vermont State Department of Education

A regular-classroom approach to special education has been operational in Vermont for nearly five years. In this program, consulting teachers assist and train regular-classroom teachers to provide successful learning experiences for children eligible for special educational services. The rationale for consulting teachers (Fox, 1972; McKenzie, 1969; McKenzie, 1972; McKenzie, Egner, Knight, Perelman, Schneider, & Garvin, 1970) has been supported by Lilly (1971) and Martin (1972). Regular-class placement for all children but the profoundly handicapped is made possible by the inservice training in applied behavior analysis and individualized

---

The work reported herein is supported in part through Title VI, ESEA, Parts B and D from the Vermont State Department of Education; Grant #OG-0-71-1637, Bureau of Education for the Handicapped, U.S.O.E.; and Grant #OG-0-70-1857 (725), Bureau of Education Personnel Development, U.S.O.E. However, opinions expressed herein do not necessarily reflect position or policy of the U.S.O.E., and no official endorsement of the US.O.E. should be inferred.

instruction that provides regular-classroom teachers with the necessary special education skills.

This paper outlines the regular-classroom, special education approach adopted in Vermont. The outline includes the following areas: the model, the training of consulting teachers, the inservice training of regular-classroom teachers, examples of services to children, the implementation of the approach in a school district, support given by the state, and an evaluation of the approach to date with an indication of superintendents' appraisals. Papers that more extensively develop aspects of the approach are listed in a bibliography.

The Model

When a child is not making satisfactory educational progress, the teacher and consulting teacher arrange for the application of more effective teaching/learning procedures. This help is given to the teacher in the form of training in the application of the special education model. The teacher learns to apply the principles of applied behavior analysis and individualizing instruction as a part of providing special education in the regular classroom.

Figure 1 is a schematic representation of the consulting teacher special education model for serving eligible children within regular classrooms.

```
                ELIGIBLE LEARNER REFERRED BY CLASSROOM TEACHER
                 BECAUSE OF MEASURED DEFICIT IN LANGUAGE,
                    ARITHMETIC, AND/OR SOCIAL BEHAVIORS

   ┌──────────────┐   ┌──────────────┐   ┌──────────────┐   ┌──────────────┐
   │MEASUREMENT OF│   │SPECIFICATION │   │DEVELOPMENT   │   │EVALUATION OF │
   │ENTRY LEVEL   │   │OF INSTRUC-   │ → │AND IMPLEMEN- │ → │TEACHING/     │
   │SKILLS FOR    │ → │TIONAL OBJEC- │   │TATION OF     │   │LEARNING      │
   │REFERRED      │   │TIVE FOR      │   │APPROPRIATE   │   │PROCEDURES    │
   │TARGET        │   │REFERRED      │   │TEACHING/     │   │              │
   │BEHAVIORS     │   │TARGET        │   │LEARNING      │   │              │
   │              │   │BEHAVIORS     │   │PROCEDURES    │   │              │
   └──────────────┘   └──────────────┘   └──────────────┘   └──────────────┘
```

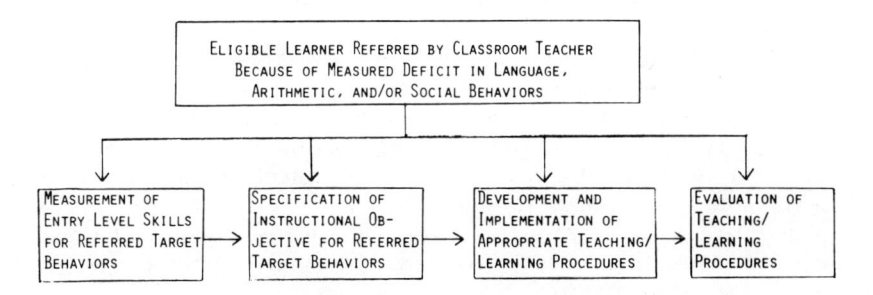

Figure 1. Special Education Model for Serving Eligible Children within Regular Classrooms

The process begins when an eligible learner has been referred by a classroom teacher for special educational services because of a deficit in language, arithmetic, and/or social behaviors. In this model, a child in a regular elementary classroom is eligible for special education services when the following criteria have been met[*]:
1. The teacher refers the child to the consulting teacher. This referral *must* include a statement indicating deficits in language, arithmetic, and/or social behaviors, and a statement signed by the teacher indicating that the referred child has a profound need for consulting teacher services.
2. *Measured* levels of language, arithmetic, and/or social behaviors, which the referring teacher has indicated are deficient, *must* deviate from minimum objectives.

Target behaviors, thus, are those indicated by the teacher in his referral. The consulting teacher begins to train the referring teacher by developing classroom measurement systems that will assess referred target behaviors that deviate from minimum objectives. Minimum objectives are those language, arithmetic, and social behaviors that all children of a particular class are expected to demonstrate at a given point in the school year.

Once target behaviors have been specified in terms of measures, the next step is to determine the referred child's entry level behaviors. A child's entry level for a particular curriculum area is his mastery of skills and knowledge in that area at the time of measurement. The entry level represents the sum total of all behaviors in the child's repertoire that are relevant to the defined target behaviors.

After the entry level behaviors are measured, an *instructional objective* can be specified. The instructional objective includes (a) a behavior that can be reliably observed by at least two independent observers, (b) a statement of the conditions under which the behavior is to be observed, and (c) a statement of the criteria for acceptable performance of the behavior (Wheeler & Fox, 1972). This instructional learning objective is the learning goal that teachers and consulting teachers both establish and commit themselves to achieve for the referred child.

Teaching/learning procedures are then developed and implemented to move the referred child from his entry level to the level

---

[*]Elaboration and justification of this definition of eligibility has been submitted to the Bureau of Education for the Handicapped, "Dimensions of the Population Served by the Consulting Teacher Program, with Data Indicating That These Dimensions Pertain to a Large Majority of Children Served by the Program." The Special Education Program, College of Education, University of Vermont, October 12, 1972.

specified in the instructional objective. In this model, these procedures involve four basic principles derived from applied behavior analysis: (a) reinforcement, (b) scheduling of reinforcement, (c) shaping, and (d) effects of antecedent stimuli.

Reinforcement procedures involve the arrangement of environmental consequences for specified behavior that lead to an increase in the frequency of that behavior. When a child is acquiring a new behavior, it is important that a reinforcer occur every time the response is made. However, maintaining a new behavior that has already been learned is best achieved by certain kinds of intermittent reinforcement. Thus, procedures for *scheduling reinforcement* become important to the classroom teacher. *Shaping* refers to the process of acquiring relatively complex behaviors through a process of successive approximations to the desired behavior. Finally, *antecedent stimuli* refer to stimuli that set the occasion for the desired behaviors; textbooks, worksheets, verbal directions, and errorless discrimination procedures effect learning.

Evaluation of teaching/learning procedures completes the model. The progress of the child from entry level to the attainment of specified instructional objectives is periodically and reliably measured. Measures of the child's progress are compared with the entry level measures, and this comparison permits an evaluation to be made of the effectiveness of the teaching/learning procedures. Procedures are judged to be effective if the child is making adequate progress toward the instructional objectives. If the measures indicate that he is not making adequate progress, then the procedures are modified.

Training Consulting Teachers

Consulting teachers are trained to implement the regular-classroom, special education model during a two-year (including one summer) training program. The trainees must be experienced classroom teachers. The typical program consists of 60 graduate credit hours, 15 hours of formal courses, and 45 hours of closely supervised practica and internship (see McKenzie, 1972, for a complete description of the consulting teacher training program).

The trainees begin the program during the summer with coursework in behavior theory and individualizing instruction, including practicum experience in a laboratory classroom. They receive daily instruction, supervision, and feedback.

During the first year, they continue the coursework and practica to broaden their skills and knowledge in the application of individualized instruction, behavior theory, and research for classroom use. The practica include extensive opportunities with and training of school personnel and consultation with the parents of eligible children.

The second year of training consists of internships in Vermont school districts. The consulting teachers-in-training work with school personnel and parents to develop effective programs to manage and educate eligible children, conduct courses and workshops for district personnel, and continue their graduate studies in University seminars.

As the trainees progress, faculty supervision is reduced until, in the latter part of the internship year, trainees are working with teachers with minimum faculty supervision. Consulting teachers-in-training are evaluated on the basis of their mastery of the minimum training objectives that have been developed by the Special Education faculty over the past five years. The objectives include such behaviors as serving children, training teachers and parents, writing reports, disseminating information (written and oral), administering the consulting teacher office in the school district, negotiating the consulting teacher budget, and conducting research. The application of behavioral techniques requires a precise record of the techniques employed. This record serves as an immediately available evaluation of the students' effectiveness in accelerating the progress of eligible children. Each consulting teacher-in-training serves approximately 30 children in meeting the training objectives during his two-year program.

Upon successful completion of the internship year, students are eligible to receive an MEd degree. They must then present their credentials to a board composed of certified consulting teachers to obtain Vermont certification as a consulting teacher.

Teacher Education Through Inservice Teacher Training

To fulfill the teacher training-based model of special education (Lilly, 1971), consulting teachers provide three levels of training for classroom teachers in the skills required to deliver special education services to eligible children: consultation, regular workshops that lead to state recertification credits, or courses that lead to University graduate credit. (See Christie, McKenzie, & Burdett (1972) for a complete description of the inservice teacher-training procedures followed and the results achieved by consulting teachers.)

Training through consultation is begun when a teacher refers a child to a consulting teacher. Using on-the-job training, the consulting teacher trains the classroom teacher in defining a behavior in observable and measurable terms; reliably measuring, recording, and graphing the target behavior; making educational decisions based on the measures; involving the child's parents in developing an instructional program; and consistently following a specified teaching/learning procedure. The consulting teacher takes a direct role in developing the referred child's instructional program; he describes the child's improvement according to the principles of applied behavior analysis and provides the teacher with attention and reinforcement as the teacher acquires special education skills.

During the inservice workshops, which lead to credits toward state recertification requirements, the skills are taught more formally. The teachers complete instructional units that emphasize the observation and measurement of classroom behaviors and the implementation of the special education model. Instruction is built around a practicum that requires a workshop participant to apply the model to at least one eligible child in his classroom. The teachers are asked to respond to introductory readings on applied behavior analysis and the rationale for the consulting teacher approach to special education. They carry out individualized instruction programs for eligible children and directly involve the parents in the development of the programs. Then they evaluate the effects of their programs through scientific verification procedures. Finally, they learn to describe special education procedures by writing and presenting the case studies of their instructional programs to their colleagues and the children's parents.

Formal University coursework is offered by consulting teachers who hold appointments as associate faculty in the special education program. The theory and practice of applied behavior analysis and individualizing instruction is emphasized, as well as the training of practice and prepractice teachers and paraprofessionals. Coursework is divided into self-paced instructional units that consist of specified instructional objectives, suggested readings to help the teacher achieve the unit objectives, and suggested practicum experiences. During weekly group and individual conferences with the consulting teacher, teachers learn to specify the terminal objectives expected of all children for language, arithmetic, and social behaviors. Teachers also learn to define and sequence those objectives that may enable children to achieve terminal objectives within a specified period of time. In addition, teachers develop reliable measurement systems to assess *every* child's rate of acquiring the specified terminal objectives. They then design individualized instruction procedures and apply consequences for those children who are not achieving at the specified rate. Evaluation of teaching/learning procedures must demonstrate that the eligible child has achieved, or is making significant progress toward, the specified objectives. Evaluations are reported through written case studies and are interpreted to parents, colleagues, and administrators.

The general goal of the described consulting and training procedures is to bring the teacher under the control of the learner's behaviors. That is, the teacher begins to make important educational decisions that are based on reliably measured changes in the learner's performance rather than on inferred mental or emotional states. An additional goal is to help teachers more directly involve the parents of eligible children in the development, implementation, and interpretation of educational programs. The success of teacher-training procedures is evaluated in terms of the applications of the special education model to serve eligible children in the regular classroom. Thus, the success of the consulting teacher's training of regular-classroom teachers depends on the pupils' progress toward acquiring important language, arithmetic, and social behaviors.

Some Applications of the Model for Serving Eligible Children Within Regular Classrooms

The following case studies are representative of the services provided by regular classroom teachers who have been trained by consulting teachers to apply the special education model for serving eligible children within regular classrooms. In these cases, classroom teachers performed all the tasks described with assistance from consulting teachers-in-training.

The procedures for determining a child's eligibility for consulting teacher services are not included in the case studies.

Bob (Coffrin, Hasazi, & Egner, 1971)

Bob was a 7-year-old second grader in a rural Vermont elementary school. He had been characterized by previous teachers as "slow to mature" and "not quite ready." Academically, his grades were below average. Socially, he was described as "shy and withdrawn." Bob was referred because he did not pay attention to his work, rarely completed his assignments, and appeared to be disinterested in school. His teacher expressed specific concern that if he continued in this pattern of behavior, he could not be promoted to third grade where more mature behaviors were required. Although the teacher noted that Bob frequently was correct in what he did, he simply did not complete assignments very often, and it was never possible to predict which day would be a "good" one for him.

To measure Bob's entry level, the classroom teacher recorded the percentage of his completed assignments for two language arts periods each day. Bob's entry level performance (Fig. 2, "Baseline") on completing assignments during the one-hour morning period was both variable and low, with a range of from 0% to 100% and a median of 60%. His performance during the half-hour afternoon period was

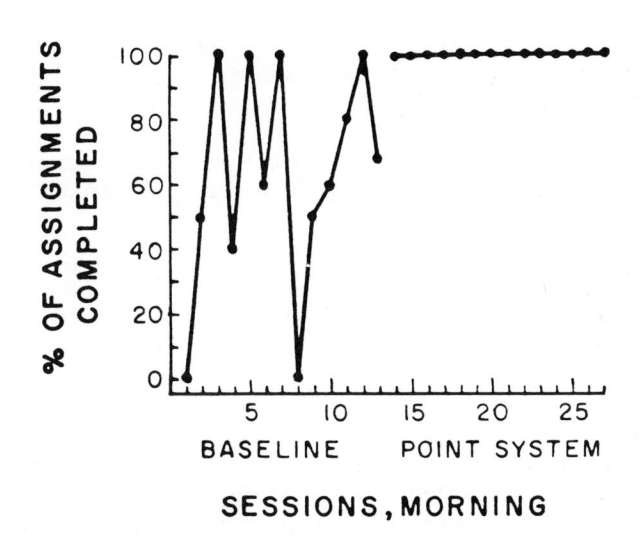

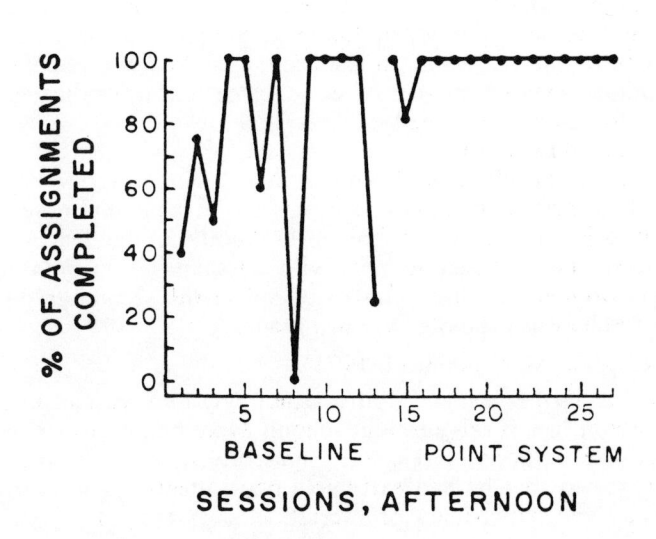

Figure 2. Bob
Percentage of Assignments Completed
During Morning and Afternoon Language Arts Period

also variable and low, ranging from 0% to 100% with a median of 75%. On several occasions, a second observer independently checked Bob's daily assignment with 100% agreement with the classroom teacher.

On the basis of Bob's entry level performance, the consulting teacher assisted the classroom teacher to specify an instructional objective for Bob as follows:

Conditions	Behavior	Criteria
Given morning and afternoon language arts assignments	Bob will complete each assignment	100% completion of assignments

The consulting teacher assisted the classroom teacher in developing a special teaching/learning procedure that incorporated a point system in which Bob earned time to be alone with the teacher as well as free time for the entire class. During the private time with the teacher, Bob could choose to read or play games with her; during the class free time, Bob could choose either games for the class, such as "Seven Up," extra recess, or listening to story records. When the point system was implemented (Fig. 2, "Point System"), Bob's performance increased dramatically. He became more consistent in completing his assignments.

During the morning period, he completed 100% of the assignment. During the afternoon period, he failed to complete all of his assignment on only one occasion. In addition, his accuracy remained at an acceptable level (a median of 80%). Post checks indicated that Bob's performance continued at this high level even though the teacher gradually withdrew the point system.

The teacher's evaluation also noted that Bob appeared to be more eager and interested in all his assignments. His parents noted that he began bringing his work home. In addition, the teacher was pleased to see Bob interacting more with classmates. Bob's more consistent performance enabled him to complete the second-grade material so that he was promoted to third grade.

Mike (Berry, Jarvis, & Paolucci, 1971)

Mike was an 11-year-old, fourth-grade boy in a regular, elementary classroom in a rural Vermont school. Mike had repeated second grade because of poor marks and "inattentiveness." His classroom teacher reported that he had extremely poor attention and academic performance and showed lack of interest.

The classroom teacher recorded the percentage of correct responses made by Mike on his daily written work in spelling, social studies, and math. Mike's entry level academic performance was extremely erratic in all three curriculum areas (see Fig. 3, "Baseline"). His accuracy averaged below 70% in each area. On several occasions, a second observer independently corrected Mike's assignments. In every instance, agreement between the second observer and the classroom teacher was 100%.

On the basis of Mike's entry level performance his classroom teacher specified the following instructional objective:

Conditions	Behavior	Criteria
Given daily written work in spelling, social studies, and math	Mike will complete each assignment	with a minimum of 90% accuracy

During a parent conference, Mike's mother reported that over a year before she had purchased a bicycle for him that was still in its carton. She had told Mike that he would be given the bicycle if his grades improved. Unfortunately, his grades had not improved and the bicycle was still in its carton.

The classroom teacher, with assistance from the consulting teacher and approval from the parents, developed a teaching/learning procedure to help Mike earn his bicycle. On each day that he received 90% correct or better in each of the three subject areas, he earned a star that was placed on a chart. Stars were later exchanged for specific parts of the bicycle. A pedal was worth five stars, the handlebars 10 stars, and so forth.

To assess the effects of the teaching/learning procedure, the teacher used a multiple-baseline evaluation procedure. The multiple baseline required that the teaching/learning procedure be implemented for only one behavior at a time. Thus, the teacher first implemented the star chart in spelling (see Fig. 3, "Contingency"). There was an immediate increase to criterion level in Mike's spelling performance (Fig. 3) with concurrent but smaller increases in response accuracy in social studies and math. After establishing that the procedure was effective in spelling, Mike's teacher began to give him stars for each day that he scored 90% or above on social studies assignments. When the effectiveness of the point system in social studies was established, the teacher gave the stars to Mike contingent upon performance on his math assignments. Mike's response accuracy averaged above 90% in all three areas until he had earned all of the parts of the bicycle. Post checks indicated that Mike continued to maintain high-level performance after he earned his bicycle and when the point system was no longer in effect.

Mike's parents were very pleased with his academic success and his much improved attitude toward school. They reported that he

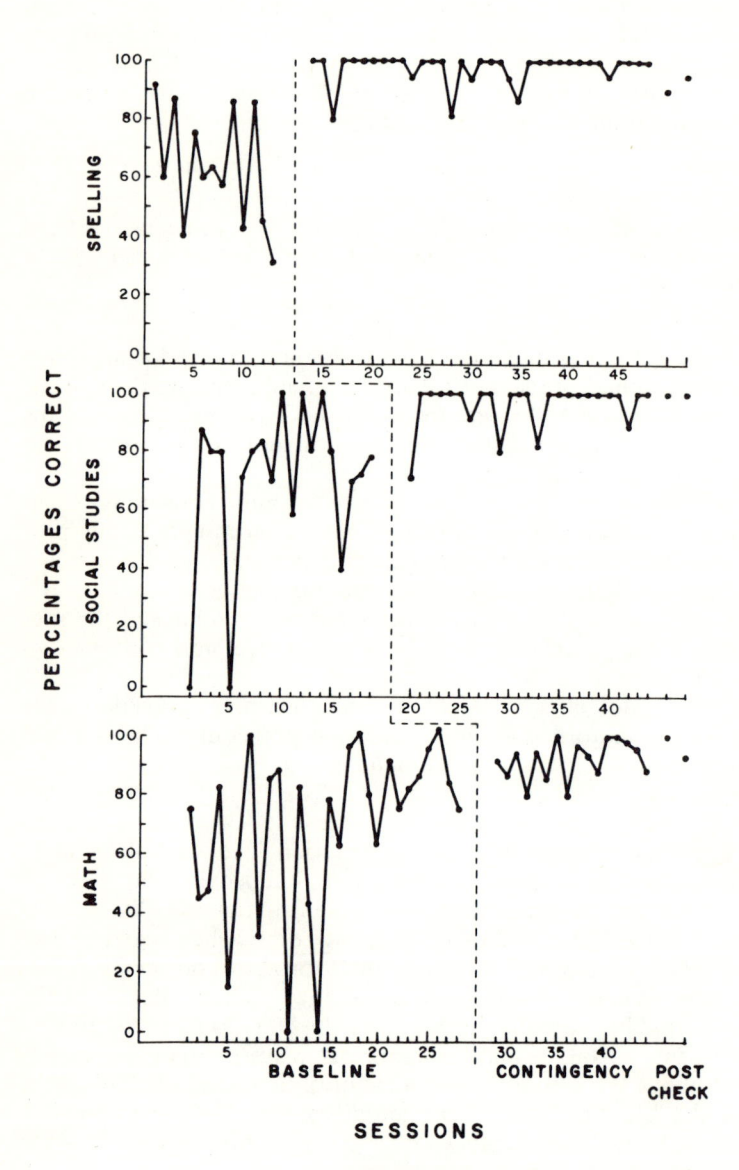

Figure 3. Mike
Percentage of Correct Responses:
Daily Spelling, Social Studies, and Math Assignments

brought home his work (something he had not done before) and took great pride in showing it to his parents and siblings. Mike's teacher reported that he was a much happier child in her classroom even though he no longer received special attention from her. Mike was promoted to the fifth grade.

Kari (Duval, Burdett, & Fox, 1972)

Kari was an eight-year-old girl in a departmentalized third-grade class in a small Vermont community. She had one teacher for language arts, one teacher for math, and another for science and social studies. She was experiencing difficulty in reading and was having a hard time keeping up with her third-grade work. Kari was inattentive and seldom completed any of her assignments. She received dexedrine and, at times, appeared dull and listless. The special reading teacher had recommended that Kari be placed in a first reader but she showed little improvement and tended to avoid reading activities. She seldom entered into voluntary group-reading activities and she was not observed using any of the various reading kits in the room. All medication was stopped when this study was undertaken.

Figure 4. Kari
Percentage of Words Recognized Correctly:
Entry Level Measurement

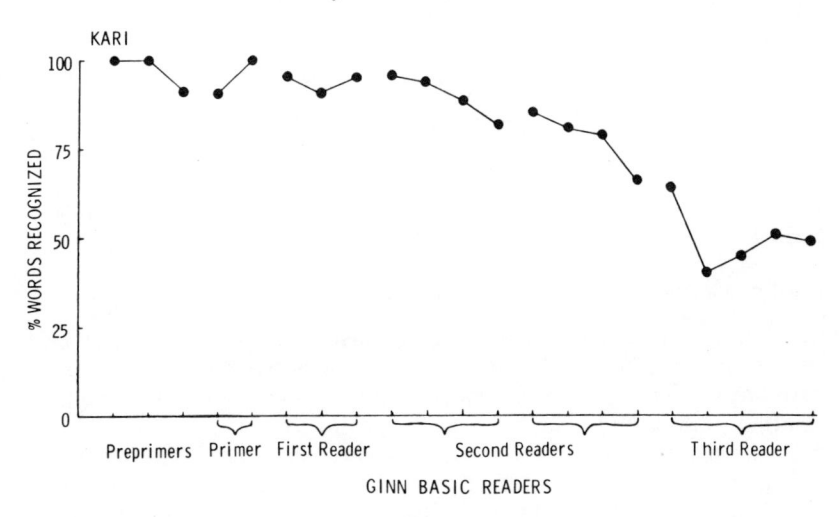

The language arts teacher measured Kari's word-recognition entry level performance for all the words in the Ginn Basic Readers* through the third-grade level. Figure 4 shows the results of the entry level measure for word recognition. Each point on the graph represents a block of approximately 50 words, except for the first three points which represent all the words in each of the preprimers.

Kari's word recognition entry level performance was quite acceptable for the first-grade words. She recognized relatively fewer second-grade words and her performance fell below 50% on words taken from the third-grade reader.

On the basis of the word-recognition entry level measure, Kari's language arts teacher specified the following instructional objectives:

Condition	Behavior	Criteria
Given all the words found in the Ginn Basic Readers through third-grade level	Kari will recognize each word upon presentation	within three seconds of presentation on three consecutive occasions

Condition	Behavior	Criteria
Given any story from the Ginn Basic Readers through third-grade level	Kari will read the story aloud	with a minimum of 90% accuracy

Condition	Behavior	Criteria
Given any story from the Ginn Basic Readers through the third-grade level	Kari will respond to comprehension questions derived from the story	with a minimum of 80% accuracy

The language arts teacher used a flashcard procedure developed by Burdett & Fox (1972) to enhance Kari's word-recognition performance. Twice each day, once in the morning during the regular reading period, and once after school while Kari was waiting for her bus, the teacher administered the flashcard procedure. The teaching/learning procedure consisted of presenting on flashcards all the words that Kari had missed on the entry level measure in the order in which they first appeared in the Ginn Basic Readers. Flashcards were pre-

---

*Ginn Basic Readers. Boston, Mass.: Ginn & Company, 1961.

sented in a stack of 10, and Kari was required to make three consecutive correct responses to each word before it could be replaced with a new word from the entry level measure. When Kari had learned all the words in a particular story from the basic reader, she was asked to read that story aloud to the teacher. Kari was *never* asked to read aloud until she had demonstrated that she could recognize each word in the story either through the flashcard procedure or the entry level measure. After she read the story aloud, the teacher asked Kari five comprehension questions derived from the story. Each reading session lasted 10-15 minutes, approximately two minutes for the flashcard procedure and approximately 10 minutes for the oral reading and comprehension questions.

Figure 5. Kari
Cumulative Number of Words
Learned During the Word-Recognition Procedure

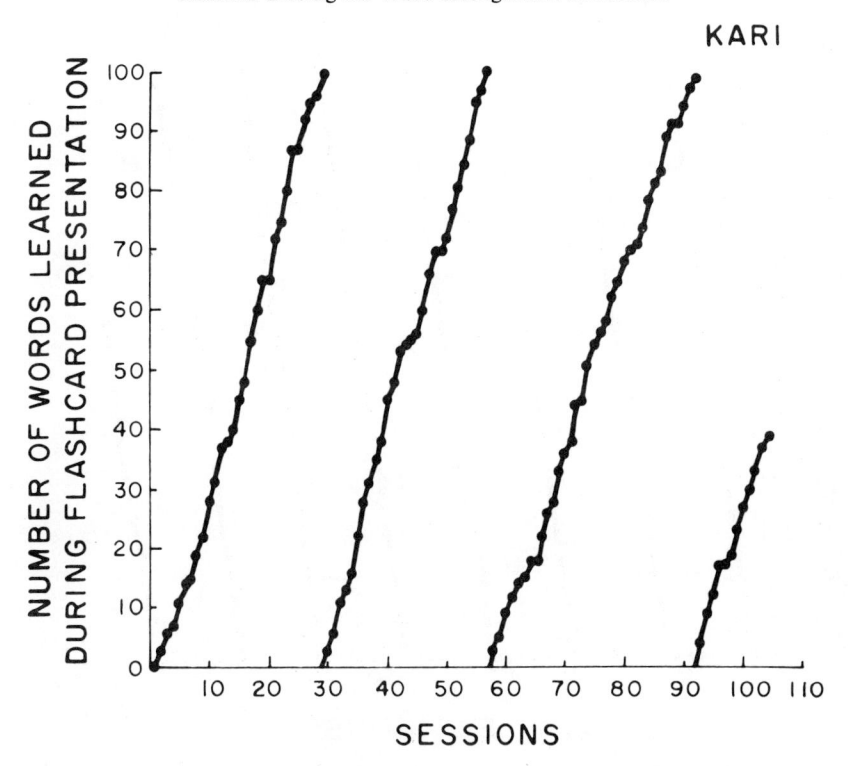

Kari responded incorrectly to each word plotted on the graph on its first presentation.

Kari participated in a total of 104 reading sessions. The actual time she spent in the reading sessions totaled approximately 10 hours. Figure 5 shows the number of words that Kari learned during the reading sessions. A learned word was one that was recognized correctly on three successive presentations. These learned words were *all missed on their first presentation* during the reading sessions. Figure 5 is a cumulative record of the number of words learned per session. The rate at which Kari learned new words is reflected by the slope of the cumulative record. A flat, horizontal slope indicates no learning, while a more vertical, rising slope indicates increasing rates. After each 100 words the graph reverts back to the baseline and continues on for the next 100 words. Thus, it can be seen that Kari learned 339 words during the 104 sessions for a word acquisition rate of 3.2 words per session.

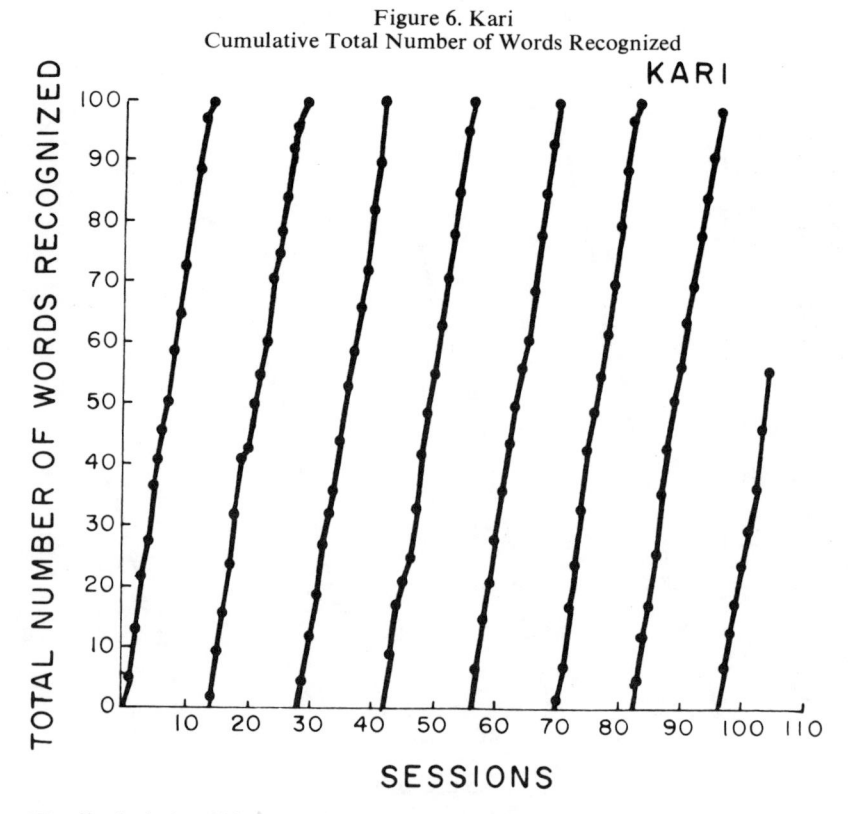

Figure 6. Kari
Cumulative Total Number of Words Recognized

The list includes 416 words that were originally missed on the entry level measure, but were responded to correctly on their first presentation during the word-recognition procedure.

In addition to the words learned during the word-recognition procedure, Kari also learned many other words during the study. Before beginning the reading sessions, she had missed several hundred words on the word-recognition entry level measure. However, when these same words were presented at a later time during the reading sessions, she recognized some when they were first shown to her as well as on the next two consecutive presentations, to meet the criterion for a learned word. Figure 6 shows the total number of words meeting criterion during the 104 reading sessions. Kari's total word count was 755 words, a rate of 7.3 words per reading session.

The additional words that Kari learned were probably the result of many factors. First, she continued to receive her regular reading instruction during the language arts class. As Kari's reading im-

Figure 7. Kari
Percentage of Correct Oral Reading and Comprehension Responses

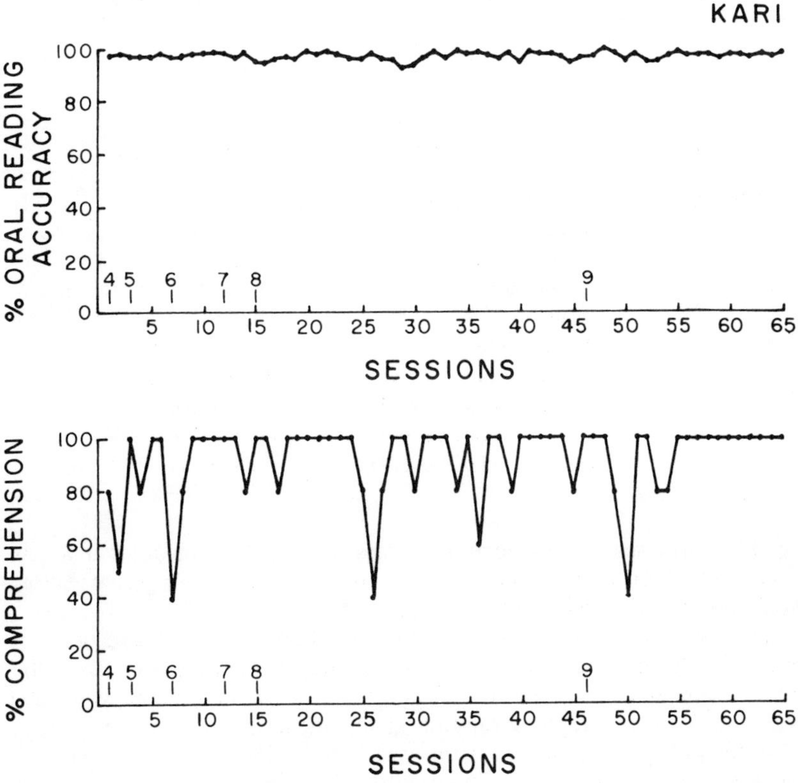

The numbers on the graph correspond to different levels of the Ginn Basic Readers (see Table 1).

37

proved, she joined the regular reading groups and was presented with many of the words that she had missed on the entry level tests earlier in the year. Thus, it is certainly possible that some new words would have been learned during these regular reading periods. Another by-product of Kari's improved reading ability was the increased reading of books other than her basal reader. The librarian reported that Kari used the library much more frequently, and her parents reported that Kari would bring books home from school and read aloud to them (something that she had not done before). Any or all of these factors could account for the additional words Kari learned during the reading sessions.

Figure 7 shows Kari's oral reading and comprehension scores. The numbers on the graph represent the different books in the Ginn Basic Reader sequence. Table 1 lists the Ginn Basic Readers from preprimers through third grade. The books are numbered in order from one through nine. Kari started reading in the fourth book of the series at the primer level; at the conclusion of the sessions she was reading in the ninth book of the series at the third-grade level.

Table 1

The Ginn Basic Reader Series from Preprimer through Grade 3

Book No.	Grade Level	Book Title
1	Preprimer	My Little Red Story Book
2	Preprimer	My Little Green Story Book
3	Preprimer	My Little Blue Story Book
4	Primer	The Little White House
5	First Reader	On Cherry Street
6	Second Reader, Level I	We Are Neighbors
7	Second Reader, Level II	Around the Corner
8	Third Reader, Level I	Finding New Neighbors
9	Third Reader, Level II	Friends Far and Near

Her oral reading performance was above 95% on all but a few occasions. Her comprehension was also excellent, dropping below 80% on only five occasions.

In the five and one-half months that Kari's teacher gave her this extra 15-20 minutes per day, Kari managed to progress from the primer through the 3^2 reader. During the latter part of the year, she was able to join a regular reading group in her classroom. She began to enter group activities with the rest of the class and was even seen working individually from the reading kits in the room. Her other teachers remarked on the change in her attitude and on her newly gained skills. She was able to participate in all third-grade activities.

Implementing a Consulting Teacher Program in a Local School District

In the initiation and expansion of a consulting teacher program, all the rules of good administrative practice must be applied at all levels of administration affecting the outcomes of the program, from the state department of education and the central office of the school district to the school principals. The school administrator who intends to manage effectively the eligible children in regular classrooms must carefully consider his strategy. It begins with the establishment of authority and responsibility and includes negotiating a written proposal. The one required by the State Department of Education in Vermont includes the following topics: needs assessment, eligibility requirements, schools and children to be served, program objectives, and activities. The proposal forces thoughtful consideration of operational procedures and it facilitates staff acceptance.

Administrators must consider objectives and limitations and be careful not to place unreasonable expectations on new special education programs. One expectation that may eventually prove to be unreasonable is the number of children that can be assigned to a consulting teacher. Experienced consulting teachers can assume responsibility for more than 40 eligible children in regular classrooms under some conditions, but establishing this number as policy will undoubtedly lead to shoddy records, poor parent involvement, and harassed special educators. If a consulting teacher wishes to increase his performance, let him thoroughly train a number of teachers before taking on more children. The consulting teacher must demonstrate progress for the pupils served. If the teacher training, or the time to complete the job is missing, the program will not succeed.

The time invested in establishing school district ground rules for this new delivery system in special education is a critical factor in determining how the elementary principal will resolve later inevitable conflicts. The building principal, who, in most cases, is the educational leader in the district, must be excited about improving pupil performance in his school. He can be expected to support a program that succeeds. However, careful discussion of the program is needed to increase the probability that he will accept the eligible child's success as the measure of the program's success. This commitment to improved learning as the basis for measuring the success of a program must be emphasized in early statements to building principals.

Administrators and special educators must plan on recognizing the good work of their teaching colleagues. One of the must successful methods has been the "Annual Conference of Behavioral Educators" conducted by the University of Vermont's Special Education Program, a forum through which teachers working with consulting teachers can report their data and research on the children they help. Trained researchers observing the quality of the work carried out by classroom teachers agree that it is truly deserving of the acclamation it receives from Vermont educators. The Department of Education publishes the results of this yearly conference in the quarterly publication, *Journal of Behavioral Education*, thereby rewarding both the contributors and the readers of these scholarly studies, which describe procedures for improving the learning of eligible children.

State Support for Local School District Consulting Teacher Programs

At the State Department of Education in Vermont, special education policies have been established to make it possible for the University and local special education programs to gain financial and staff support. The Department of Education has adopted pupil eligibility requirements for children educated in regular classrooms. The consulting teacher program is now an approved program and is funded at 75% of the salaries of the consulting teacher and his technical assistant under the State special education budget.

The University and the State Department of Education developed an unusual certification for consulting teachers: A heretofore unused certification regulation that permitted competency-based certification by a peer board was reactivated. A Board of Consulting Teachers was established and, at present, recommends to the State Department of Education the certification of each person who is ultimately approved as the educational specialist called a consulting teacher.

The adoption of the consulting teacher model as an approved program in special education brought the Department of Education face to face with some critical questions. Could a child who is not tested on any of the acceptable psychoeducational instruments be accepted as an "eligible special education child?" Did the Department of Education really mean to accept competency-based certification? Positive answers resulted because of the cooperative planning between the State Department of Education and the University.

Evaluation of the Consulting Teacher Program

The consulting teacher's skills have been found to be effective in both open and traditional classroom designs, as long as the following conditions exist:

> The teacher must be willing to provide the pupil with appropriate tasks to which he can and does respond.
>
> The teacher must wish to know what daily successes the child is achieving on each assignment.

The teacher must value and reward the child's improved performance.

The teacher must provide the quiet place that some eligible children need for "time-outs" from activity.

It goes without saying that the better organized the learning experience, whether in an open or traditional model, the easier it is to plan learning programs for eligible children. In either case, consulting teachers have demonstrated the skills to facilitate the progress of eligible children.

Evidence of these skills is found in the fact that some 400 Vermont teachers have received inservice training in individualized instruction and applied behavior analysis from consulting teachers. That such training is effective is demonstrated by reliably measured changes in the learning behaviors of some 1,000 children eligible for special education. Many teachers so trained have generalized their newly acquired skills to children not eligible for special education with a resultant acceleration of their learning.

Superintendents of schools have been generous and honest with their comments on this departure from traditional special education. Their analysis of the program is reflected in some of the comments made in recent conversations with one of the authors (J. S. Garvin).

"One of its great strengths is the caliber of the training program. It starts with their outstanding selection process for applicants."

"They dig in and work and resolve problems. Their techniques are extremely successful. It works!"

"One thing I like is that they don't tag kids. The way I see it, the consulting teachers do a really nice job."

"It got us away from the idea that we can't work with the child in the classroom and we ought to figure out a way to get rid of him."

"This is my twenty-first year in the business. I have never seen anything like the positive attitude they have toward the children."

"All the teachers except one were willing to do scientific verification of children's progress."

"One of the weaknesses is that there aren't enough consulting teachers."

"We need them for all our new teachers who are filled with vim and vigor and haven't learned yet how to manage a classroom."

"Teachers can easily feel threatened. But when success becomes obvious, it's hard to fight it. One of my teachers who had been particularly uptight about the program said, 'Hey, we better start using this program!'"

"It almost seems like some of my teachers aren't ready to face up to what learning is really about. There is more resistance when they do not have this level of readiness."

"I know from others that there can be problems in building the correct image. I haven't found this. Of course their competence sometimes brings resistance. We started with two willing and able teachers and it gradually spread around the building. You can't change a whole school in one year."

Even more important than what superintendents say about the consulting teacher program is what they are doing about it, of course. As of this writing, two positions are immediately available for every consulting teacher-in-training. Consulting teachers currently may be found in 9 of the 54 superintendencies in the State of Vermont. This record is especially meaningful when one realizes that the first consulting teachers completed their training only two years ago! An additional 24 superintendencies have requested consulting teachers, with the result that the University plans to double the number of consulting teachers-in-training from 16 to 32 by 1974.

Parents are very supportive of the approach; hundreds of them send positive letters to teachers, consulting teachers, administrators, and school board members and they make positive comments to teachers. Perhaps the support can be attributed to the fact that parents are directly involved in the special services provided to their children and the careful accountability advocated by the approach.

Taxpayers, state legislators, officials in the Governor's office, and school board members have provided the highest level of support—financial—to the program. The data and accountability emphasis of the consulting teacher program has great appeal to them. Also appealing are the preliminary studies that show the consulting teacher approach in Vermont to be, at minimum, an average of $200 per school year per child less expensive than special education services provided by resource teachers or a special-class approach (for a cost analysis see McKenzie, 1969).

Basing a special education program on successful changes in the deficit behaviors of eligible children is a brave undertaking. Moreover, the behavioral approach stresses that learning deficits need not be permanent and that language, arithmetic, and social behaviors can be accelerated to the point that the eligible child is no longer eligible for, nor requires, special education services. The case studies presented demonstrate the success of regular-classroom teachers in applying this special education model within their classrooms. As long as consulting teachers continue to provide classroom teachers with success, the approach will remain a very real and very effective alternative to special-class placement.

References

Berry, C., Jarvis, C., & Paolucci, P. E. Mike: Bicycles and schoolwork—a good combination. Unpublished case study. Special Education Program, College of Education, University of Vermont, 1971.

Burdett, C. S., & Fox, W. L. Measurement and evaluation of reading procedures: Word recognition, oral reading and comprehension. Unpublished manuscript. Special Education Program, College of Education, University of Vermont, 1972.

Christie, L. S., McKenzie, H. S., & Burdett, C. S. The consulting teacher approach to special education: Inservice training for regular classroom teachers, *Focus on Exceptional Children*, October, 1972.

Coffrin, L., Hasazi, S., & Egner, A. N. Bob: Completed tasks. Unpublished case study. Special Education Program, College of Education, University of Vermont, 1971.

Duval, J., Burdett, C. S., & Fox, W. L. Kari. In C. S. Burdett & W. L. Fox, *Measurement and evaluation of reading procedures: Word recognition, oral reading, and comprehension.* Unpublished manuscript. Special Education Program, College of Education, University of Vermont, 1972.

Fox, W. L. The consulting teacher program. Unpublished manuscript. Special Education Program, College of Education, University of Vermont, 1972.

Lilly, M. S. A training based model for special education. *Exceptional Children*, 1971, 37, 745-749.

Martin, E. W. Individualism and behaviorism as future trends in educating handicapped children. *Exceptional Children*, 1972, 38, 517-527.

McKenzie, H. S. (Ed.) *The 1968-1969 Yearly Report of the Consulting Teacher Program: Vol. I.* Burlington, Vermont: Special Education Program, College of Education, University of Vermont, 1969.

McKenzie, H. S., Egner, A. N., Knight, M. F., Perelman, P. F., Schneider, B. M., & Garvin, J. S. Training consulting teachers to assist elementary teachers in the management and education of handicapped children. *Exceptional Children*, 1970, 37, 137-143.

McKenzie, H. S. Special education and consulting teachers. In F. Clark, D. Evans, & L. Hammerlynk (Eds.) *Implementing behavioral programs for schools and clinics.* Champaign, Illinois: Research Press, 1972, 103-125.

Wheeler, A. N., & Fox, W. L. *Managing behavior: Part 5, Behavior modification: A teacher's guide to writing instructional objectives.* Lawrence, Kansas: H & H Enterprises, 1972.

Additional case studies of eligible children served on the consulting teacher program are available from the authors.

Bibliography
Consulting Teacher Program

Burdett, C. S. Minimum expected objectives and the ideal school. Unpublished manuscript, Special Education Program, College of Education, University of Vermont, 1972.

Burdett, C. S., & Knight, M. F. *The 1969-1970 Yearly Report of the Consulting Teacher Program: Chittenden South Supervisory School District.* Burlington, Vermont: Special Education Program, College of Education, University of Vermont, 1971.

Christie, L. S. Home consequation of in-school behaviors. Paper presented at the 50th Annual Convention of the Council for Exceptional Children, Washington, D.C., 1972.

Christie, L., Egner, A., & Lates, B. J. (Eds.) *A very special education for all children.* Montpelier, Vermont: Office of Federal Programs, 1972.

Cleveland, M. D., Humphreys, S., Schneider, B. M., & Fox, W. L. *The 1969-1970 Yearly Report of the Consulting Teacher Program: Chittenden Central School District.* Burlington, Vermont: Special Education Program, College of Education, University of Vermont, 1971.

Egner, A. N., Burdett, C. S., Knight, M. F., McKenzie, H. S., Paolucci, P. W., & Perry, J. Some methods for daily measurement of reading, writing, and arithmetic. *Thought Into Action.* Burlington, Vermont: College of Education, University of Vermont, December, 1970.

Egner, A. N. Consulting procedures for Wells, P_1. Unpublished manuscript, Special Education Program, College of Education, University of Vermont, 1971. (a)

Egner, A. N. History of special education in Vermont. Unpublished manuscript, Special Education Program, College of Education, University of Vermont, 1971. (b)

Egner, A. N., Burdett, C. S., & Fox, W. L. *Observing and measuring classroom behaviors.* Austin, Texas: Austin Writers Group, Inc., 1972.

Egner, A. N., Paolucci, P. W., Perelman, P. F., Fox, W. L., & McKenzie, H.S. *The 1970-1971 Yearly Report of the Consulting Teacher Program: EPDA Chittenden Central School District.* Burlington, Vermont: Special Education Program, College of Education, University of Vermont, 1972.

Fox, W. L., McKenzie, H. S., & Hanley, E. M. The consulting teacher approach to training consulting teachers. Paper read at the Teacher Training Conference, University of Kansas, Lawrence, Kansas, April, 1972.

Fox, W. L. Consulting teacher program. In L. Schwartz, A. Oseroff, H. Drucker, & R. Schwartz (Eds.) *Innovative non-categorical and interrelated projects in the education of the handicapped: Proceedings of the special study institute.* Tallahassee, Fla.: Florida State University, 1972, 30-33.

Hall, C. Acquisition of creative writing skills. Unpublished manuscript, Special Education Program, College of Education, University of Vermont, 1971.

Hall, C., Conlon, M., & Hanley, E. The effects of a peer correction procedure on the arithmetic accuracy of two elementary school children. In G. Semb (Ed.), *Behavioral analysis in education:* 1972, in press.

Hanley, E. M. Review of research involving applied behavior analysis in the classroom. *Review of Educational Research,* 1970, 40, 597-625.

Hanley, E. M. Results of a parent workshop program. Unpublished manuscript, Special Education Program, College of Education, University of Vermont, 1972. (a)

Hanley, E. M. (Ed.) *1972 Fiscal Year Report, Consulting Teacher Program, University of Vermont, Title VI.* Burlington, Vermont: Special Education Program, College of Education, University of Vermont, 1972. (b)

Hanley, E. M., & Perelman, P. F. A report of the Winooski model cities paraprofessional training program. In E. A. Ramp & B. L. Hopkins (Eds.) *A new direction for education: Behavior analysis, 1971.* Lawrence, Kansas: The University of Kansas, 1971, 158-190. (a)

Hanley, E. M., & Perelman, P. F. *The 1969-1970 Yearly Report of the Consulting Teacher Program: Winooski School District.* Burlington, Vermont: Special Education Program, College of Education, University of Vermont, 1971. (b)

Knight, M. Home based learning programs for handicapped preschool children. Paper presented at the 50th Annual Convention of the Council for Exceptional Children, Washington, D.C., 1972.

Knight, M., & McKenzie, H. S. Elimination of bedtime thumbsucking in day care and home settings through contingent reading. *Journal of Applied Behavior Analysis,* in press.

Knight, M. F., Hasazi, S. E., & McNeil, M. E. A home based program for the development of reading skills for preschoolers. In E. A. Ramp & B. L. Hopkins (Eds.) *A new direction for education: Behavior analysis, 1971.* Lawrence, Kansas: The University of Kansas, 1971, 223-233.

Lates, B. J., Egner, A. N., & McKenzie, H. S. Behavior modification of the academic and social behaviors of first-grade children, or what happens when educators turn on. In E. A. Ramp & B. L. Hopkins (Eds.) *A new direction for education: Behavior analysis, 1971.* Lawrence, Kansas: The University of Kansas, 1971, 191-222. (a)

Lates, B. J., Egner, A. N., & McKenzie, H. S. *The 1969-1970 Yearly Report of the Consulting Teacher Program: Burlington School District.* Burlington, Vermont: Special Education Program, College of Education, University of Vermont, 1971. (b)

McKenzie, H. S., Clark, M., Wolf, M. M., Kothera, R., & Benson, C. Behavior modification of children with learning disabilities using grades as tokens and allowances as back up reinforcers. *Exceptional Children,* 1968, 34, 745-752.

McKenzie, H. S., A report on the University of Vermont's consulting teacher program: Some measures of and contingencies for some school behaviors. Paper presented at the First Annual Kansas Symposium on Behavior Analysis in Education, Lawrence, Kansas, 1970. (a)

McKenzie, H. S. (Ed.) *The 1968-1969 Yearly Report of the Consulting Teacher Program, Volumes I and II.* Burlington, Vermont: Consulting Teacher Program, College of Education, University of Vermont, 1970. (b)

McNeil, M., Hasazi, S., Muller, A., & Knight, M. Open classrooms: Supporters of applied behavior analysis. In G. Semb (Ed.) *Behavior analysis in education,* 1972, in press.

Orzell, D., Armstrong, S., & Egner, A. Shaping creative writing for a first-grade boy. *Journal of Behavioral Education,* 1971, 1, 5-7.

Paolucci, P. W., Knight, M. F., & McKenzie, H. S. *The 1969-1970 Yearly Report of the Consulting Teacher Program: South Burlington School District.* Burlington, Vermont: Special Education Program, College of Education, University of Vermont, 1971.

Perelman, P. F. Elimination of isolate behavior of a girl in a learning disability class. Paper presented at the 50th Annual International Convention of the Council for Exceptional Children, Washington, D.C., 1972.

Pigeon, G., Cleveland, M., Ashley, L., Fox, W., & Egner, A. Teaching basic number concepts for a first-grade repeater. Unpublished manuscript, Special Education Program, College of Education, University of Vermont, 1971.

The use of categorical labels, which are derived from the psycho-medical orientation of educational assessment and programming, is rejected both in theory and practice in the DPT program, as is the dichotomous conceptualization of education as "regular" and "special," and of children as "normal" and "exceptional." The DPT serves all children experiencing difficulties in learning and/or behavior who are referred by their teachers.

Although the DPT is the point of first referral for problems of learning and behavior in schools in which the program functions as defined, the DPT works closely with other specialists to ensure that any needs beyond the reasonable scope of the regular-class teacher are not neglected, and that all resources of the school and community are mobilized when needed on behalf of the children. If a child evidences problems in vision, hearing, or speech, appropriate specialists are consulted. In the same way, the school psychologist, visiting teacher (school social worker), reading consultant, or school nurse is called in if a problem seems to be within his area of competence.

The basic viewpoint of the DPT program is that regular education and special education, as now constituted, share a common responsibility to ensure the optimal educational experience for every child. In order to carry out this responsibility the capacity of regular-class teachers to provide successfully for a diversity of children's needs must be improved. The expansion of teacher abilities requires the on-site consultative services of a specialist-teacher who can function with humanistic concern for both children and teachers and who possesses the necessary knowledge and skills to facilitate positive change in the classroom through the realistic assessment of each child's needs and strengths and each teacher's capabilities and resources.

The Diagnostic/Prescriptive Teacher program was first developed in 1966-67 (Prouty & Prillaman, 1967) and, subsequently, it was implemented with success in some urban, suburban, and rural schools. DPT programs have functioned successfully at the elementary and intermediate (junior-high) school level in all socio-economic settings and in a variety of cultural environments. Prototype programs at the high-school level are being initiated in the 1972-73 academic year.

The organizational structure of a school (open classroom, self-contained, departmentalized, single-grade, multi-grade, ungraded, etc.) is not seen as a crucial variable in the success of the DPT. Clearly, what is significant is the degree to which the school's faculty accepts (or comes to accept) the worth of individualized instruction. DPTs are trained to anticipate a variety of organizational structures in schools and they soon learn, through experience in the training program, that the values held by the teachers and principal are of far more importance than the physical facilities or organizational structure of the school.

The training program for Diagnostic/Prescriptive Teachers is limited to experienced teachers and is a 36-semester-hour graduate sequence that leads to the MA degree. The core of the program is some 675 clock hours (15 semester hours) of intern and practicum experience in Diagnostic/Prescriptive Teaching. The student starts out under the direct supervision of a qualified DPT as an intern and finishes with a 15-week practicum as a full-time DPT solely responsible for an entire school.

Humanistic psychology and education theory are the bases of the program. In addition, the students study educational research and evaluation, specialized instructional techniques, and materials. The emphasis of the course work is on informal approaches to educational diagnosis, group process and change agent skills, personal growth techniques, and the Diagnostic/Prescriptive Teacher operational model.

The DPT model is highly specific. It provides the DPT with both the structure by which delivery of service is achieved and a clear role-definition aimed at the prevention of fragmentation or distortion of program goals. The DPT operational model follows:

1. Referral: The classroom teacher submits a written referral—a simple, one-page form—of the child seen as posing problems. An anecdotal description of the problem and a summary of the referring teacher's efforts to that point to adapt the program to the child, are required.
2. Observations: The DPT observes the referred child in his regular-class environment one or more times.
3. Referral Conference: The DPT confers with the referring teacher to update referral information, clarify their respective roles and responsibilities in the case, and arrange suitable times for the referred child to come to the DPT's room for diagnostic teaching.
4. Diagnostic Teaching: Informal, small-group work is conducted by the DTP with the referred child to determine successful teaching techniques and materials based on the child's needs and strengths.
5. Educational Prescription: A written educational report is prepared; it recommends well-defined techniques and materials to the referring teacher and describes in detail their use with the child.
6. Prescription Conference: Explanation and open discussion of the Prescription with the referring teacher result in modifications that are mutually agreeed upon and culminates in a schedule for demonstration by the DPT.
7. Demonstration: The DPT takes over the referring teacher's class to demonstrate elements of the Prescription in the total class environment.
8. Short-Term Follow-Up: The DPT makes periodic visits to the referring teacher's room to offer suggestions, provide encouragement, and give demonstrations as they are needed.

9. Evaluation: The referring teacher completes a single-page evaluation form 30 days after receiving the Prescription, indicating progress to date.
10. Long-Term Follow-Up: The DPT continues periodic checks with the referring teacher. Only when *both* DPT and referring teacher view the child's progress as satisfactory is the case closed.

In each of the 10 steps of the operational model, the DPT maintains appropriate records and logs. The school principal receives, as they are completed, a copy of the Referral, Prescription, and Referring Teacher's Evaluation; he also is kept informed of the status of all cases in the Long-Term Follow-Up.

Throughout the process, the DPT does not engage in remediation, tutoring, or counseling, except as it may occur coincidentally to the Diagnostic Teaching procedure. The referred child is not removed from his regular class for more than one hour per day, nor is final responsibility for his instruction or supervision ever removed from his regular-class teacher. The DPT has no supervisory or administrative responsibility for or authority over teachers; he shares fully in the nonteaching responsibilities of the school faculty and is paid according to the teacher salary schedule. The DPT is assigned a centrally located, well-equipped classroom within the school and he works with children and teachers throughout the day on an appointment or scheduled basis.

Concern for the possible stigmatization of children sent to the DPT room by appointment has led to three innovations by DPTs in the field which are calculated to counter such negative effects. First, DPTs tend to name their room the "Activity Room" or to allow children to select a name of their own choosing. Second, DPTs plan open times in their rooms (before school, after school, free periods) when any children may come in to talk, examine and play with the informal games and materials, or care for various pets kept within the room. Third, the DPTs arrange for periodic "referral" to the room of "ringers," that is, selected children who have a clear reputation for success and leadership within the school. In addition, DPTs find it relatively easy to respond openly to children's questions concerning their roles as their efforts are focused on the child's strengths and interests, rather than deficits. In practice, the DPT's room is sufficiently nonstigmatizing to be viewed by children as a reward for successful behavior or achievement.

Although the DPT seeks to assist the referring teacher in developing an individualized instructional program to meet the needs of the child within the regular classroom, full recognition is given to the possibility that some children cannot be adequately provided for in a particular classroom under a particular teacher. In such cases, the DPT, in consultation with the principal, may recommend the reassignment of the child to another class in the same or a different grade; in unusual cases, the DPT may confer with the director of special education on possible special-class placements.

One further role of the DPT should be noted. Frequently, it has been possible to return children from special education to regular classes. Such "phasing-in" must be done with care, on an individual basis, and with adequate follow-up service. The arbitrary return of numbers of children from special to regular classes by administrative decree without careful planning and preparation is not recommended in the DPT program in any case. The undesirable consequences of such actions become magnified as one moves up the age scale. In "phasing-in" procedures, the DPT depends upon referral from the special-class teacher. If the child is viewed as having good potential for successful placement in a regular class that is responsive to individual differences, the DPT identifies a regular-class teacher who is sensitive to the problem and then, with the referring special-class teacher, he develops a timetable and strategy for preparation and reassignment.

Often, the DPT will arrange for "ringers" from the regular class to be part of the group with which the referred child works, thus developing friendships to ease the transition. When deemed appropriate, the child is transferred from the special class to the selected regular class in the same school. If it is the child's home school, the process is completed with follow-up. However, a second transfer is often required as many special-class children are bussed out of their home schools to a special class elsewhere. In such cases, the child is placed in a regular class in his home school only after he has had a well-established period of success in his first regular class and the DPT in his home school has identified and prepared a regular class for his arrival.

For those who may be interested in such a "phasing-in" or "mainstreaming" process, the following outline* may be useful:
1. Special-class teacher identifies and refers child with good prognosis for regular-class placement.
2. DPT, following model, prepares the receiving regular-class teacher in same school.
3. Child enters regular class with DPT follow-up.
4. First DPT contacts the DPT in the child's home school, beginning preparation for return to the home school.
5. When success experiences are deemed sufficient, child is transferred from the regular class in his current school to a regular class in the home school.

---

*S. John David, Division Superintendent of Schools, Fairfax County, Va., first suggested this procedure which has proven to be successful.

6. Home-school DPT provides follow-up support.

A DPT's skills include the ability to (a) analyze correctly the behavior of adults and children: (b) utilize successfully informal teaching techniques and materials to diagnose children's needs and capabilities; (c) create realistic, well-organized, easily-understood educational prescriptions; (d) develop and maintain good rapport with teachers and principal; (e) work cooperatively with a range of other ancillary service specialists; and (f) engage in difficult and frustrating tasks over a long period of time with minimal external support or reinforcement.

Diagnostic/Prescriptive Teachers also need a strong sense of personal and professional commitment to the needs of children and they must possess unusual strength in self-direction to be successful. The role of a DPT is lonely, demanding, sometimes frightening, and with little recognition and a heavy work load. The redeeming feature of the role, for those who are successful, is that it provides a practical vehicle whereby the individual who is truly interested in effecting positive change in schools for both teachers and children may do so.

The criteria used in the evaluation of the program are explicit in the following questions asked in each school:
1. Is the DPT following completely and without variation the operational model?
2. Are all children now, with rare exception, functioning successfully in their regular classes?
3. To what degree and in what ways are regular-class teachers making changes in their teaching techniques, environments, and materials to accommodate individual needs?
4. How is the DPT influencing change?
5. What is the evaluation of the DPT program by the teachers? by the principal? by the DPT?
6. How successfully are children functioning who have been served by the DPT? Particularly, how well are they integrated socially within the class group and what is the nature of their learning behavior?

Summarily, the DPT's value is best judged by his capacity to facilitate positive change in regular-class environments and procedures with benefit to all children but with focus on those children who might otherwise be denied the opportunity for education with the majority of their peers.

Support for the DPT Program from school administrators and other professionals in the schools has been heartening. Requests from school principals for Diagnostic/Prescriptive Teachers in their schools has exceeded both local budgetary resources and the university training capacity in every year since the program's inception. Supervisors of special education, coordinators of services, school psychologists, visiting teachers, speech and hearing specialists, and reading consultants, as well as senior, central office, and administrative staff, have provided valuable and sensitive support for the development of DPT Programs.

The development of the program also has been supported strongly by parent organizations at crucial times. They have testified before board-of-education meetings, made direct contact with school-board members and provided information on programs at the local school level. Particularly interesting is the degree of positive interest that has been evidenced by parents whose children are not now and probably will never be categorized as "exceptional." The concern for broad, humanistic practices in special education that lead to the maximum integration of all children in a common educational environment seems widespread among both parents and educators.

The DPT Program, first implemented in schools in the metropolitan area of Washington, D.C., has since been successfully initiated in selected schools in South Carolina, West Virginia, both southeast and southwest Virginia, Georgia, and New York. Plans have been made for new DPT Programs to start in at least three additional northeast states during the 1972-73 academic year. Some programs continue to depend upon Federal support, others have both local and Federal funds, while still others are supported entirely by local and state resources.

More rapid expansion of DPT Programs is inhibited by two major factors: In some states, certification procedures have not kept pace with the rapidly evolving state-of-the-art in special education. As a result, traditional certification in psychomedical categories persist. In such environments, school districts are faced with the painful choice of following outmoded staffing and service models or risking the loss of state supplementary funds for special education.

The obvious dilemma at the state level is also clear. Contemporary special education roles and philosophy, eliminating as they must the clear line of demarcation between "regular" and "special" children, pose very real political and economic problems for state legislatures that have learned to think and act in a more traditional special education context. Some states have already moved to facilitate positive development in contemporary special education practices but others must depend upon responsible input from the profession in the political sphere before progress in certification standards can be expected. This area of concern applies, of course, to a wide range of innovations in special education and is by no means limited to the DPT Program.

A second factor that tends to inhibit more rapid DPT Program proliferation is the lack of qualified DPT graduates in sufficient numbers. At present, only three university training programs follow the

DPT Model.* The need for more rapid movement toward the development of innovative, noncategorical programs in special education has been recognized through increasing support at the Federal level. The need for training advanced graduate students in noncategorical special education, when met, should effect significant long-term changes in university training programs.

In the interim period, the use of Teacher Education Centers and Education Renewal Centers to provide specialized training of Diagnostic/Prescriptive Teachers is wholly feasible. A significant pool of trained and experienced Diagnostic/Prescriptive Teachers now exists, many with advanced graduate education and successful experience in teacher training. Although DPTs are hardly in abundant supply, a strong nucleus of thoroughly competent specialists in DPT are not presently employed in DPT training.

A word of caution seems very much in order here, however. There are, at present, a number of sound, carefully developed school consultant models in special education. If serious, totally unproductive, jurisdictional, and ego-oriented disputes are to be avoided, it is essential that the profession take the time to start an open exchange of experiences and knowledge that will lead to the development of some common principles of program design. Such investment *now* can lead to the development of optimal educational practices for all children, which is clearly what we are all about. The U.S. Office of Education has provided valuable leadership in this area but more must be accomplished if the job is to be done.

The process by which a conceptual model is translated into field operations is seldom free of difficulty. When the conceptual model has as one of its goals the introduction of change in long-standing policies and practices of public education, the difficulties become a virtual certainty. The DPT Program has been no exception.

The appearance of a new professional role in the public schools has the potential of introducing disequilibrium within the system, with consequent anxiety and hostility among those already occupying the structure. DPT Programs have had this effect in certain instances, although to a far less degree than had been anticipated. Obviously, the initiation of an innovative program has the greatest chance of success in places where the climate is most supportive of change. In the DPT Program, at least, we have found that the support of the school principal is extremely important for and, in most cases, vital to the success of the DPT in his school. We have learned that a conference between the principal and the DPT should precede

---

*The George Washington University, College of William and Mary, The Citadel.

the placement of a program in that school, with either party having the option of declining the placement.

Another concern, the jurisdictional conflict arising out of the introduction of a new professional role in the schools, is most rationally dealt with through open discussion and with the clear definition of goals, roles, and responsibilities. The success of this strategy depends to a significant degree upon the philosophical set of the other specialists who are involved. To the degree that they see themselves as consultants to teachers in order to facilitate modifications in classroom environments, the likelihood of dispute is minimized; and such has been our most frequent experience.

A third area that must be considered is the reaction of regular-class teachers, which has been found to vary. If the DPT functions with equal concern for the human needs of the teachers as well as the children, and is competent in providing practical assistance through educational diagnosis, recommendations, classroom demonstrations, and follow-up, and if the program is clearly understood by the faculty, our experience has shown that the great majority of teachers will accept and, indeed, welcome DPT service.

The role of a DPT is demanding and difficult. The turnover rate among DPTs is not now a major concern but extensive interviews with DPTs as well as numerous informal interactions, leaves no doubt that a majority feel themselves to be isolated and generally denied adequate psychological support in their work. Two approaches to dealing with this very real problem are first, the initiation of planned, frequent DPT inservice meetings within the school systems and second, the establishment at relatively frequent intervals of a postgraduate seminar for practicing DPTs. In time, it is hoped, the rapidly growing number of school consultants in special education will be reflected in regional and national professional organizations with all of the resultant opportunities for communication and interaction. This widespread concern has clear implications for the training of DPTs.

Traditional, categorical special education has long enjoyed a strong and vocal constituency among parents in support of its programs. The development of new models of service in special education requires continuing communication with that constituency if intelligent and effective support is to continue. In our experience, principals and other school administrators have been extremely effective in communicating with parent organizations. This responsibility must be met if school boards and school administrators are to provide resources necessary for innovative programs.

The development of an innovative training program requires a university environment that is open to change and accepting of evolution in design, because the design may move ahead of local or even national practices at a given time. Not only a courageous department chairman and helpful colleagues are needed but also students who have a strong desire to participate in and contribute to positive change in American education. At The George Washington University we have been blessed with all of these, as well as with many intelligent, creative colleagues in the schools our DPTs serve. The first priority for anyone considering major departure from traditional practices should be to ensure that he has a working base within which change, with all its trials, is accepted and respected.

Reference

Prouty, R. & Prillaman, D. Diagnostic teaching: A modest proposal. *Elementary School Journal*, 1970, 70, 265-70.

The following partial bibliography has been useful in providing our students and interested colleagues in the schools with the backgrounds of some of the issues in special education today:

Brabner, G. The myth of mental retardation. *Training School Bulletin*, 1967, 63, 149-152.

Christoplos, R., & Renz, P. A critical examination of special education programs. *J. Special Education*, 1969, 3, 371-378, 409-410.

Cronin, R. E. (Paper Delivered at Miami CEC) Special education for the seventies and beyond: A redefinition, April 20, 1970.

Deno, E. Special education as developmental capital. *Exceptional Children*, November 1970, 229-236.

Dunn, L. Special education for the mildly retarded—is much of it justified? *Exceptional Children*, 1968, 35, 5-24.

Engel, M. The tin drum revisited. *J. Special Education*, 1969, 3, 381-384.

Falcone, J. F. The diagnostic classroom. *Catholic Educational Review*, 1969, 67, 139-144.

Harshman, H. Toward a differential treatment of curriculum. *J. Special Education*, 1969, 3, 385-387.

Harvey, J. To fix or to cope: A dilemma for special education. *J. Special Edution*, 1969, 3, 389-392.

Johnson, J. L. Special education for the inner city: A challenge for the future or another means for cooling the mark out? *J. Special Education*, 3, 241-251.

Kauppi, D. The emperor has no clothes: Comments on Christoplos and Renz. *J. Special Education*, 1969, 3, 393-396.

Lilly, M. S. Special education: A teapot in a tempest. *Exceptional Children*, 1970, 37, 43-49.

_____ A training based model for special education. *Exceptional Children*, Summer 1971, 745-749.

Miller, J., & Schoenfelder, D. A rational look at special class placement. *J. of Special Education*, 1969, 3, 397-403.

Newsletter: "Principals Evaluate DPT Program," Oct. 1, 1971, 2:1. DPT Program, Charleston, S.C. Schools.

_____ "National Conference on Diagnostic/Prescriptive Teaching," Feb. 1, 1971, 1:2, DPT Program, Charleston, S.C. Schools.

_____ "Dr. Ronald A. McWhirt Asst. Superintendent for Special Services, explains how Diagnostic Teaching Developed in Charleston," Nov. 1, 1970, 1:1. DPT Program, Charleston, S.C. Schools.

Nelson, C., & Schmidt, L. The question of the efficacy of special classes. *Exceptional Children*, Jan. 1971, 381-384.

Prouty, R., & Prillaman, D. Educational diagnosis: In clinic or classroom? *Virginia J. of Education*, November 1967.

Reger, R. The questionable role of specialists in special education. *J. Special Education*, 1966, 1, 53-59.

Rhodes, W. Presidential Address, Toronto 1966. *Council for Children with Behavioral Disorders*, 1966, 4, 1-8.

Trippe, M. Educational therapy. *Educational Therapy*, 1966, 1, Special Child Publications, 29-50.

Valletutti, P. Integration vs. segregation: A useless dialectic. *J. Special Education*, 1969, 3, 405-408.

Inquiries about the Diagnostic/Prescriptive Teacher Program are welcomed. Training materials including course outlines, bibliographies, film lists, unpublished handbooks and papers, and so forth, will be sent on request. The preparation of a DPT Program multimedia training package will be completed in June 1973 and will be available on a loan basis at that time.

The University of Connecticut's Classroom Specialist Model

One of the papers adding fuel to special education's soul-searching was a 1970 article by Stephen Lilly entitled "Special Education: A Teapot in a Tempest." In this and other statements, he contends that responsibility for the instruction of the handicapped should be clearly placed with the regular-class teacher with little or no "out" provided by segregated placement possibilities. Dr. Lilly maintains that once an alternative is present, children will be perceived to need it, pressure to use the alternative will develop, and it will be used. He believes that the regular-class teacher becomes more open to inservice learning when a responsibility is irreducibly his or hers, and he proposed a training-based model for special education (Lilly, 1971).

A program for training personnel to help regular-class teachers develop the skills needed to work from such a premise had been developed at the University of Oregon by Stan and Wilma Shaw. Dr. Lilly's observations of this program and interactions with the Shaws while the three of them were on the University of Oregon staff contributed to his conceptualization of what he calls the "Zero Reject Model." All three have moved into other positions but they continue to test the potentialities of the "Zero Reject" assumption. Others are also testing similar service conceptions.

The Shaw paper was published in its original version in the October, 1972, issue of the Journal of Special Education (*Vol. 6, No. 2*). The paper, included here by special arrangement with the authors and publishers, suggests the implications of taking the Lilly position seriously.

Further commentary on Dr. Lilly's proposition is provided by Dr.'s Phillip and Carol Cartwright of the EPDA-Special Education project at Pennsylvania State University in a paper titled, "Gilding the Lilly: Comments on the Training Based Model for Special Education." This article, which appeared in the November 1972 issue of Exceptional Children in a slightly different version, describes some of the specific components for a training-based model that has been developed in the Penn State approach.

References

Lilly, M. S. A training based model for special education. *Exceptional Children*, 1971, 37, 745-749.

_____ Special education: A teapot in a tempest. *Exceptional Children*, 1970, 37, 43-49.

The Inservice Experience Plan: Changing the Bath Without Losing the Baby

Stan F. Shaw
Assistant Professor, School of Education
University of Connecticut

and

Wilma Shaw
Former Instructor, Special Education
University of Oregon

As educators become increasingly more aware of the learning needs of children, the range of individual learning differences within the regular classroom becomes more and more apparent. Changes in school organization and curricula, the development of a more advanced teaching technology, provision for more adequate preschool education—all are directed toward dealing with individual learning needs.

Education is experiencing a revolution, yet eight million elementary- and secondary-school children in America today will not learn to read adequately. One child in seven is limited in his ability to acquire essential reading skills. Within the American educational system, an estimated 15 percent of otherwise capable students experience difficulty in learning to read (Reading Disorders, 1969). "This difficulty is of sufficient severity to impair seriously the overall learning experience of these students and their ultimate usefulness and adaptability to a modern society" (Reading Disorders, 1969, p. 8).

A recent report of the Western Interstate Commission for Higher Education (Special Education, 1970) stated that of the more than one million children in the West who need special-education services, 625,000 receive no help with their learning difficulties. No longer do we doubt that mildly handicapped children—those experiencing significant learning difficulty—are currently enrolled in regular elementary classes (Dunn, 1963; Geer, 1969).

How does this information affect the goals of special educators? More specifically, what are the various alternatives by which educators may serve those children who are experiencing learning difficulty and who are not now being served? And which of these alternatives has the highest probability of minimizing—indeed, preventing—the high incidence of learning failure among children who experience learning problems?

The current alternatives—special-class settings, remedial services, resource facilities, diagnostic-prescriptive services or a combination of any of these—share two operational characteristics that make it improbable that they will prevent learning failure. First, each removes the mildly handicapped child from the regular classroom for all or part of the school day; thus the classroom teacher is encouraged to relinquish direct responsibility for the child's learning in the problem area and to become dependent on the personnel providing the special services to the child. Second, the major objective of each is direct service to the child, an emphasis that does not encourage change in the classroom teacher's teaching behaviors and, again, fosters dependence on special-service personnel. In addition to these limitations, educators are confronted with significant evidence that the alternatives have not been effective in assisting children who are experiencing learning difficulties (Schiffman, 1964). The current literature indicates that correction strategies to remedy specific learning problems appear to follow not the medical "restoration to normalcy" model but, rather, a "continued support" model (Bateman, 1966).

It is imperative that special and general educators now find the means to teach effectively the mildly handicapped child in the regular classroom setting where the classroom teacher can have the direct responsibility for each child's instructional program. A strategy that realizes the prevention of learning difficulty and the correction of previous problems in the regular classroom is needed.

An example of the strategy is computer-assisted instruction which has been demonstrated in programs such as Project Plan (Weisberger & Rahmlow, 1968) and Individually Prescribed Instruction (Bolvin & Glaser, 1968). However, these programs are impractical for the average school district because they are very expensive and, even if a district elected to pay the price, the services could not be made available for every child on an immediate basis as needed.

Computer-assisted instruction is similar to the alternatives discussed earlier in its assumption that the classroom teacher cannot adequately meet the basic educational demands of every child in his classroom. Through our services to children, we special educators have accepted this assumption. Perhaps of more importance, we have induced the classroom teacher to depend on supporting services. Although current evidence indicates that the classroom teacher may not be responding adequately to the basic educational demands of every child, no evidence indicates that he cannot become self-sufficient in teaching the basic skills.

Consider, then, another strategy: that of enabling the classroom teacher to become relatively self-sufficient, competent to teach and direct in the basic skills areas all children in his charge, even those who are experiencing learning difficulties—the mildly handicapped.

Implementing a New Strategy

One fundamental requirement of any plan designed to implement the strategy of making classroom teachers relatively self-sufficient is that tactics developed should be consistent with the terminal objective. Hence, any type of child-centered supporting service (instructional or behavioral) in the basic academic skills cannot be included, nor can any teacher-centered supporting service that is not consistent with the objective of self-sufficiency. Having fulfilled this first requirement, another strategy consideration naturally emerges: If teachers are deprived of such supporting services and cannot meet the basic skills demands of pupils, then tactics must be developed to enable them to do so.

Such a series of tactics, an inservice experience plan, is outlined here. Unlike those remedial, resource, or diagnostic-prescriptive services that are child-centered, this plan is teacher-centered. It focuses on those aspects of the teacher's classroom program that he perceives as inadequate. In contrast to a diagnostic-prescriptive service in which an individualized instructional plan is developed for a pupil and then transmitted to the classroom teacher for implementation, the inservice experience plan enables the classroom teacher actually to experience the diagnostic-prescriptive process, and to learn and transfer the skills required in that process. Therefore, the implementation of a child's learning plan in the classroom is probable because it has been developed "on the scene" by the classroom teacher.

Administrative arrangement

Inservice experience is initiated by an administrative arrangement for participating schools. All special services, exclusive of speech therapy, are terminated, and provisions for special-class referral and placement are discontinued. The inservice experience plan does not in any way affect those special classes already established but, as a preventive strategy, it seeks to preclude future referrals from the regular system. This arrangement induces the school administration to accept full responsibility for the education of every child in the regular classroom. Under these conditions teachers should have the option of participation or transfer. Thus, most teachers who choose to participate elect to support this arrangement and its assumptions.

The role of the classroom specialist

Having established the opportunity for self-sufficiency, the process of inservice experience begins. The primary agent in the process is a classroom specialist; his major function is to arrange inservice learning experiences for classroom teachers in the building. The shared objective of the classroom teacher and specialist is the successful modification of any classroom problem-situation referred by the teacher. The modification plan developed by the two must satisfy the condition that it be an "in the classroom" strategy that is implemented by the classroom teacher. At no time does the classroom specialist work directly with a child, unless it is to demonstrate a technique or the use of a material for the classroom teacher. An underlying assumption of the inservice experience plan is that no child in the regular classroom need fail if he has been taught adequately. Also, the plan assumes that no teacher need fail if he has experienced adequate inservice learning, whether independent of or through a program such as the one described subsequently.

Competencies of the classroom specialist

The role of the classroom specialist requires both a high degree of professional competence and interpersonal skill. Problem situations referred by classroom teachers usually require the specialist to be competent in the areas of diagnosis and evaluation, instructional techniques, classroom organization and arrangements, and behavior management. He should also be knowledgeable in curricula materials, practice, and independent learning activities. Experience in relating to and communicating with peer-professionals should be another of his competencies. He should demonstrate confidence in classroom-teacher ability and in the concept of teacher self-sufficiency. While he must consistently communicate and represent the criteria for acceptable performance, he must also realize that various levels of performance are to be expected; thus he accepts and makes provision for them as approximations of his standard. Without this realistic attitude, the classroom specialist cannot be a flexible and effective teacher trainer.

Persons demonstrating these competencies are already available. Many are currently employed as special- or regular-classroom teachers. In addition, numerous university programs are developing inservice or graduate training models that emphasize these very competencies (McKenzie, Egner, Knight, Perelman, Schneider, & Garvin, 1970). The combination of professional competence and interpersonal skill should characterize the classroom specialist.

The Inservice Experience Process

The role of the classroom specialist is to arrange inservice learning experience for teachers who have referred a problem situation. Upon referral the classroom teacher and specialist work together to pinpoint or identify the pertinent elements of the problem situation. In the area of diagnosis, for example, the teacher and specialist together may investigate the decoding-skills sequence in beginning reading as a prelude to considering ways of measuring performance in them. If behavior management is the problem situation area, the classroom specialist may suggest some observation guidelines to assist the teacher in pinpointing the problem. In the area of classroom organization, the specialist may provide some criteria to be considered in math grouping and to help the teacher define his objectives for each participating child. The process of pinpointing should be one of teacher definition: specifying the characteristics of the problem and, in so doing, learning which questions to ask and what information to use in formulating the questions on pinpointing. Throughout this process, the classroom specialist's role is determined by the stated needs of the teacher. In some instances, he may actually participate in the pinpointing process but, in others, he may suggest only some pinpointing strategies to be tried.

Once the characteristics of the problem situation are identified, the teacher and specialist investigate and evaluate a number of alternative strategies that may be used to modify the problem situation. Tactics are then developed according to the teacher's stated goals. Once again, the role of the classroom specialist varies according to the stated needs of each teacher. In almost all situations, however, a function of the classroom specialist is to obtain for the teacher pertinent information on the effectiveness of the strategies being considered and materials that may be used to implement the strategies. The teacher may then become better informed about the advantages and disadvantages of the various alternatives, and he will be better equipped to choose the strategy that will provide success for himself as well as for his students. Another important outcome of this process step is to develop in teachers awareness of research information and its use in classroom practice.

Having determined a strategy and developed tactics to modify the problem situation, a teacher is now ready to implement his plan. The classroom specialist serves in several capacities during this phase, demonstrating the use of materials or modeling an instructional technique that the teacher wishes to learn. Regardless of these and other functions, a primary role of the classroom specialist at this point is to encourage and assist the teacher in evaluating the effectiveness of his plan. Is it successfully modifying the problem situation? How is it affecting student performance?

A number of evaluation methods may be considered by the teacher and specialist. The classroom specialist can be of further assistance in providing the necessary equipment and materials to be used in the evaluation. This stage of inservice experience is, perhaps, the most crucial step in teacher learning because without evaluating his tactics in terms of student performance, a teacher cannot determine the effectiveness of his decisions and implementation skills. The evaluation tools that he selects, therefore, should provide him with information on the elements of his plan that are working effectively and those that are not. Without some measures of effectiveness, the entire inservice experience could be wasted. The role of the classroom specialist should be to encourage such evaluation, as well as to assist in the analysis of the data and in the subsequent modification of tactics, if it is necessary.

This process of classroom adviser-teacher interaction is the full cycle of a problem-situation referral. Certain steps within that process may be eliminated according to teachers' stated needs; inservice experience can be provided only in those areas for which teachers request it. Whereas one teacher may refer a problem situation at the first stage (pinpointing), another may successfully specify the characteristics of the problem but still need information and inservice experience on the strategies and tactics to use. Another staff member may request experience in pinpointing, proceed with the next stages independently, and then request inservice experience in the evaluation segment.

One basic characteristic of the inservice strategy is the gradual progression toward self-sufficiency; the classroom teacher determines the areas in which the classroom specialist and inservice experience may be useful to him.

Teachers' stated needs should also determine the classroom specialist's schedule. In some instances, he or she may be devoting 15 minutes daily to one problem situation and three hours weekly to another. If a teacher should request extensive inservice experience in classroom organization and arrangement through a problem-situation referral, the classroom specialist may spend two or three mornings in that classroom to demonstrate and model learning routines and organization patterns.

The classroom specialist should also evaluate referrals in order to identify similar inservice experience needs and then to provide group experience or training opportunities whenever possible. Such sessions would function as opportunities for in-staff sharing of competence as well. The classroom specialist might further develop such constructive communication by providing information to staff members on problem situations, strategies tried, and subsequent student performance results. The primary function of the classroom specialist, however, should be focussed on the problem-situation referral process. By arranging for and participating in inservice learning experiences, the classroom specialist is an agent in the teacher's progression toward self-sufficiency in the basic skills.

Opening Tactics

Although teachers are induced to refer problem situations when special services are terminated by administrative arrangement, they may not necessarily believe in the classroom specialist and the program. Acceptance can be gained, however, by a demonstration of the immediate usefulness of inservice experience. Teachers could be asked, prior to school opening, to submit one problem statement or question relating to their first day (or week) of classes. Questions might be limited to classroom organization and arrangement, informal diagnostic procedures, screening techniques, or any other area that seems to pose a problem during the first week of school. The classroom specialist would then suggest a number of ways to deal with the problem effectively, with the condition that each teacher submitting a problem situation try one of the specialist's suggestions and then share the results with him. Such a strategy, providing it is adequately structured and the question areas are well defined, could provide immediate assistance to a teacher at a time when it is needed by most, and initiate a working relationship with the classroom specialist.

In addition, the role of the classroom specialist and the process of inservice experience should be adequately understood by all staff members. Although this understanding will develop as inservice experience is demonstrated throughout a school building, clear and ample communication on objectives and process should be in effect before school begins.

Conclusion

The inservice experience plan is a strategy aimed toward the improvement of services to mildly handicapped children in the regular classroom. If it is successful, the benefits are not limited to such children alone but are evident throughout the entire range of individual learning differences. Like all other strategies, however, the inservice experience plan is of little value unless it is tried and evaluated. The basic criterion for evaluation should be student performance. Although such data will indirectly measure teacher performance, other criteria for measuring change in teaching behavior may also be used (Brophy & Good, 1969a, 1969b). Some advantages of the strategy already have been cited. The ultimate success of the inservice experience plan, however, depends on three basic assumptions: (a) a teacher can change his teaching behavior; (b) he can become self-sufficient in teaching the basic skills; and (c) he wants to be competent in these areas. If these assumptions are not valid, the inservice experience plan is not a valid strategy. If, however, such assumptions are acceptable, then educators may finally realize a self-fulfilling prophecy of success.

References

Bateman, B. D. Learning disorders. *Review of Educational Research*, 1966, 36, 93-119.

Bolvin, J. O., & Glaser, R. Developmental aspects of individually prescribed instruction. *Audiovisual Instruction*, 1968, 13, 828-831.

Brophy, J. E., & Good, T. L. *Teacher's communication of differential expectations for children's classroom performance: Some behavioral data.* Report Series No. 25, Research and Development Center for Teacher Education, University of Texas, Austin, 1969. (a)

Brophy, J. E., & Good, T. L. *Teacher-child dyadic interaction: A manual for coding classroom behavior.* Report Series No. 27, Research and Development Center for Teacher Education, University of Texas, Austin, 1969. (b)

Dunn, L. M. (Ed.) *Exceptional children in the schools.* N.Y.: Holt, Rinehart & Winston, 1963.

Geer, W. C. Testimony. Hearings before the General Subcommittee on Education, Committee on Education, Committee on Education and Labor. Washington, D.C.: USGPO, 1969.

McKenzie, H. S., Egner, A. N., Knight, M. F., Perelman, P. F., Schneider, B. M., & Garvin, J. S. Training consulting teachers to assist elementary teachers in management and education of handicapped children. *Exceptional Children*, 1970, 37, 137-143.

Reading disorders in the United States. Report of the Secretary's National Advisory Committee on Dyslexia and Related Reading Disorders. Washington, D.C.: U.S. Department of Health, Education, and Welfare, 1969.

Schiffman, G. Early identification of reading disabilities: The responsibility of the public school. *Bulletin of the Orton Society*, 1964, 14, 42-44.

Special education for the general educator. Boulder, Col.: Western Interstate Commission for Higher Education, 1970.

Weisberger, R. A., & Rahmlow, H. F. Individually managed learning. *Audiovisual Instruction.* 1968, 13, 835-839.

Section II

Resource Teacher Programs

Much of the current concern about how special education service is rendered and which children should receive it stems from what many educators regard as the unfair segregation of disadvantaged students into special classes for the educable mentally retarded on the basis of test scores that may be questionable evidence of actual learning ability. Statistics quoted in the 1968 report of the President's Committee on Retardation led many educators to conclude, as Wilton Anderson (1971) did, that "special education has been aimed at children more often short-changed by society than by nature" (p. 7).

Some cries of alarm from special educators were even stronger. Lloyd Dunn expressed the sense of urgency felt by some of the persons who are close enough to the problem to sense its seriousness.

> The prices for our past practices have been too high for handicapped children. Our children are being stigmatized with disability levels. Our children are not getting the needed stimulation and challenge provided by being with more able students. Our children are not being expected to achieve at a high enough level (perhaps they should all be taught as though they had IQ scores above 120). I feel so strongly about the wrong we are perpetuating that, know what I'd do, if I were a blue-collar worker from the slums, and especially if I were an Afro- or Mexican-American (or of some other non-Anglo-Saxon middle class background), and the schools wanted to label my child educable mentally retarded (or some such disability label) and place him in a self-contained special class—I would go to court to prevent the schools from doing so. I say this because I want you to know how deeply and sincerely I feel that the child with a mild to moderate handicap has been exploited. I feel this—as a special educator, and as a citizen concerned about equal rights and equal education opportunity for all children (Dunn, 1967).

The Judge Skelly Wright decision (1967), which triggered the abolition of the track system in District of Columbia schools, was based on the judgment that such tracking was "discriminatory toward the racially and/or economically disadvantaged, and therefore in violation of the fifth amendment of the Constitution of the United States." Subsequent litigations support the need to find services that do not further disadvantage the already disadvantaged. As a result, education agencies have intensified their search for alternative ways of serving all children.

Many programs have been initiated to maintain handicapped children in regular classes through resource teacher support. Resource teachers are not a new phenomenon in educational practice. Curriculum specialists who provide help to regular teachers in basic skill or content areas, such as reading, math, art, music, or physical education, have often been called "resource teachers," "consultants," or "helping teachers." They have been used in special education programs for many years.

When special education resource teachers move about to serve several buildings, they usually have been called itinerant teachers. Sometimes they conducted resource room service for a particular type of handicapped child, and the children needing their kind of help were transported to their stations for the service. But the practice meant that children were removed from their neighborhood peer groups and resulted, sometimes, in less than optimal integration conditions because a disproportionate number of handicapped children were assigned to one building.

Special educators, now, are systematically testing three propositions to eliminate the earlier discriminatory patterns of service.

1. *Building-based service:* A special education resource teacher (or more than one) who is a staff member in a school building may relieve some of the service delivery problems that occur when a variety of categorical specialists interrupt schedules, are not around when problems arise, or transport children out of their home schools. To facilitate this resident specialist approach, people are testing the validity of the following proposition:

2. *A general, special education, resource teacher.* When a resource teacher serves only one category of child, too few of such children may be in a building to justify the specialist's continuous presence. However, if the resource teacher possesses certain basic competencies, he/she may be able to teach effectively a wide range of handicapped children in the school they would normally attend and thus ease some of the scheduling, monitoring, and transportation-related separation problems noted in the first proposition.

3. *Indirect service:* If a teacher possesses broadly applicable generic competencies, he/she may be able to make a beneficial impact on more children by working indirectly—helping the child's regular teacher, parents, classroom aides, peers, or others to carry out a more effective plan—rather than directly with the children themselves. In the latter case, impact is limited by the specialist's available time; also, the possibility of influencing institutional practices is lowered.

A recent paper by Jenkins (1972) provides a good analysis of the features that are being combined in different ways in designs of resource systems. The article also provides some data on the relative effectiveness of various pupil-teacher ratios in working with handicapped children.

Because of the variety of ways in which resource teachers may work and the variable range of their potential impact on the overall structure of related service delivery systems, it is difficult to make a neat distinction between the kinds of functionaries described in Section I and the "resource teacher" programs described in this section. These reports have been separated simply because the authors term them "resource teacher" programs and there is much national interest these days in serving handicapped children through resource systems as an alternative to separate special classes.

Another project testing the feasibility of training and using a general (cross-categorical) special education resource teacher is at Florida State University (Tallahassee), under Dr. Louis Schwartz. This BEH-funded special project is not described in this monograph but details of it are available in the following references.

References

Anderson, Wilton. Who gets a "special education." In Reynolds, M. C. & Davis, M. D. *Exceptional children in regular classrooms.* Leadership Training Institute, University of Minnesota, Minneapolis, Minnesota, 1971.

Dunn, L. M. Is much of special education (as we have known it) obsolete? Ray Graham Memorial Address delivered at the Eighteenth Annual Convention of the Illinois Council for Exceptional Children. Chicago, October, 1967.

Jenkins, J. Dimensions and attributes of resource systems serving handicapped learners. Southwest Regional Resource Laboratory, New Mexico State University, Las Cruces, New Mexico. Unpublished working paper, 1972.

Schwartz, L. A clinical teacher model for interrelated areas of special education. In Innovative non-categorical and interrelated projects in the education of the handicapped. Proceedings of a Special Study Institute, Florida State University Department of Habilitative Sciences, Tallahassee, Florida, 1972.

Schwartz, L. A clinical teacher model for interrelated areas of special education. *Exceptional Children*, 1971, 37, 565-571.

Schwartz, L. An integrated teacher education program for special education—a new approach. *Exceptional Children*, 1967, 33, 411-416. (a)

Schwartz, L. Preparation of the clinical teacher for special education: 1866-1966. *Exceptional Children*, 1967, 34, 117-124. (b)

Schwartz, L., & Oseroff, A. Clinical teacher competencies for special education: An individualized performance-based teacher-education curriculum. Florida State University, Tallahassee, Florida, 1972.

University of Washington: Precision Teaching Methods in Regular Elementary and Secondary Classrooms

Haring and his associates at the University of Washington, focussing on developing classroom applications of behavior analysis principles, have facilitated the incorporation of precision teaching practices into special education programs. Although they were highly controversial initially, and are still so to some degree, behavior analysis approaches have been judged by special educators currently to be one of the most significant developments in recent special education history (Jordan & MacDonald, 1971).

The persistent demand of behaviorally oriented workers—"show me your data"—challenged mental health workers and special educators to document their ability to deliver whatever benefits they claimed for the methods they advocated. The effect of the challenge from professional peers, along with rising public demand to show benefits received for dollars invested, has had a profound effect on both the thinking and practice in service fields.

University of Washington workers have been faithful to their own principles in their practices. Consequently, the reports presented here describe the practices and provide data on the outcomes of their use.

BEH funds supported the categorical training programs in special education at the University of Washington as well as the training programs for non-categorical resource teachers. EPDA Special Education funds helped to support the inservice training for regular teachers reported here.

Quite logically, we think, most programs aimed at minimizing the need to separate handicapped children from the educational mainstream have focussed their experimentation at the elementary level. Haring's initial work was in this area. He and Miller, however, trained regular secondary teachers in precision teaching methods and they found the results to be highly gratifying for both children served and other school staff.

Reference

Jordan, June B., & MacDonald, Phyllis. *Dimensions: Annual survey of exceptional child research activities and issues,* 1970. Information Center on Exceptional Children, 1971.

Improved Learning Conditions for Handicapped Children in Regular Classrooms

Norris G. Haring
Director, Experimental Education Unit
Child Development and Mental Retardation Center
University of Washington

The importance of keeping moderately handicapped children in regular classrooms wherever possible is becoming more and more evident. Often, these children have such highly individualized learning problems that the teacher may be required to pinpoint a problem and to select or develop appropriate instructional materials for its remediation. At the same time, the teacher needs to handle the behavior problems that often accompany learning deficiencies. The ordinary classroom teachers, ideally, are able to handle these problems and to manage the regular instructional programs of the classroom as well. The fact that they have often found it difficult to do so is shown by the rise of special education as a discipline and the impetus to place problem students in special classes. Unfortunately such classes have not always been an ideal solution to the children's problems. However, asking teachers to retain these pupils in their regular classrooms places an intolerable burden on them, unless they receive some special help. Resource teachers can provide the needed assistance.

The resource teacher can be seen as an itinerant special assistant to teachers who have students with "exotic" problems. An analogy might be drawn between the resource teacher and the medical specialist: Both are trained as experts in particular areas and each works with a generalist—teacher or practitioner—to provide a program of total care for the population they serve. Until such time as we can make specialists of all teachers, that is, provide all teachers with the skills to cope with the widest range of educational problems, the resource teacher is a necessary and economical interim solution to a serious problem.

The resource teacher benefits the financially pressed education system by eliminating the need for certain self-contained special education classes; at the same time, he spares the mildly handicapped student the added stigma and disruption of removal from his regular class for special placement. Over half the children with special learning or behavior problems are classified as functionally mentally retarded. In about three-fourths of this population, the mental retarda-

---

This project was supported in part by funds from the Bureau of Educational Personnel Development, U.S. Office of Education, Department of Health, Education, and Welfare, Grant No. OEG-0-9-577001-3580(725).

tion is the result of socio-environmental influences. The children in this group are mildly retarded and they are very capable of acquring basic academic skills and making adequate social adjustments, if the community setting is appropriate. But, how appropriate a community setting is a special class? The opportunities for intellctual stimulation are diminished when the only model of elevated functioning is the teacher. If indeed, the children's retardation occurs because of deprived environments, then the replication of that deprivation in their official learning situations compounds the problem.

The problem itself may become more critical if, as states begin to implement legislation to provide education for all children—including those with all degrees of handicap—special classes are forced to accommodate the more seriously handicapped children, because then regular classes will be pressured into finding room for the borderline children whom the special classes can no longer serve.

Another source of pressure is the rising call for accountability. More and more pressure is being applied to teachers to produce demonstrable gains in their classes. Yet teachers who lack the means to meet these demands, for whatever reasons, cannot be abandoned to failure. If the teacher's professional training has not already equipped him with the requisite skills, the profession has an obligation to train or assist him to meet these increased expectations.

> The teacher should be made to realize that others on the team are prepared to help him if he is having difficulties in managing the behavior problems and academic deficits of his students. . . .
>
> Accountability should involve a team approach in which *all* members, and not merely the teacher alone, are responsible. Otherwise, each problem escalates, creating a more complicated problem in which parents, administrators, and teachers have only extra work to do instead of relieving one another of aspects of the burden. In other words, given the fact that there are problems, a mature approach would emphasize solving the problem cooperatively rather than giving red marks for failure to those who are beset by difficulties (Hayden & Haring, 1972, pp. 436-437).

According to recent statistics (Martin, 1972), the number of teachers trained in special education is woefully inadequate. Many of those now functioning in special education classes are not even certified specialists. Once again, trained resource teachers can provide necessary assistance to such teachers. They can work directly with children who have learning problems and, at the same time, train regular-classroom teachers to use the skills they have acquired.

EEU Training Project

The project discussed here was conducted in one rural, one suburban, and one urban school under the direction of the Experimental Education Unit (EEU), Child Development and Mental Retardation

Center, University of Washington. Its purpose was to train regular-classroom teachers as special education resource teachers who would return to natural school settings and be able not only to manage the academic and social behavior problems of moderately handicapped children, but to act as resource teachers to the regular-classroom teachers as well. Thus, by providing regular teachers with special assistance, school districts might be able to maintain students with less profound degrees of retardation or emotional disturbance in regular classrooms.

Three school districts—Monroe, Clover Park, and Seattle (Asa Mercer Junior High School)—referred teachers for training in the program. At Monroe, the rural district, the training phase concentrated on team teaching for mentally retarded elementary- and middle-school children. When the teachers returned to the classroom, they worked with mentally retarded children and with children who had academic and behavior problems. At Asa Mercer Junior High, the urban school, disadvantaged minority students had serious behavior problems that were manifested by their dropout or suspension status. Clover Park is a suburban school district; its five elementary schools were served by two generations of trainees in this program.

In the first year, a total of five teachers were trained for the Clover Park District, four teachers were trained for the Monroe District, and two were trained for the Seattle District. In the project's second year, six new trainees were concentrated at Clover Park and at the Experimental Education Unit. In addition, two teacher aides were trained at Monroe and one at the Experimental Education Unit. The continuation of the project is now underway at a junior high school in suburban Mercer Island, where teacher aides are being trained.

Rationale for Training Sequence

In order for a teacher to know that he has transmitted a skill, a student must demonstrate that skill—he must act, do, perform. Learning by doing is the governing principle that we adhered to in designing our training program for resource teachers. Just as driving a car requires more than learning the contents of a driver's manual and knowing the rules of the road, so being able to face a classroom of children and having the skill to help any one of them requires more than text books or courses; it requires supervised practicum experience.

Our training program builds on the usual student-teaching experience in several ways. On the basis of previous experience, the program staff agreed on certain terminal objectives for each trainee: the acquisition of skills in setting behavioral objectives, taking continuous performance measurements, applying reinforcement principles to manage behavior, individualizing instruction, and programmed teaching. These clearly defined terminal objectives permitted an easy evaluation of the program's success at the end; they were also useful for formative evaluation, enabling the trainees and the trainer to know at any time how far the trainees had progressed toward acquiring the specified skills. Further, the trainer could alter the program to assist the student in difficulty. The meaning of an individualized program is that it changes to meet the needs of the student as he progresses through it. A prerequisite for that alteration is a knowledge of what needs to be changed. The following discussion of the training program explains the rationale for any particular steps or procedures in the sequence.

Population Served

The training sequence carried out at one of the three project settings—the suburban Clover Park School District—and at the University of Washington is an example of the applicability of precision teaching techniques to the training of skilled teachers. The training sequence varied slightly at each of the three project locations, but the Clover Park experience exemplifies the procedures well and stands as evidence of the workability of the program. Furthermore, the population in the Clover Park District is particularly worth discussing. Clover Park has a highly transient, military-impacted population with an unusual concentration of children with academic and social behavior problems; the children had a wider range of handicaps than did children in other project schools. Most of the target children at Clover Park exemplified a critical national problem—the moderately handicapped child in the regular classroom. If, as we have noted, 75% of the retarded children in this country belong to the group of mildly retarded or handicapped students, then any success in improving their instruction is of particular interest. The finding (Deutsch, 1965) that culturally deprived children display a cumulative deficit wherein early small deficiencies lead to inferior learning that, in turn, increases the size of the deficiency, underscores the need to alleviate the learning problems of these children as early as possible. If these problems are not attended to, the child faces a difficult adjustment as an adult. Edwin Martin (1972) estimated that,

> Only 21 percent of handicapped children leaving school in the next 4 years will be fully employed or go on to college. Another 40 percent will be underemployed, and 26 percent will be unemployed. An additional 10 percent will require at least a partially "sheltered" setting and family, and 3 percent will probably be almost totally dependent.

The Basis for the Training Program: Precision Teaching

Some past teachers have defined the goal of the teaching process as "providing the student with exposure to a wide range of information and experience" or as making sure that his school experience makes him a "well-adjusted, mature adult." These definitions have two major flaws:

1. They do not specify precisely what information and experience should be provided, or what *observable* symptoms of "adjustment" and "maturity" will tell the teacher that his efforts have been successful.

2. They do not identify any specific procedures or steps for the teacher to follow in order to reach the goal.

If, for no other reason than the practical one of offering more guidance to the teacher, one could wish for a definition of teaching that specifies exactly the goal or purpose of the teaching act and the specific steps to be followed in carrying it out. In fact, such a definition has been implicit (at least) for years: All teaching involves a series of acts whose purpose is to change a pupil's behavioral repertoire from a state of relative incompetence to one of relative competence. "For centuries schools have accepted the fact that they must *change* their students (e.g., change them from 'non-readers' to 'readers'; from 'non-adders' to 'adders') . . . ." (White, 1971, p. 5).

It is true that some teachers and some schools in the past (perhaps even a few in the present) have felt that teaching is strictly an either/or matter of *presenting the material* to be learned; whether the pupil changed his behavior sufficiently to *acquire* the information or skills the teacher presented resulted more or less from his "motivation" or "interest." But things have been changing. As the critical role of the environment in determining the behavior of individuals has become more and more evident (e.g., Skinner, 1971), teachers and schools have become more and more convinced of the need to manipulate the instructional environment in order to change the behavior of their pupils.

If the environment is maintaining a given behavior in a student, then it makes sense to change the environment if a change in behavior is desired. And, if teaching is concerned with changes in behavior in this sense, it cannot be a black-or-white, on-or-off process: It is a matter not only of presenting or not presenting material, but of presenting it more or less *well* and with appropriate environmental alterations to promote specified changes in pupil performance. At present, we are less inclined to place "responsibility" for learning on the student and more inclined to view teaching as a *process by which the teacher arranges the environment to make learning more likely.* The teacher of today is in the "hot seat" as far as learning goes: He is the one most likely to be held responsible for how well or how much his pupils learn.

How is the teacher to reach the goal of making learning more likely—or even inevitable? The answer to this question cannot really be given until another question has been asked and answered, that is, "What is the goal?" Until the teacher knows exactly where he should be when he is at the end of his travels, he is in no position to map out a route for getting there.

The first problem, then, is to specify exactly what *observable behaviors* will be accepted as evidence that learning has indeed taken place (Mager, 1962). The condition of *being* knowledgeable or *being* mature has no precise meaning until the "symptoms" of these conditions have been specified to leave no doubt about them. A student, for example, has a "knowledge of German" if he can translate without help passages of unfamiliar German prose at a rate of 100 words per minute. This specification might not suit every German teacher; nevertheless, it serves as a model of exactitude that every Geman teacher might use in setting his own specifications.

If teaching is concerned with *changing behavior*—and in order to change a student's behavior or to know what will constitute a change in his behavior—we must specify what observable behaviors will constitute evidence that a change has taken place. But then the criterion is only partially satisfactory. It is possible that the student may already exhibit the criterion behaviors; if so, teaching can hardly be said to *change* anything. So, teaching must really have more than one measurement if one is to know exactly how successful it has been. At the very least, the teacher must know exactly what the student is able to do before the course of instruction begins, and what he is able to do after it.

If the teacher waits until the end of a course before evaluating his methods' success, he has obviously waited too long. The students will be gone and the new students may or may not profit from any alterations the teacher decides to make. In any case, the teacher who relies exclusively on before and after pictures of teaching effectiveness is in the position of perennially closing the barn door after the horse is stolen. What the teacher needs, clearly, is an ongoing measure of effectiveness that permits him to alter unsuccessful methods or materials while the student is still able to profit from the alterations.

Now we can specify a definition of precision teaching: It adds to the old, familiar term "teaching" a new adjective that signifies precision and accuracy in measuring progress toward the goals of instruction. And the novel methods of precision teaching are not really methods in the usual sense at all; rather, they are tools by which the teacher can measure the effectiveness of any methods he is now using or may adopt in the future.

Precision teaching has a number of advantages. Not only do precise, ongoing measures of the child's performance give the teacher information about which instructional measures have been successful, but how successful the measures will be in the future. Although the measures are difficult and time-consuming for the teacher to carry out by himself, they are simple enough for kindergarteners and first-graders to chart their own data (Bates & Bates, 1971). Another benefit is that the very process of involving the child in measuring his own progress may be rewarding to him, and will surely lead to his better understanding of the contingencies in his environment—of the connections between his behavior and its consequences. A child who can understand that much is in a better position to take over the management of his own behavior. Ultimately, all teachers agree about one goal of instruction: making the child independent of a teacher and able to function without instruction. Because precision teaching promotes that goal, it represents a valuable addition to traditional instruction.

Precision Training for Precision Teachers

The resource teacher must know first of all how to teach. As elementary as the statement may sound, it seems to be overlooked in many instances in which "specialists," who often have no classroom experience, help teachers. In order to teach effectively, the resource teacher must be able to identify the sequence of skills that the child should acquire in order to reach a terminal objective. A teacher so trained will probably be able to generalize his skills from subject matter to subject matter, should the rapid changes in curricula students today are seeking make the ability to shift necessary.

Our Clover Park trainees were all elementary school teachers who were enrolled in MA programs at the University of Washington. At the end of their project training, they returned to their home schools as resource teachers. During the summer of 1969, they were given an intensive, four-week, supplementary, didactic program that emphasized techniques of precision teaching, behavior management, instructional program planning, and performance recording and evaluation. (For a discussion of the topics covered see Haring & Phillips, 1972; Kunzelmann, Cohen, Hulten, Martin, & Mingo; and Haring, 1971.)

The critical phase of the training was a 16-week supervised practicum experience based on 12 training exercises in the Clover Park School District training sites. Had the resource teachers not had controlled practicum experience under the direction of an experienced teacher, they would have returned to their home schools as unpracticed apprentices. The staff preferred that trainees complete their practicum experiences during intensive training and then provide skilled service to their schools and to the children there.

Exercises 1 through 4 were designed to give the trainees practice in modifying a disruptive social behavior. Social behavior is first in the sequence because the child's behavior must be under control before he can profit from instruction. Further, a social behavior that disrupts a class may be more readily identified and remediated than an academic behavior deficit that requires the teacher to have programming and other skills. With Exercises 5 though 8, the trainees began the modification of academic performance.

The first eight exercises required the trainees to work with only one student at a time, first to modify a disruptive social behavior and then to remediate an academic deficiency. The staff believes that working with one student under the strict control of the trainer is a necessary introduction to more complicated intervention.

Beginning with Exercise 9, trainees worked with a group of from four to six children in the training center school to remediate their academic difficulties in the group setting. As the children in Exercise 9 began to function successfully, trainees began to work with them in the regular classroom and with the room's teachers (Exercise 10). In Exercise 11, the trainee extended the program to one academic area for the entire class. The exercise was a major task for the trainees, some of whom were faced with classes of 37 or 38 pupils. To institute a contingency management and performance recording system in such a class was the final evidence that the trainees were highly skilled resource personnel.

With Exercise 12, the trainees were at the end of their intensive training period. To facilitate their assumption of the roles of resource teachers in their home schools during the 20-week "Re-entry Phase" of training, they were asked to carry out Exercise 12, which consists of

1. compiling a complete project report form; and
2. summarizing (a) their own expectations for their future roles, and (b) one of their training projects for discussion at a faculty meeting to be held in their own schools the week following the intensive training period's end.

The emphasis in the training program is on data-sharing skills. Resource teachers whose work will involve cooperation with a child's classroom teacher and perhaps his parents must be able to explain not only the child's performance problems, but ways to remediate them. Further, to enlist the cooperation of others working with the child, the resource teachers must be able to explain the reasons for their procedures and to teach others to take over portions of these responsibilities. During the entire training period, the project staff made many visits to the trainees' home schools to prepare administrators, teachers, and parents for the advent of the resource teachers and to enlist their cooperation. Obviously, rapport between teachers and resource teachers is necessary for a successful working relationship.

20 Week "Re-entry Phase"—Training Sequence

1. The trainees continued course work in special education MA programs at the University of Washington.

2. The trainees assumed more and more of a full-time resource teacher role in their home schools, although they were under the continued "care" and "maintenance" of the project trainer.

3. The project trainer made two half-day visits per week to the resource schools.

4. The trainer continued collecting the same data on the trainees' performance that he amassed during their intensive training period.

5. The trainer continued adjusting the training program to meet the trainees' individual needs so that they would all meet the terminal objectives of the project.

Procedures

When a child requires intervention by a resource teacher, the regular classroom teacher fills out a referral form that has been designed by the resource teachers. It is written concisely and specifically to prevent any differences in interpretation and covers reading, arithmetic, cursive penmanship, spelling, classroom behavior, and general testing; referrals are made in any of these areas for remediation or enrichment. In addition, the teacher can select as many specific areas within the larger ones for the student as he considers necessary to bring the child's performance up to a satisfactory level.

The resource teacher uses probes to assess the student's present level of functioning. (A "probe" may consist of a sample page of a reading text or math workbook.) The classroom teacher and the resource teacher then agree on a criterion for a successful project. In the agreement they state the specific terminal objectives for the student. After the student reaches the goal, the contract is terminated. The teacher, however, has the option to "recontract" the student if he needs work in other areas. At the time of this agreement, the resource teacher schedules weekly conferences to facilitate communication with the regular-classroom teacher and to evaluate together the data displayed on the student's six-cycle graphs. They discuss changes in program, arrranged events, reinforcers, contingencies, and the total learning environment. Through these conferences, the resource teacher attempts to convey an understanding of the student's abilities, the resource teacher's role, and the procedures implemented.

Occasionally, the resource teacher works with the child on a one-to-one basis in the resource room for part of the day. Occasionally, too, the resource teacher manages several children at a time in the resource room, or continues to provide individualized programs for children who work on them in their regular classrooms.*

This program is different from the self-contained special education programs to which most classroom teachers are accustomed. Formerly, teachers either managed a "problem child" themselves, using their accustomed methods, or referred him to another class. This program demands changes in the regular teacher's behavior and, therefore, it requires tact and careful planning from the resource teachers. The goal of this program is two-pronged: The resource teachers use their training to meet the children's requirements and to train classroom teachers in the procedures the resource teachers learned in their own training. Clearly, if they alienated teachers, they would never have an opportunity to improve the performance of students or teachers.

The resource teachers are able to involve the regular-classroom teachers in the project with minimal difficulty, however, partly because of the resource teachers' tact and planning and partly, too, because the regular teachers have the desire for both new teaching techniques and, even more urgently, help in managing students with learning and behavior problems. The resource teachers help them to alleviate their present difficulties and to learn to deal better with future ones. Sending the child to a special-education classroom merely helps with the present moment's problems and teaches the regular-classroom teacher nothing.

Results of Training Program

The training program has been effective in urban, suburban, and rural settings. Clearly, the training sequence can produce resource teachers who are able to maintain children adequately. The trainees felt secure enough in their skills to train others; in some instances, community volunteers, parents, and teachers' aides were able to initiate individual projects with students after preparation by the resource teacher.

The success of the training program is indicated by the following results:

1. The trainees, who scored from 40 to 75 percent correct on pretest measures of their skills as precision teachers, virtually all scored 100 percent at the end of their training.

---

*[Editor's note: The submitted manuscript contained 10 individual student project reports that illustrated interventions carried out by the resource teachers in each of the following areas: academic subjects (math, reading, and spelling); and social behavior (talk-outs, hitting others, etc.). They were omitted because of space limitations. The reports are available from the NCIES Special Education L.T.I. office or from the author.]

2. Because of services provided by our first group of trained resource teachers, two self-contained special-education classrooms in the Clover Park district were closed; school district administrative personnel requested continuation of training services for a second generation of resource trainees the following year at district expense.*

3. By the end of the project's second year, first and second generation trainees had completed 883 academic and 43 social interventions. They had worked with 561 students, whom they returned to regular classrooms, and with 113 teachers. In addition, they had completed 141 assessments of students who, they found, required no intervention.

4. All Clover Park trainees continued to function successfully as resource teachers during the 1971-72 school year and the school district hopes to expand the program in the future.

The goal of the project, as originally stated, was to train teachers who would assist regular teachers in systematically instructing children in a regular classroom over the two-year period—children whose academic or social problems marked them as candidates for special education. The staff hoped to demonstrate the viability of the teacher-preparation program in increasing the effectiveness of any classroom teacher. This program differed from other teacher-preparation programs only in its emphasis on systematic instruction based on principles of behavior management and programmed learning, and in its use of the continuous measurement tools of precision teaching.

The project is an example of one of the best methods devised to date of meeting the needs of moderately handicapped children. Each resource teacher who worked with the children in our project saw an average of 41 children, more than four times the number that a teacher in a self-contained classroom can manage in a year and more than seven times the number set as a management goal in the original proposal for all three school districts, during both years of the project. Additionally, the resource teacher was a resource for classroom teachers and, in many cases, even for "normal" children; the classroom teachers were often so pleased with the work their "problem children" were doing that they requested individualized programs for other students on an informal basis. We feel, therefore, that not only the project goals were realized but that some serendipitous results were achieved also.

Finally, consideration should be given to the long-range economic implications of a program that maintains students in school and provides them with skills that will ultimately make them employable.

---

*Now, two years later, a total of 5 self-contained classrooms in Clover Park have been closed, and a sixth will be closed this year.

It is estimated that a special education for one individual for 12 years costs about $15,000 (Martin, 1972). Presumably, that figure can be lowered if "special education" is provided by a resource teacher who can serve many children.

References

Bates, S., & Bates, D. F. ". . . and a child shall lead them": Stephanie's chart story. *Teaching Exceptional Children*, Spring, 1971, 3:3, 111-113.

Deutsch, M. The role of social class in language development and cognition. *American Journal of Orthopsychiatry*, 1965, 25, 78-88.

Haring, N. G. A strategy for the training of resource teachers for handicapped children. In M. C. Reynolds & M. D. Davis, *Exceptional children in regular classrooms*. Minneapolis, Minn. LTI/Special Education, University of Minnesota, 1971.

Haring, N. G., & Phillips, E. L. *Analysis and modification of classroom behavior*. Englewood Cliffs, N. J.: Prentice-Hall, 1972.

Hayden, A. H., & Haring, N. G. The improvement of instruction through evaluation. In N. G. Haring & A. H. Hayden (Eds.), *The improvement of instruction*. Seattle, Wash.: Special Child Publications, 1972, 432-452.

Kunzelmann, H. P., Cohen, M. A., Hulten, W. J., Martin, G. L., & Mingo, A. R. *Precision teaching: An initial training sequence*. Seattle, Wash.: Special Child Publications.

Mager, R. F. *Preparing instructional objectives*. Palo Alto, Calif.: Fearon Publishers, 1962.

Martin, E. W., Jr. Individualism and behaviorism as future trends in educating handicapped children. *Exceptional Children*, 1972, 38:7, 517-525.

Skinner, B. F. *Beyond freedom and dignity*. N.Y.: Alfred A. Knopf, 1971.

White, O. Working paper no. 1. The "split-middle": A "quickie" method of trend estimation. Eugene, Oregon: Regional Resource Center for Handicapped Children, College of Education, University of Oregon, March, 1971.

Precision Teaching in Regular Junior-High-School Classrooms

Norris G. Haring

*Director, Experimental Education Unit
Child Development and Mental Retardation Center
University of Washington*

and

Don Miller

*Coordinator, EPDA Special Education Project
Experimental Education Unit
University of Washington*

Variables Influencing Performance (VIP) was a one-year cooperative venture between the Mercer Island School District and the Experimental Education Unit (EEU) at the University of Washington. The project had two goals: (a) to instruct unresponsive junior-high-school youth more effectively and (b) to provide project staff with experience in applying precision teaching to such students. Three very powerful instructional variables were used: (a) arranging and implementing the necessary steps to individualize instruction for the children, including training the VIP teachers to rearrange instructional materials; (b) establishing systematic procedures to reinforce children's correct responses; and (c) instructing the teachers in more precise ways of measuring the performance of each child regularly throughout the course of the project. A key to the study's success was the frequent use of an equivalent measure that permitted changes to be made on an individual basis as they were needed.

The VIP staff consisted of four teachers who had been selected from eight volunteers and four half-time adult aides. The teachers received six inservice salary credits for their participation. Both teachers and aides were given basic training in precision teaching twice a week after school for the first quarter; thereafter, individual conferences

---

The project reported herein was supported in part by the Bureau of Educational Personnel Development (Grant Number 00-7001). The VIP staff gratefully acknowledge the cooperation of Dr. Paul J. Avery, Superintendent of Mercer Island School; Mr. Carl Marrs, Director of Pupil Personnel Services; Lynden Watts, Principal of North Mercer Junior High School, and the four teachers who put forth so much extra effort to help their pupils and their profession: Mmes. Christine Dybas, Shirley Frederico, and Jan Wilson, and Mr. Tom Garrison.

were held during the teachers' preparation periods. (The individualized conference approach was preferred.)

The following topics were covered in the formal training sessions:
1. Behavioral objectives.
2. Pinpointing.
3. Observation.
4. Measurement.
5. Recording.
6. Analysis of data.
7. Intervention strategies.

Development of Classroom Techniques

After the basics of precision teaching were acquired, their application to teaching problems was dealt with in individual conferences. Although all the teachers had the same three basic problems—how to individualize the presentation of material, obtain meaningful data from the material, and reinforce appropriate behaviors—each had unique problems because of differences in subjects taught and class composition. The classes taught by the teachers were eighth- and ninth-grade mathematics (Garrison); seventh-grade mathematics (Wilson); eighth- and ninth-grade English (Frederico); and speech and personal writing for the seventh, eighth, and ninth grades (Dybas). The ways in which the teachers, in conjunction with the project director, solved their problems are the interesting story that emerges from this investigation.

The teachers were encouraged to make their decisions on the basis of continuous data. To obtain these data on a child who is progressing through his material, the teachers were introduced to the use of probes. As used in this project, "probes" are short, daily tests, which are equivalent but not identical to each other and consist of items or questions that cover several small steps the pupil is supposed to learn; the items are repeated in cycles on the page so that he has several opportunities to show his grasp of each step or objective to be reached. As the child progresses in skill and knowledge, his accuracy and rate of performance are reflected in his responses. Observed improvement can be considered reliable as the same instrument is used to measure his progress. Although the probe as a concept is similar to pretest/posttest strategy, which is summative, it has the additional advantage of formative measurement, which allows corrections to be made before the end of a unit or topic. Probing also is easily applied to convergent thinking tasks at the skill level. It is potentially applicable to divergent thinking tasks at a higher cognitive level but difficult to use. The adaptation of probes to such tasks is an exciting problem that needs more work.

Probing, even at this embryonic stage of its development, served the project well. It solved the measurement problem in the areas of convergent thinking and, at the same time, it provided practice. With the implementation of the probing procedure, the number of academic projects grew rapidly because, in part, the basic academic skills of many pupils at the junior-high-school level are still inadequate and, in part, some of the new behaviors that must be learned there still have characteristics of convergent thinking and skill.

The algebra teacher rewrote his entire course; it now has an instructional sequence for the type of problem to be solved, sample practice problems, probes, and a criterion test. The sequence of pupil progress through a unit is demonstrated in Figure 1. The adult aide assisted the teacher in keeping track of each pupil's progress and producing necessary materials. Because the aide was not able to help tutorially, a high-school student and some junior-high pupils who had finished the course previously were recruited to provide the assistance. One student tutor also timed the probes. In this class situation, the teacher functioned less as an information-dispenser and more as an environmental manager; he made sure that pupils stayed on course and had the necessary materials and help.

The problem of reinforcement was solved in two ways. First, if a pupil finished ahead of schedule he was given free time. Second, if the pupil behaved very well, his class schedule was rearranged so that he could leave school early. Both rewards proved to be very powerful reinforcers. The staff also considered permitting a pupil who earned the time off to go elsewhere during the assigned class period but the administrative and attendance problems associated with the idea were not solved at the time, although they could be.

The other math teacher* developed the individualized teaching sequence illustrated in Figure 2. The probes that she gave to her classes took about five minutes and were generally administered at the beginning of each period. The reinforcements were quiet, free-time activities such as macrame, reading, drawing, cards, checkers, and so on.

---

* This teacher worked with the EEU to develop a computer system that would generate math problems to specification for practice or as probes.

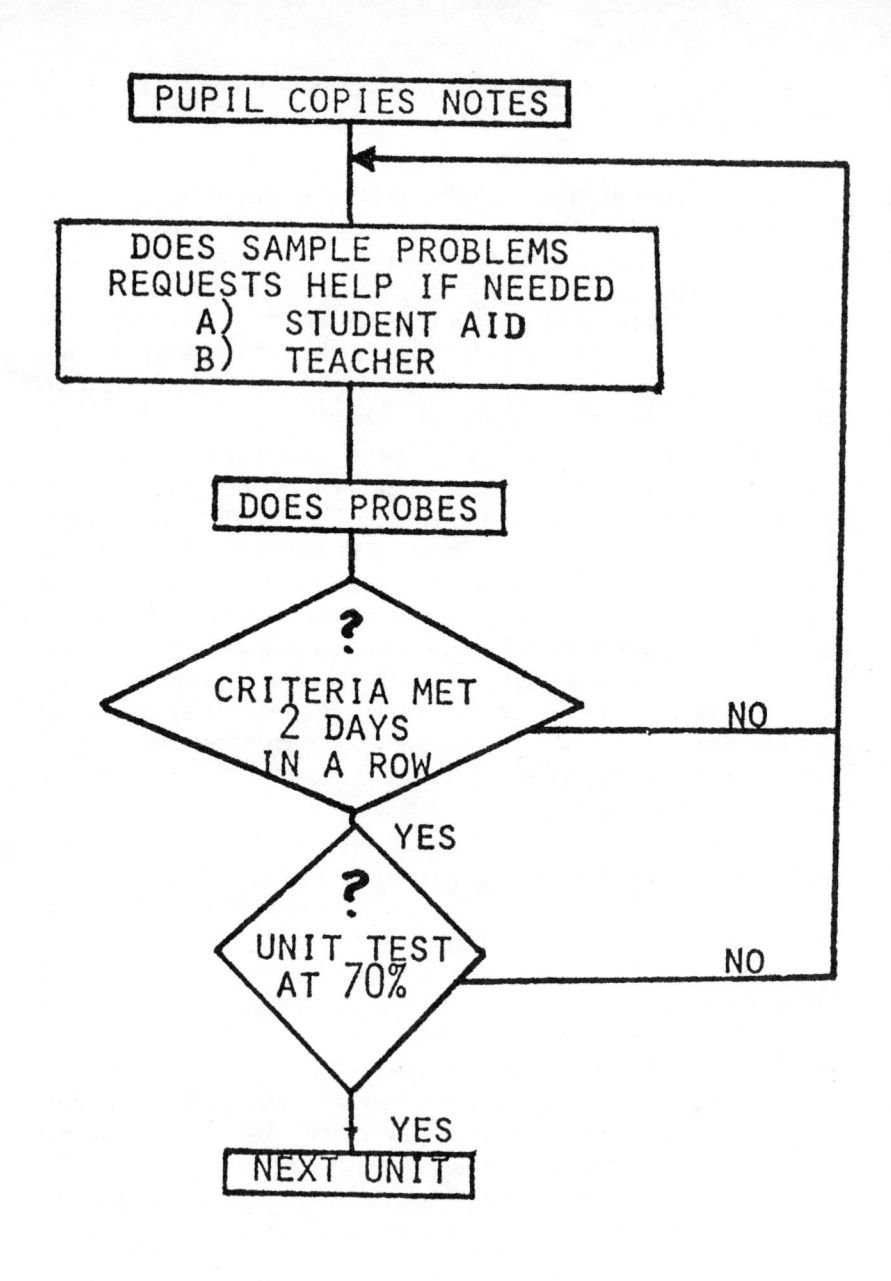

Figure 1. Flow Chart of Individualizing Procedures Used by Algebra Teacher

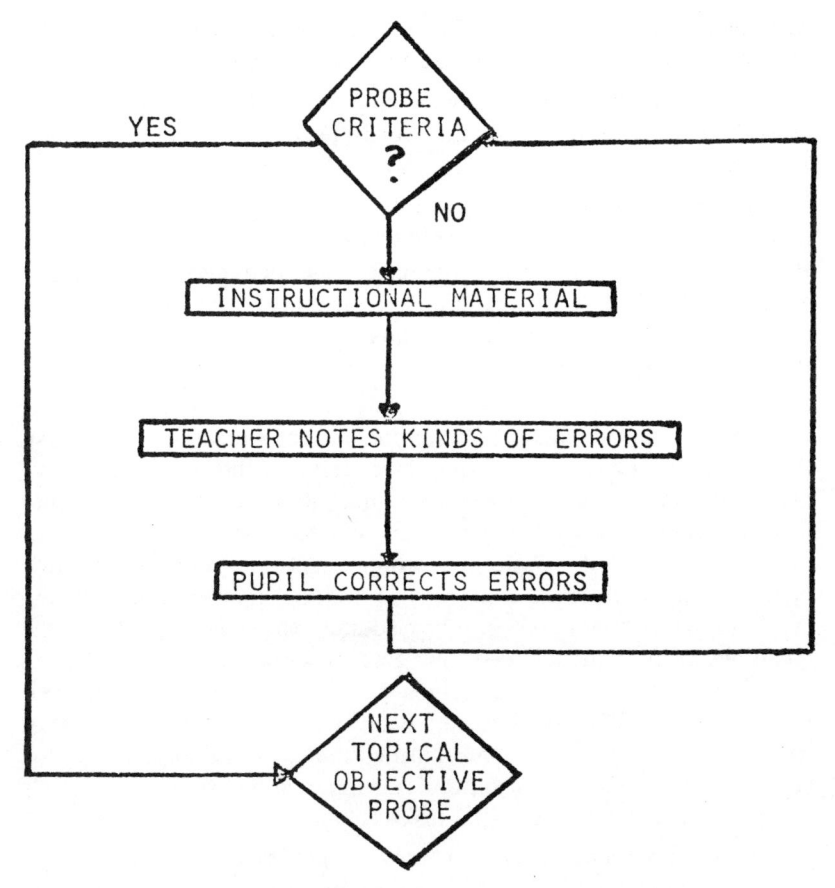

Figure 2. Flow Chart of Individualizing Sequence
Used by Seventh Grade Math Teacher

The pupils of both math teachers expressed appreciation for being permitted to progress at their own rates. The teachers agreed that such progress was desirable but they found that some pupils had to be prodded to move on.

English teachers had different problems and different solutions. They used precision teaching techniques for three parts of the curriculum: vocabulary, spelling, and punctuation. One teacher used her aide to develop appropriate word lists for the pupils according to individual ability. The children were tested on them until they could meet the accuracy and rate criteria. Each child was given time to study his list before he was probed; then his errors were corrected, a record was made of the words he had missed, and his correct and error rates were plotted on a graph for his and the teacher's information.

Another method that has been suggested is to compile a pupil's individual spelling list from the words he misspells in his writing assignments.

Pupils worked on word lists while the rest of the class worked on writing assignments. The aide could handle two children at a time, one studying while the other was being tested; she spent about five minutes with each. Interestingly, the pupils volunteered for the aide's attention and she soon had a waiting list of those who wanted to work on their spelling or handwriting.

The same English teacher used two different techniques for the presentation of problems in punctuation and capitalization. In the first, she dictated sentences for the pupils to write; in the second, she gave the pupils mimeographed sheets containing strings of words that would form correct sentences if they were punctuated and capitalized appropriately. The second technique had the advantage of permitting a free operant but it had the disadvantage of multiple interpretations. However, ambiguity could be averted by adding explanations to clarify the meanings of the sentences or to indicate its properties, such as a question. The teacher also gave regular writing assignments. After recording the types of errors that had been made (capitalization, use of periods, apostrophes, etc.), she returned the corrected papers and discussed his progress with each pupil. Commercially produced materials were also available for remedial tasks.

In this classroom, the reinforcers were grades; success in improvement, as shown on the chart; and the opportunity to play *Spill and Spell*, a commercial spelling game.

The second English teacher employed slightly different techniques to work on the same problems. In spelling, she instituted a buddy system, pairing the pupils by like ability. Each child took turns drilling the other for three-minute periods and kept a record of his performance which the aide checked. Two couples, one slow and one fast, constituted a team that competed against other teams. The status of each was displayed on a scoreboard. The combination of slow and fast couples made the team competition more equal and utilized the cooperation/competition model for motivation. In the drill sessions, the pupils had not only to spell a word correctly but provide a synonym for it. There was very little noise in the room during the drills. The prize was a trip off campus with the teacher during class time to get ice cream cones; leaving school with the teacher was probably the greater reward as ice cream was available in the school vending machines.

In punctuation and related skills, the teacher gave an assigned topic for the children to write on for five minutes. In addition to recording the data as the first English teacher did, she gave extra points to pupils who used words or their synonyms from the spelling lists they were studying; the pupils called her attention to such words by underlining them.

Results

The effectiveness of the VIP project can be assessed in many different ways: changes in teacher behavior, changes in pupil behavior, experience and knowledge gained by the EEU staff, and the impact on the school in general. All were useful indicators.

The impact on the pupils was assessed three ways. First, for each pupil who was of concern to the teacher, data were taken and charted on either social or academic behavior or both, thus giving a continuous formative evaluation measure to guide the teacher in helping him. The child was compared to himself and to criteria established for his behavior. By the third quarter, the teachers were no longer concerned with inappropriate social behaviors. The number of academic behaviors reaching the criteria rose to a high of 593 (all academic behaviors for all pupils in the program) for the third quarter. Although the data for the entire year are incomplete, a conservative estimate would be that for the four quarters, over one thousand academic behaviors reached the criteria. No data were collected for the fourth quarter. The estimate of 1,000 was derived by adding the second-quarter count of 190 to the third-quarter count of 593, and assuming that the fourth-quarter count was at least 217.

The second assessment method was a classic large N design. It was used to determine the effect of the probes in Wilson's seventh-grade math class. The pupils were given a test that she had administered to her class the previous year and a one-tailed T test for significant difference was applied. The previous year's class and the study class also were compared on their sixth grade standardized test scores (no seventh-grade standardized test scores were available). Although no significant differences were found between the classes on the sixth-grade standardized scores, the study class scored significantly higher[*]

---

[*] $p = .01$

on the teacher-made test that was given to both groups in the seventh grade. However, probes alone may not have accounted for the difference in the scores as aides were present in the project classrooms.

The third method of assessing pupil response was by questionnaire. Three-quarters of the study children indicated that they would recommend their classes to friends and one-third said that they considered frequent charting of class performance helpful. Many children verbally expressed their preference for the individualized approach and none said he did not like it.

Changes in teacher behavior were based on the teachers' classroom activities that they documented in their weekly reports to the project coordinator. Only 39 pupils were charted in the first quarter but the number eventually rose to 155. With time, phase changes or changes in independent variables also increased, along with the use of reinforcers. Teachers developed materials that were useful for the techniques they employed and, as reported earlier, each adapted the theory to make it an individual, operational procedure that made her/him more creative. The results of the questionnaire given to the teachers indicate that the methods they developed during the year-long project will be continued.

The impact on the school has been impressive. The algebra teacher has been appointed chairman of the math department and he is changing the departmental procedures to approximate the techniques—particularly, criterion advancement coupled with a more individualized approach—he learned on the project. The English teachers have been trying to influence their department similarly as many of their colleagues come to them for help and advice.

More than the target school gained from the VIP project; EEU also has profited. The staff developed probes more fully in both English and math and, thereby, better practical skills in and general knowledge of probing. Work has been started and is now partially completed on writing computer programs to generate curriculum materials according to teacher specification. The teacher performance monitoring system developed in the VIP project is having an effect on future plans of EEU for the same activity. The EEU also gained from these teachers some practical "tricks of the trade" that it hopes to share with other teachers in both the EEU and the field.

Cautions in Instituting Similar Projects

The following considerations should be kept in mind by anyone who is planning to initiate a project like VIP:

1. The maintenance of good school-community relations.
2. The maintenance of good staff-to-staff and staff-to-administration relations.
3. A tendency to assign to project teachers all the pupils other teachers cannot or will not handle. The tendency may become an acute problem.
4. The data load on teachers, which must be bearable.
5. If pupils are allowed free time out of class, they should have some explicit place to go during that time.
6. Means of keeping track of pupils with respect to the content of their courses and achievement must be implemented if the project is to be successful.

Items one and two in the list may require frequent clear communication and discussion. In the VIP project, clearance for the four teachers was secured from the school board through the central school administration. Parents were called upon individually and the PTA was also informed of the project. Two controversial issues—whether or not "bribes" were used in behavior modification and whether or not students would develop dependence on extrinsic reinforcers—were anticipated and dealt with satisfactorily before they became points of contention.

To protect the teachers in a project from being assigned all the problem pupils, a "trading" procedure could be set up so that the teacher who wished to move a child out of her class would have to take another in return.

The data load on a teacher can become very heavy. Possible solutions are not to collect data on every pupil all the time; to collect them only on individuals who need it and only when they need it; to get the pupils to do their own charting; and to ask the aide to assist when necessary. When the pupils do the charting themselves, their charts must be checked for accuracy. However, checking can be done on a random basis and accuracy can be shaped through appropriate reinforcement.

When pupils have earned free time and are allowed to leave class, they must have a definite place to go: home, another class, job, or a volunteer agency. In all cases, the arrangements must be cleared in advance and they must be checked after they are in operation. The privilege of free time is easy for children to abuse, but it is a very powerful reinforcer that usually repays the staff's efforts to manage it.

Teachers can keep track of pupils by noting the sequence of objectives in the grade books and recording the time each pupil has achieved a goal. Another method is to use the chart to record all changes.

Whenever people attempt change, problems will usually follow; but the more the problems can be anticipated and planned for, the more smoothly the change will go. The procedures developed in the VIP could well apply to other situations to one degree or another. In this project, teachers had half-time aides; however, after teachers have been trained, adult aides easily can be replaced by pupil aides. Probes, admittedly, are easiest to develop in the skill areas. Although limitations in their use were found, two factors should be noted: (a) many skills in many topic areas permit the approach to apply, and (b) even though the development of probes for divergent thinking is not easy, teachers should not give up working on the possibility. The attempts are especially important if teachers, who profess to teach creativity, problem solving, and cognitive development, are to answer present and future questions about their accountability.

In essence, the VIP project was a behavioral-objective, formative, data-based program that involved taking advantage of appropriate parts of the environment to assist individual pupils to acquire useful behaviors. Hopefully, these attributes will be found applicable to any educational project.

University of Minnesota—Minneapolis Public Schools

Minnesota special educators have encouraged integrated education for handicapped children for many years. Their concern has been not whether integrated education is desirable for children with different learning needs—they assume it is—but for which children education within the regular mainstream can be effective and for which ones it does not appear to be the best solution. Their search is supported by a sympathetic state education administration and by service consumers who believe that the normalization principle is a reasonable basis for a service design.

The two programs reported here represent joint efforts of the Minneapolis public schools and the University of Minnesota to study the key question systematically. The two institutions recognize that all the required instructional and assessment technology is not yet available but, through the projects, they hope to develop the more effective instructional support systems and the more suitable assessment techniques that will permit a better exploration of the problem. Their experience reveals a good deal about the kinds of problems that are likely to be encountered when better opportunities for handicapped children are promoted within the educational mainstream of any school system. These projects are just two of many efforts undertaken by the two institutions to improve special education services.

The two projects were selected for presentation here because first, they deal directly with the problems of regular-special education service interface that are the central concern of this monograph, and second, they describe intervention models that have broad applicability to basic structural change. Both studies have been supported by different combinations of Federal, state, and local funding.

The Harrison School Center:
A Public School-University Cooperative Resource Program

Richard A. Johnson
Director of Special Education
Minneapolis Public Schools

and

Rita M. Grismer
Coordinator, University Training Programs
Minneapolis Public Schools

Up until the mid-1960's, special education programs in the Minneapolis area, as in most other parts of the country, were characterized by the traditional and singular reliance on special-class placement for most atypical children referred for service. Indeed, throughout the country, in recent history, special classes established for the educable mentally retarded have been used as catch-basins for large numbers of pupils who are not seriously handicapped but are culturally different, poor, or otherwise personally disadvantaged. One of the reasons for the practice is the use of generally inappropriate selection criteria and assessment techniques. Another is the university and college training programs; their curricula, coursework formats, and special-class practica have tended to produce special education teachers and leadership personnel who are special-class oriented.

In recognition of the mutual responsibility and interdependence of public schools and colleges in creating change within the schools, the Special Education Departments of the Minneapolis Public Schools and the University of Minnesota designed and implemented a program to change the extant service and training system. The first step was the development of a Public School-University Cooperative Resource Program in a Minneapolis Elementary School. It has two basic goals:

1. To develop a prototype to provide additional, nonspecial-class alternatives for the placement of children who are typically labeled educable mentally retarded, and to modify programs in the other 68 city elementary schools in accord with the prototype.
2. To establish a University practicum setting that (a) provides students-in-training with the necessary competencies to become more flexible, individualized teachers of EMR children who can function in a variety of service delivery settings, and (b)

develops a pool of teachers to work within the resource program format.

Inherent in the definition and implementation of these goals are some basic premises that were agreed upon by both agencies.

1. The prototype would be developed as a resource for EMR children whose primary placement would be in a regular, elementary-school class rather than a special class.

2. In order to be of the most benefit to public-school children, the model must be transferable to other elementary schools in the city. Thus the program was designed, to a major extent, to be implemented with funding typically available to the elementary schools rather than to be dependent for success on new dollar resources.

3. The school and the University must establish joint systems of case management for special education children. Without a mutually defined and controlled system of case management, the changing of typical placement practices would be difficult at best.

4. University students placed within this model would be provided with an orientation to prescriptive education and to teaching by individual, instructional objectives.

5. With the stated intent of transferring the model to other Minneapolis schools, this cooperative program would help provide a pool of appropriately trained teachers for the resource model staff needs, and also would provide employment opportunities for University graduates in similar settings as other school systems modified their service delivery systems.

The definitions of goals and premises led to the decision to implement the cooperative project by appointing a full-time project director to represent both agencies at the selected project site. As defined in the formal agreement, the project director is an employee of the public school system and holds an appointment as an Instructor at the University of Minnesota. An administrative-level position was established in the Department of Special Education of the Minneapolis Public Schools to permit the project director to operate on an administrative level with the building principal and to be a visible member of the special education leadership team. The project director's position represents a contractual relation between the University and the public schools for purposes of mutual program development. His title, "University Training Programs Coordinator," was chosen deliberately to avoid restricting the impact of the model over time to any one special category or site location.

Since its inception, the Cooperative Resource Center has been viewed as a service delivery prototype. As such, it includes the continuous defining and redefining of operational procedures and philosophy that are necessary to keep pace with current trends, rapidly changing practice and technology, and local developments in the mainstream of education. The Center was established in September 1968 and it was allocated resources that were deemed necessary for its development. It was assigned to the Adams Elementary School, an inner-city school with a population of approximately 400 regular children and 30 to 40 EMR children. Initially, the Center was provided with one regular classroom, one certified EMR teacher who had previously served as a special-class teacher within the building, and a limited amount of new materials and equipment. Using the guidelines that had been developed for Minneapolis Special Learning Disabilities Resource Programs, the population was selected, student teachers were assigned, and the process of regular-class teacher involvement was begun.

Unfortunately, as the year progressed, the school neighborhood began to decline rapidly in population because of the construction of freeways and a general deterioration of the neighborhood. With the decrease in pupil enrollment, it became obvious that the Resource Center would not have an adequate or representative base population and that, ultimately, the school would be closed. Consequently, at the beginning of the second year, the Cooperative Resource Center was relocated at the Harrison School. In retrospect, the move was as much an advantage as a disadvantage because it permitted the long-term effect of some human and strategic errors in the initial year of operation to be minimized.

The Harrison-University Cooperative Resource Center

The school is located in a disadvantaged and racially imbalanced area; large numbers of children reside in low-income Federal housing and more than half are from one-parent families. The total school population is about 750.

The Resource Center consists of one double-sized classroom that contains private instruction booths, a variety of equipment, and an array of educational materials that have been accumulated over the four years of operation. Two certified special education teachers and the project director comprise the professional staff. Five or six practicum students are assigned each quarter by the University's Department of Special Education for training. At any one time, the Resource

Center population includes 30 to 40 children. The staff has the basic responsibility of maintaining each child as a participating member of his regular class. Thus, a wide range of services for children and a great deal of communication with regular education personnel are required.

Case Management

If mildly handicapped children are to benefit from educational experiences in regular classrooms, regular education personnel must be involved in program planning; the responsibility for decision-making must be shared to minimize conflict between special educators and regular teachers.

At Harrison School, special education placement decisions are made by the Student Support Team, which consists of a psychologist, the principal, the school social worker, the special education teachers and the regular-class teacher. The needs of the individual child and the alternative services available are both considered by the team. If a resource program seems most appropriate for the child, he is given an initial placement period in the Resource Center; if not, he is assigned to one of the other levels on the "Cascade of Services" model (Deno, 1971).

The initial placement in the Resource Center, which consists of a half-hour every day for two to three weeks, is a period of testing and evaluation. Psychological, neurological, or physical examinations are made, if necessary, and the child's problems and the available services are discussed with the parents by the social worker. At the conclusion of this placement, a case-planning conference (essentially the same people as are on the Student Support Team) is convened to evaluate the collected data on the child. All facets of the child's background, behavior, strengths, and weaknesses are discussed and specific instructional and behavioral goals for his educational progress are developed. The roles of both the resource and regular teachers in meeting these goals are delineated and a specific educational prescription and schedule are established. All subsequent activities follow the prescription, which is reviewed at least twice each year by the Case-Planning Team.

Individualized Instruction

Based on the prescriptive plan, Resource Center personnel individualize instruction for the daily 30 to 90 minutes that the child is scheduled in the Center. The staff provide a highly supportive atmosphere, acceptance of the child's current academic and social behavioral level, and reinforcement for his smallest bit of progress. They try to help him develop appropriate social behavior, learn to work independently when possible, acquire academic skills, and participate in regular-class discussions and activities. To accomplish these goals, individual performance objectives are used. Objectives for all facets of the child's behavior are defined and specifically stated, and criterion performance levels are established. The development and use of instructional objectives has been judged by the staff to be an invaluable procedure for implementing educational prescriptions. Mager (1962) and others have provided reference models for the development of instructional objectives.

The Resource Center program uses various techniques to develop a child's learning strengths. For example, a programmed reading format is used for the children who need a highly structured, step-by-step approach, and a basal reading series is used for the child who needs a more traditional approach. Every attempt is made to match the most appropriate educational materials to the child's learning characteristics. Furthermore, all available educational media and ideas suggested by creative teachers that might stimulate the child's interest are employed in developing learning experiences for the Center's clients. Thus, instructional tapes, original games, slides, transparencies, progress charts, and teaching machines are often-used aids.

Support to the Regular Classroom Teacher

As stated earlier, the resource teacher is responsible for providing a special education client with skills that enable him to participate in the regular class. Since 30 to 90 minutes per day of individual remedial programming cannot realistically accomplish this goal, the regular-class teacher needs support to maintain the child in the room. The team prescriptions, therefore, are constructed to apply not only to the child's needs but also to any difficulties that the regular-class teacher may have in increasing the child's coping behavior.

Some of the children placed in the Resource Center manifest disruptive, uncontrolled behavior; consequently, a number of regular-class teachers are understandably hesitant about accepting responsibility for them. If special assistance is readily available, however, the teachers lose their hesitancy and the result is that continuing regular-class placement for the child becomes far more viable. Until behavior modification programs become effective in helping a child control his behavior, the Resource Center may be designated by the Team prescription as a "crisis" room for him. Crisis programs are carefully monitored and eliminated as soon as possible, however.

Because regular-class teachers are not usually oriented toward modifying instructional activities to match unique learning styles, it is the role of the resource teacher to adapt activities to the specific performance level of a learner. The resource teacher assists the classroom teacher in the specific planning and development of classroom units and activities so that the mildly handicapped child can participate more effectively in the regular class. Classroom teachers at Harrison have used these Center services extensively, particularly in the areas of social studies, science, and health.

Time in the resource room is scheduled to coincide with the unique and identified needs of the child. If a child does not read well enough to function in a regular-class reading group, for example, he may be sent to the Center during the reading period. Resource Center personnel, therefore, must be flexible and able to modify their time schedules to accord with the varying schedules followed in the regular educational program.

Continuous Evaluation

The entry level team prescription and individual instructional objectives are only the beginning point for helping the child. Ongoing monitoring and systematic evaluation procedures are integral to the resource program. Each child's activities and progress in the Resource Center are recorded daily in his personal log as part of the pupil-progress evaluation process. In addition, the child's instructional objectives are reviewed and rewritten at four-week intervals. The original team prescription, the rate of progress in each area, and the effectiveness of the instructional materials are monitored and reconsidered in these reviews. If, at any time, the team prescription is judged dysfunctional in major aspects, the Case-Planning Team is reconvened and a new educational prescription is developed. The original prescription and the appropriateness of the Resource Center placement are reviewed for each child at least twice annually by the Case-Planning Team.

The University Training Component

The Resource Center, in addition to providing a basic service option for handicapped children, also provides a practicum setting for students enrolled in the Department of Special Education at the University of Minnesota. This training capacity evolved with the development of the Resource Center model and is a significant departure from the traditional student-teaching experience.

The basic orientation of the training program is individualized instruction. Each quarter, five or six students spend 20 hours per week for 12 weeks in the Center as trainees. Each student is assigned his own case load of children and he/she is given the responsibility of writing individualized programs for them. The programs are monitored continuously by the permanent Resource Center staff.

Although students assigned during the first several years were undergraduates in the area of mental retardation, the Resource Center is gradually shifting its training focus to students in the Special Education Resource Teacher (SERT) program, a new training program at

the graduate level for general cross-categorical resource teachers.*
Concurrently, the Department of Special Education at the University
is phasing out the undergraduate training program.

The University and public school staff who are involved in the development of the SERT program are currently in the process of defining the competencies necessary for general resource teachers toward the establishment of a competency-based program. In line with this goal, the Harrison Resource Center has structured five basic training modules in which each assigned student-in-training participates.

Diagnostic Techniques Module

Before an individualized program can be outlined for any child, his specific educational status must be determined. Consequently, the administration and interpretation of a variety of standardized diagnostic instruments are taught in the diagnostic techniques training phase. Students are directly assisted in the interpretation of the assessment tools and in the application of the data derived from them to the development of specific teaching strategies. Also important to the development of individualized plans is the use of informal observation and assessment inventories. During the diagnostic techniques training phase, therefore, the student is assisted in acquiring a set of skills that enable him, for example, to delineate significant behaviors, chart unacceptable behaviors, interpret informal reading inventories, and utilize time sampling and other observational techniques.

Instruction by Objectives Module

Most of the students who were assigned to the Resource Center for field training in the past were unfamiliar with the basic ingredients of instructional objectives and they had little or no practice in writing specific performance objectives. Thus, instruction and practice are given in the writing of relevant performance objectives that are appropriate to the individual needs of a child as determined by the assessment process.

The student uses the daily log that is kept for each child as a tool for evaluating the progress toward the objectives developed for him. Only those activities directly related to the written objectives must be considered. The lack of or insufficient progress toward the objectives is viewed as the problem of either inappropriate instructional techniques or inappropriate objectives, but not as the child's problem. Weekly conferences are held with each student-in-training on the progress being made. At the end of each four-week period, the student is required to evaluate the child's objectives, review their relevance and

---

* See, in this monograph, "The Seward-University Project: A Cooperative Effort to Improve School Services and University Training," by S. Deno and J. Gross.

progress, and rewrite them as necessary. Both the child's and the practicum student's progress are monitored throughout this process by the Center staff.

Remedial Instruction Module

The Resource Center has available a large selection of various educational materials for study and experimentation by the students-in-training. Time is alloted to the students to review these various materials, define their best uses, and evaluate their effectiveness. Also, and more importantly, the students are given instruction and field training in the interrelation of the various materials to the specific teaching strategies learned in their formal coursework, and they are assisted in matching materials and strategies to the specific educational needs of individual children. As a major culminating activity, trainees are required independently to select and apply appropriate methodology and materials to each child, based on the assessment information they have gathered.

Behavior Management Module

Many of the children enrolled in the Center have had adjustment problems. The documented problems are analyzed by the staff during the informal observation phase of the assessment procedure. As children with adjustment problems are more likely to be rejected in some sense by the regular-class teacher, systems to extinguish these behaviors must be included in the instructional objectives. Therefore, appropriate contingency management plans are developed and monitored by the Resource Center staff and they are made an integral part of the regular-class maintenance process. Students-in-training are responsible for modifying such behaviors by learning to apply contingency management systems.

One of the most persistent problems observed in children assigned to the Resource Center is in the area of self-concept. Long-term failure, previous rejection by peers and/or adults, and other factors contribute to lowered self-concept. Admittedly, the area is a difficult one to define and treat. However, in their interactions with all the children in the Resource Center, the trainees are encouraged to be particularly reinforcing in their approach, to emphasize continuously strengths and progress, and to attempt to communicate sincere respect and interest.

Consultative Skills Module

Students-in-training are asked to participate fully with the Student Support Team in the process of placement as well as case planning. Their responsibility for presenting information to the team increases through their training until they become fully functioning representatives of individual children. The process of "teaming" is important to the Resource Center concept and students are taught various teaming skills.

In addition to the training in consultative skills that are required for an effective Student Support Team member, the trainees are also taught the consultative strategies and skills that are necessary to assist regular-class teachers. Students are required to meet with each child's regular-class teacher on a weekly basis. While attempting to develop positive relationships with members of the school staff, students are asked, in cooperation with the regular-class teacher, continually to monitor the progress of a child and to advise the teacher on areas in which the child may be encountering difficulties in his regular-class activities.

A great deal of Resource Center staff time is devoted to assisting and counseling students in the strategies and skills necessary to consult with regular-class teachers. For many, maintaining a position of listener, reinforcer, and helpful expert is difficult and requires much guided practice.

Current Goals and Directions

As stated earlier, the Harrison Resource Center training and service delivery model has, since its inception, been the subject of an ongoing redefinition of process, procedures, and population. Perhaps the most notable change in direction, which is presently in progress, is the recent reorganization of administrative structure and leadership resources in the Division of Special Education of the Minneapolis Public Schools (Johnson & Gross, 1973). The new leadership structure should result in the delivery of services to mildly handicapped children without excessive use of categorical labels—a concept that has been under consideration for several years in Minneapolis and other parts of the country. The newly developing SERT program was generated from this same concept, and it represents another aspect of the Minneapolis Schools-University Cooperative efforts.

In keeping with these recent local events and trends, the Harrison Resource Center, although originally designed to serve educable mentally retarded children, now includes learning-disabled and hearing-impaired children, also. A continued effort to place children according to their learning needs and teacher competencies rather than labels is being maintained.

In summary, this cooperative project between the Minneapolis Public Schools and the University of Minnesota, operating out of a single Minneapolis elementary school, has helped to create major changes in both the school's service system and the University's training program. Since its inception in 1968, for example, the Harrison project has served as a reference model for the Minneapolis effort to decrease reliance on special-class services and to offer support without segregation to many children previously described as EMR. In addition to serving as a model for resource rooms for the educable mentally retarded, the Harrison Resource Center has provided many of the staff for a score of such programs. Currently, some 30 to 40 percent of all elementary-school-age EMR children served by the Minneapolis Schools are placed in resource rooms or are receiving tutoring services in lieu of segregated special classes. When the Harrison School project was started in 1968, 100 percent of the children labeled EMR were in special classes.

Clearly, the most important ingredient in the success of the Harrison Resource Center Project has been not dollars or physical plant but the formal cooperation of the two participating agencies in planning, setting goals, and day-to-day operation. This cooperation between the public schools and the University has generated innovations and, perhaps more importantly, the diffusion of the innovations.

References

Deno, E. Strategies for improvement of educational opportunities for handicapped children: Some suggestions for exploitation of EPDA potential. In M. C. Reynolds & M. D. Davis, *Exceptional children in regular classrooms*. Minneapolis, Minn.: Leadership Training Institute/Special Education, University of Minnesota, 1971.

Johnson, R. A., & Gross, J. C. Restructuring special education leadership systems—the Minneapolis plan. In *Special education leadership systems: Decategorization and the courts.* Proceedings of the 1st and 2nd Minneapolis Leadership Conferences, in press, 1973.

Mager, R. F. *Preparing instructional objectives.* Palo Alto, Calif.: Fearon, 1962.

The Seward-University Project:
A Cooperative Effort to Improve School Services and University Training

Stanley Deno
*Associate Professor, Special Education Department
University of Minnesota*

and

Jerry Gross
*Assistant Director for Program Services
Special Education Division
Minneapolis Public Schools*

The Seward-University Project is one of the activities in which the University of Minnesota has collaborated with a local education agency of the state (The Minneapolis Public Schools) to find ways of serving handicapped children effectively without the undesirable social effects produced by separation and labeling. Its purpose is two-fold: to improve both the quality and quantity of special educational services available to the children at Seward Elementary School, and to increase both the opportunity for and effectiveness of preservice and inservice education for teachers.

The project originated in an agreement between the Special Education Division of the Minneapolis Public Schools and the Department of Special Education at the University of Minnesota. The substance of that agreement was that the University would provide resources to the public schools for the development of a special educational service system organized around the concept of what a child needs to learn, rather than a psycho-diagnostic label such as "mentally retarded," "emotionally disturbed," "learning disabled," and so forth. In return, the University would be provided space in a public school in which to develop the special educational service system and to organize preservice and inservice practicum (or internship) opportunities for teachers.

After exploring several schools, an agreement was reached early in the Fall of 1971 among the Seward School staff, the Special Education

---

This project was assisted by a Special Projects grant from the Bureau of Education for the Handicapped awarded to the University of Minnesota in 1971. The funds were used to facilitate the development of site capabilities and the design of the training-evaluation activities. Other aspects essential to realization of the overall project conception were financed from other resources, including the school system and the University.

Acknowledgement must also be made of the key role, in the establishment of the project, of Mr. Robert Monson, Principal of Seward School; his cooperation reflects his long interest in the education of exceptional and other children.

Division of the Minneapolis Public Schools, and the Department of Special Education of the University of Minnesota to establish the cooperative project at Seward, and University personnel moved onto the site on November 1, 1971. According to the agreement, the program of special services developing at Seward is the responsibility of the community and the school; the University is the consultative assistant in program development. A continuing activity of the University is the organization and reporting of information to the school at all stages of program development, and the development of recommendations for program changes.

The Special Education Program at Seward

In the Spring of 1972 a plan for developing flexible, integrated, and cross-categorical special education services was adopted by the Seward staff. The elements of this plan are as follows:

Goals, Objectives, Procedures

Goal 1.0. To provide each child within the Seward district with maximum opportunity to participate in the mainstream educational experience without the potential stigma of diagnostic labeling.

   Objective 1.1. To integrate all children within the school boundaries into the regular school program.

      Procedure 1.11. All children in the Seward District are assigned full time to regular classrooms.

      Procedure 1.12. Instructional special education personnel (teachers and aides) are assigned to provide direct (in classroom) assistance to all the regular-classroom teachers; in this cooperative role, their functions are to supervise children, prepare materials, and conduct instruction for any handicapped children encountering learning and adjustment problems.

   Objective 1.2. Traditional special education labels are not used to organize programs. Specialized support services are organized around functional handicaps.

      Procedure 1.21. The labels "educable mentally retarded," "emotionally disturbed," "learning disabled," and so forth, are used only for program evaluation and reports at the administrative level. Seward works with the Special Education Division of the Minneapolis Public Schools to reduce the necessity for such labels.

      Procedure 1.22. Modification in the modal instructional program for individual children is organized around individual assessment of a child's progress through curriculum sequences (particularly reading and mathematics) and on social requisites. Individual program modifications are directed toward improving a child's progress on the minimum requirements of the modal program. All modifications are regularly monitored and they are terminated upon a child's successful re-entry in the modal program.

Goal 2.0. To develop an effective and coordinated special educational support system.

   Objective 2.1. To develop a building-level management system to create individually effective program modification.

Procedure 2.11. A building-based team, appointed by the principal and the Division of Special Education, decides which children are eligible for program modifications through Special Education Services. Once a decision has been made to modify an individual child's program, responsibility for the development and management of the modification belongs to the special education staff in the school but the regular class teacher retains the responsibility for the child's progress.

Objective 2.2. To maintain only those administrative and physical arrangements that are necessary to develop individual program modifications.

Procedure 2.21. At the beginning of the school year, all special educational personnel work in regular classrooms and assist in creating individual program modifications within the regular classroom. Decisions to modify individual programs and decisions on the effectiveness of modifications are based on measures of discrepancy between minimally acceptable performance and actual performance of the individual student.

Procedure 2.22. Should an individual program modification within the regular classroom not succeed in reducing a measured discrepancy, a series of program options are created as they are necessary to optimize the child's progress. Program options are intended to be temporary and established only when needed, and all options that remove the child from the mainstream are reviewed by the building team. For example, a resource room or special class may be organized to provide more individually appropriate reinforcement for behavior that is prerequisite to learning (sitting, completing work, etc.) for as long as it is required. As soon as the program is no longer useful to the children, it is dropped. Special education personnel must be prepared to create, dissolve, and recreate instructional arrangements as they are required to modify individual programs.

Goal 3.0. To create continuing opportunities for educational personnel to learn how to work with children who are academically and socially handicapped.

Objective 3.1. To establish Seward as a site for practicum-based training in developing individualized instruction programs for handicapped children.

Procedure 3.12. The Department of Special Education at the University of Minnesota assigns six graduate students at a time to take their practicum at Seward School. These students are not a a supplement to but a replacement for the services ordinarily rendered by special education personnel at Seward. The permanent special education staff at Seward supervises the efforts of practicum students in developing individual program modifications.

Objective 3.2. To develop an instructional staff in special education that can successfully operate the Seward Special Education and Training Program.

Procedure 3.21. The Special Education staff at Seward are appointed on the basis of the following criteria:
1. Willingness to work at making an integrated, cross-categorical system flexible and effective.
2. Willingness to function in a program jointly managed by the Minneapolis Public Schools and the University of Minnesota.

Procedure 3.22. The special education staff at Seward participate in a year-long training program during which they develop their skills in individualized programming for handicapped children and in supervising instructional personnel interested in developing individualized instructional programming skills.

Objective 3.3. To organize and implement inservice programs in individualized instructional programming for regular and special educational personnel.

Procedure 3.31. Arrangements are made for regular and special education personnel to visit and work in the Seward program as part of an ongoing effort to increase their skills at accommodating handicapped children within the regular school program.

Procedure 3.32. University credit courses and professional growth courses are regularly offered in the school by Seward and invited staff.

The Program Modification System

The special education program that is evolving might best be described as an individual program modification system. Its key resource is three Special Education Resource Teachers* who develop and continuously evaluate program modifications for individual handicapped children. Although it is referred to as a *resource system*, it is not a *resource room* program. All efforts are made to individualize the child's program within the regular classroom; he is removed for tutoring or small-group activity in a separate resource room as little as possible. These efforts place a heavy burden on a SERT's interpersonal and resource management skills, as well as on his or her direct instructional skills, since much of what a SERT must do requires cooperative planning and management.

The basic sequence of events in program modification are depicted in the flow diagram of Figure 1.

Several features of the system are worth emphasizing:

1. SERTs are much more heavily involved in the diagnostic process than teachers usually are, and for that reason they must have knowledge of psychological or medical diagnostic procedures and social-work evaluations, and be skilled in formal and informal educational diagnoses.

2. Since the SERT coordinates the assessment of the child, marshalls resources, communicates with staff, and manages paraprofessionals, much more of her time must be reserved for these activities instead of for direct instruction. (This point is difficult to establish with both SERTs and their colleagues.)

3. Whenever necessary, responsibility for decisions is shared. However, only program modifications that involve separating the

---

* The individual teacher is referred to as a SERT.

child from his regular classroom for more than one hour per day need to be reviewed and recommended by the Building Special Services Team. (Since most individual program modifications do not require separation, red tape is reduced.)

PROGRAM MODIFICATION SEQUENCE

Person(s) Involved	Event
Classroom Teacher	Request for Assistance
Special Services Team (SERTs and Title I Resource Teachers)	Does referral have potential for SERT* assistance? — No → Title I Resource or other assistance
SERT	Assessment of academic and social status of child
Building Special Services Team	Should child be recommended for special education program? — No
SERT	Special Education Program implemented ← Program Revised
SERTs	Is planned program working? — No → Can building resources be provided to help Child?** — No → Refer to special station
SERTs and Manager	Program Management shifted to child, teacher or volunteer
SERTs and Manager	SERT Assists Manager or Resumes Control — No ← Can manager maintain program effectiveness?
SERT and Manager	Continue program until objectives are met
Building Special Services Team	Has program been successful? — No
	Terminate and Follow-up

**Building Special Services Team Decision

*Special Education Resource Teacher

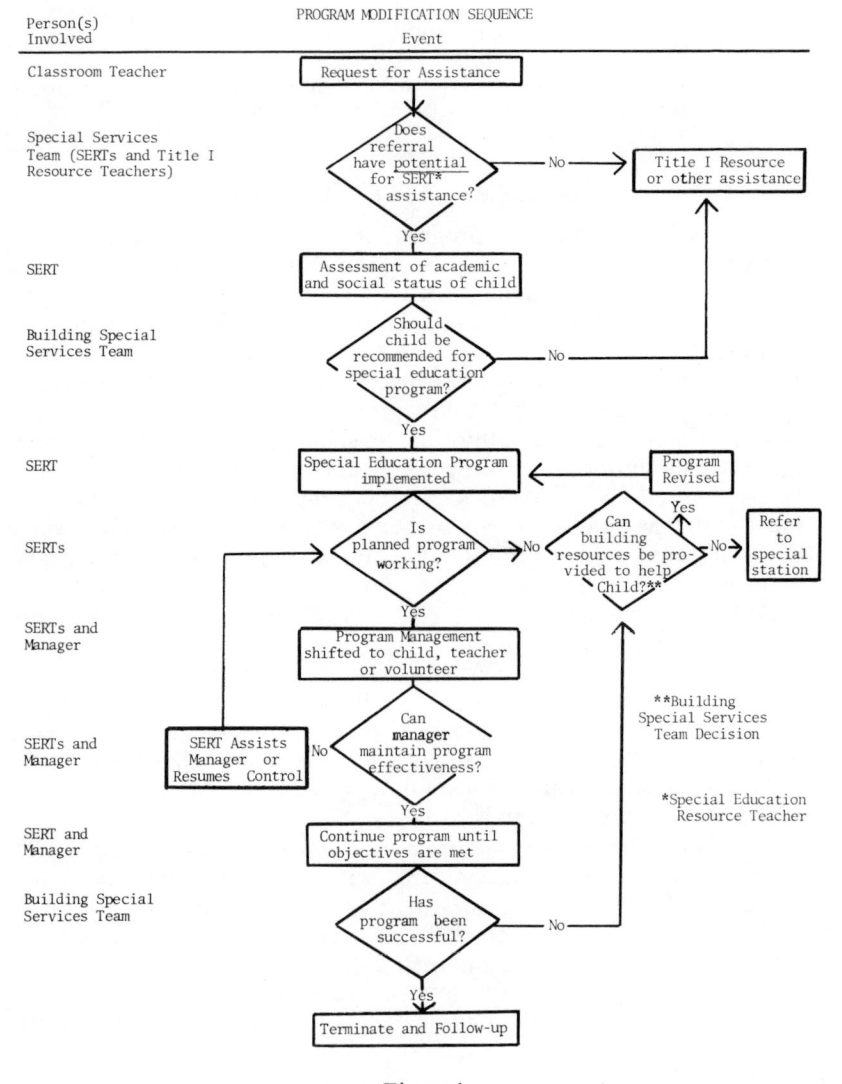

Figure 1.

4. SERTs are involved in direct instruction primarily during the assessment procedures and the development of an effective program modification. SERTs must be skilled in using alternative methods and materials to develop effective instructional programs.

5. The pressure is, and always should be, on turning over direct instruction and management of an effective program to the child, the regular-classroom teacher, a peer, or a paraprofessional. Thus the SERT is free to develop additional effective individualizations instead of being restricted to a static caseload.

6. The progress of handicapped children is monitored by the SERTs. They are responsible for charting the progress of all handicapped children on a regular basis, whether or not they are directly instructing the children themselves. The program is committed to ensuring the children's success, not necessarily to directing instruction. Regular and continuous monitoring of progress is the basis for establishing this accountability.

Increasing Inservice and Preservice Professional Education Opportunities at Seward

The education of professional and paraprofessional personnel proceeds in many ways, at many times, and at many places. In the past, the primary vehicle for education organized by the University of Minnesota was the campus-based course, with internship and practicum placements arranged for the students in professional programs.

Campus-based courses and internship assignments, although workable, have not been convenient and they probably are not so effective for developing professional competence. The major shortcoming of campus-based training is that the teaching faculty are separated from the interns at the most critical time—when the intern is working directly with children. University laboratory schools and clinics were developed to overcome this problem but most have not been successful because the arrangement has been artificial, both physically and in terms of the school or clinic population.

The inservice and preservice education component of the Seward-University Project is based on the assumption that training can be improved if the University will move to the schools rather than trying to move the schools to the University, which is what has happened at Seward. The following descriptions suggest the number of different kinds of preservice and inservice educational opportunities that are being developed:

1. *University Credit Courses.* Each quarter, beginning in the Winter of 1972, graduate students in University programs and

public school teachers are enabled to enroll in one of the several University practica or lecture courses offered at Seward School. All efforts are carefully supervised by qualified University personnel and coordinated with the regular school staff.

2. *Professional Growth Courses.* Professional growth courses sanctioned for credit within the Minneapolis schools are offered regularly in conjunction with University courses. Aides, as well as teachers, have been eligible for participation in these courses, which are supplemented by University personnel.

3. *Staff Development.* As a part of the revision of the special educational services at Seward, University personnel have worked formally and informally with the school staff to rethink educational goals, programs, and human relationships. This process, perhaps more than all the formal coursework, has extended the competence of everyone involved.

4. *Advanced Graduate Training.* University graduate students have participated in all phases of developing both the special educational services and the inservice and preservice educational programs. These experiences are probably best described as apprenticeships in which graduate students work side by side with school-University personnel.

5. *Parent Education.* A part of the current plan is the development of a parent-education series in child management which will be supervised by faculty from the University's Departments of Special Education, School Psychology, and School Social Work.

The professional education component of the Seward-University Project is best viewed as an attempt to develop a suitable facility for training special educational personnel, rather than as a training program. This particular effort was undertaken out of the need to create a practicum situation in which preservice and inservice personnel in the field of special education could practice resource teaching in a special education program that, instead of organizing its instructional services around the traditional categories of handicap, gives personnel in training an opportunity to organize and deliver service across all categories of handicap. University involvement in the development of such a setting was necessary because existing resource programs in the region tended, and continue, to be organized around categories of handicap. Area schools utilize resource teachers but they are specifically identified and function as "resource teachers" for the "vision impaired," "hearing impaired," "retarded," "learning disabled," and so on. Although the possibility of a "general" (i.e., cross-categorical) special education resource teacher has been considered in this state for some time, the majority of program administrators have tended to operationalize the concept under an increasingly narrow conception of "resource teacher for the learning disabled" (sometimes referred to hereabout as "broom closet tutors!").

By working directly with the Division of Special Education of the Minneapolis Public Schools to select a school and develop the Seward-University project, the University was able to create the kind of operational special education program within a building that is needed to provide cross-categorical resource-teaching practicum experience for its trainees. At the same time, the public school was given the opportunity to test feasibility under more favorable conditions than the school can usually supply alone.

The process of developing the program at Seward Elementary School has resulted in a useful training station for University students to practice serving as resource teachers who can provide assistance across all categories of handicap. More importantly, perhaps, experience in the process of developing this site helped all parties to identify problems that are likely to be present whenever an attempt is made to eliminate categories and segregation in special education programming. In the next section there are described some of the problems or issues that have arisen in the development of the program.

Some Outcomes

We began with the assumption that the best way to improve the interface between regular and special education is by organizing instructional services around the substance of a common goal: the developmental tasks that represent the criteria of success for children in their school settings. We accepted the premise that society established public education services to promote individual development in order that society may be developed and maintained. The tasks included under the rubrics of "basic skills" and "social competence" are those that have been stipulated explicitly or implicitly by society to be necessary for its maintenance. While it may be true that success on most school tasks benefits the child as an individual, society supports the schools primarily to promote those successful performances it rewards. Such an argument brings us to what has become the central perspective governing practice in the Seward-University Project:

> The handicapped child's "problem" is not his physical or mental disability as traditionally defined; it is the discrepancy between his performance and either the implicit or explicit performance desired from him by his society.

It is important to note that performance on many tasks required in schools is not necessarily inherently desirable; rather, performance on those tasks is "desired" by others who are in a position to determine for what the child will be rewarded. The distinction is important because it leads to a search for the criteria of successful performance in the desires of the society of which the child is a part, rather than in the developmental characteristics of groups of children. Elementary as the point may seem, most of the problems faced in the development of the Seward-University Project turned out to be, and still are, associated with the need to identify the performance discrepancies that make the special child deviant in the eyes of some significant person or group. As project implementers we found ourselves faced with the same kind of need to test what constitutes effective reality as that which children themselves confront. What are some of those problems?

Associated Problem A: The Search For Desire

The first set of difficulties encountered by special educational personnel trying to identify the child's problem is in determining what performances are desired. The task is not easy. It may be helpful to others seeking to go this route to consider some of the reasons why it is so difficult.

Whose desires are important? In searching for desired performance, the most obvious step would seem to be an assessment of society in general to determine what the majority consider to be the school tasks in which children ought to succeed. This step is essentially that taken in developing a hierarchy of values which, when synthesized, might form the educational philosophy of a particular school district. (Such a set of comprehensive goal statements has been developed by the Center for the Study of Evaluation at UCLA as a part of their needs-assessment kit for elementary-school programs.) A survey of all or of a representative group of the parents and teachers in a school or district could establish priorities among a set of goal statements, and the most representative priorities for that social microcosm might then be determined. The "desired performance" base would then have been established *a priori*.

This approach to determining desired performance is reasonable only to the extent that each "smaller society" (the significant others in the individual child's life space) actually mediates differential consequences for performance on those tasks. That is, do the individual child's teacher and parents actually apply positive and negative sanctions for differential success on the hierarchy of values made explicit by the survey of parents and would not be the case if individualized goal-setting really obtained. The point is that anyone who cares about a child's ability to cope with the world probably holds some preconceived expectations for that child; we should attempt to be more explicit about these expectations and not allow them to remain implicit. ("The unexamined desire is not worth having?") It is extremely difficult for a SERT to work in a context in which desired performance is unstated and attempts to make desires explicit are thwarted by defensive teachers, administrators, or parents. A point well learned by University students training at the Seward-University Project is that any time a child is identified as having or being a problem, some incongruity between desired and actual performance *can* be identified.

Forgotten Desires. One of the most frustrating tasks facing the resource teacher in the development of successful programs for integrating or remediating handicapped children is to bring the forgotten desire to the surface. A real advantage of making explicit the discrepancy or discrepancies at the heart of an identified problem is that acceptable intervention and agreements can be made so that upon the attainment of prescribed levels, the child can become the full responsibility of the regular-education mainstream.

Perhaps one of the most difficult problems facing special education systems is how to "get out of business" with the individual child. Some have gone as far as specifying maximum periods of time during which a child may be the responsibility of special education (Gallagher, 1972). If discrepancies are monitored carefully, the magnitude of the discrepancy can serve as the variable controlling service responsibility. Unfortunately, in many instances, after the SERT has helped to reduce the agreed upon discrepancies and seeks to turn total responsibility over to the classroom teacher, forgotten desires are remembered. New discrepancies are now identified as needing reduction. Very likely, some of the forgotten desires are truly forgotten; in some instances, however, it appears that the desires are newly created rather than only now remembered.

Associated Problem B: The Measure of Performance

Identifying the desired performances is, of course, only the first step in describing the discrepancy that is the basis of referral. Any attempt to be reasonably systematic about reducing the discrepancies demands that the SERT develop some quantitative representation of the magnitude of a discrepancy. Without such measures, communication among interested persons on objectives and evaluations of progress can become mired in personal subjective judgments and disagreements. Quantitative representations give the resource teacher a firmer grasp of the problem and provide a basis for all subsequent decisions on the success of an intervention.

One problem faced by personnel attempting to integrate special children is an apparent need by members of the educational establishment to measure children's performances esoterically. The diagnostic process involved in most educational interventions is perhaps the most elaborately developed portion of special education interventions systems. The diagnostic process that follows the referral of a problem child in most special education systems includes extensive medical and psychological variables. Further, the educational diagnoses usually advanced rely heavily upon descriptions of hypothetical central processing mechanisms or performance categories that are logically, rather than empirically, derived. The multiplicity of instruments used to describe the strength and weaknesses of the learning-disabled child ordinarily are of the first type, while the standardized tests used to describe achievement in basic skills are of the second.

Quantitative representation of children's performances developed from such measurement practices has one serious shortcoming that diminishes its value in the planning of programs to successfully integrate handicapped children: The measurements do not describe the child's performance in terms of the task requirements of the specific sub-society of which the child is a part. Consequently, such descriptions mean nothing to the significant people in that child's life. Many of the more esoteric descriptions confuse more than they clarify. Our experience has been that the simplest way to monitor progress in the curriculum facilitates communication of the results and also works as well as the more complicated methods in providing continuous feedback on the success of an intervention.

The basic conceptual scheme for representing academic discrepancies in the project is presented in Figure 2. It is a time series record of pupil performance; cumulative progress on an ordered series of tasks is plotted on the ordinate, and successive calendar days are plotted on the abscissa. The heavy diagonal line represents desired performance, which is made explicit by the SERT through interviews, analysis of curriculum requirements, and direct observations in the classroom. The line is always a straight diagonal because for any unit of time spent in school (the abscissa), an equal unit of developmental progress (the ordinate) must occur for a child to progress at a minimally acceptable rate (i.e., so he will not be considered deviant, or "falling behind"). The specification of the units of developmental progress, which must relate in a straight line to time in school, is a major task for the SERT. However, once developed in a curriculum area (reading, for example), it can be used repeatedly for assessing and representing a child's progress, setting objectives, and evaluating interventions.

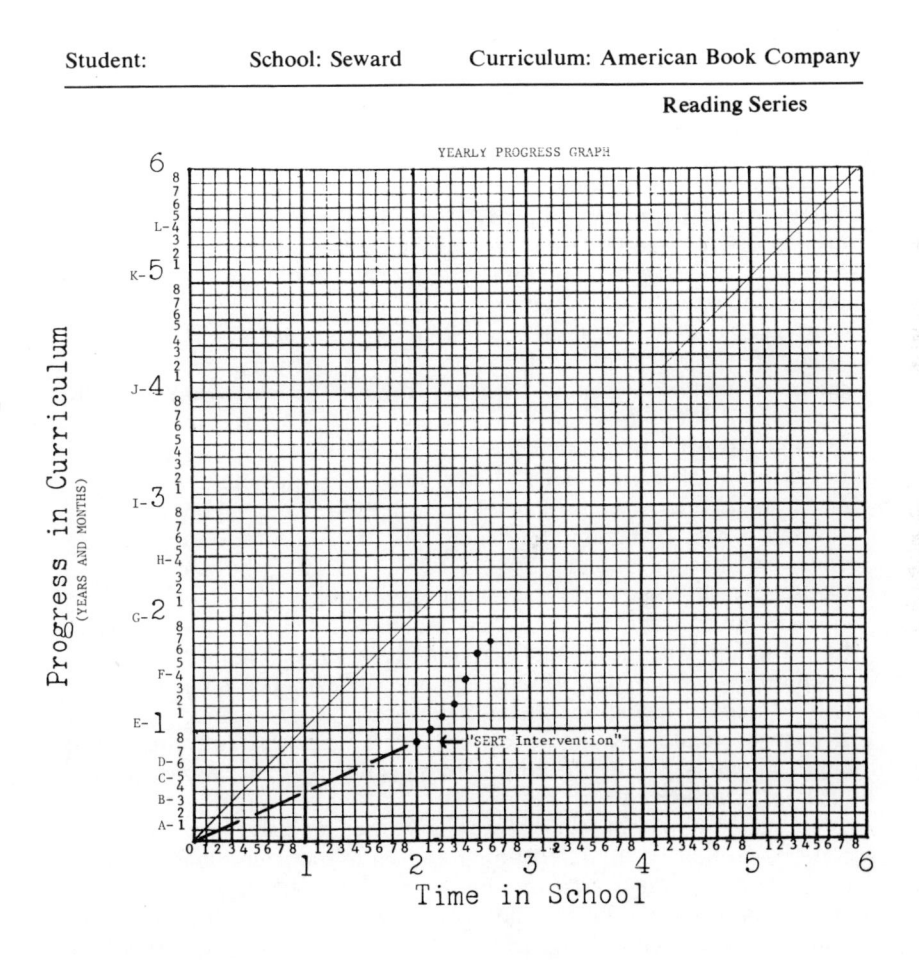

Figure 2. A Time Series Record of Pupil Performance

The dotted line on this chart is the hypothesized performance of an individual child. The extent of his discrepancy can be observed at any point along the abscissa. The hatched line is an extrapolation from past progress and represents the base rate against which an intervention can be judged. The desired performance line serves as the target. Any progress rate after intervention that exceeds past performance can be considered successful and any actual performance line that, when extrapolated, intersects with the desired performance line suggests the point in time at which program responsibility may be returned to regular education. The discrepancy chart illustrated in Figure 2 can be constructed any time that an ordered sequence of tasks can be identified. In structured curricula, for example, task sequences are predetermined at the time the curriculum is developed. Sequences can be identified in published curricular materials or through teacher interviews and classroom observations.

Although the discrepancy chart can be used whenever a developmental sequence can be identified, many performance discrepancies are not easily placed in a sequential context, particularly, the social behaviors that mark a child as "different" in the classroom. More likely, a child is identified as socially discrepant because certain undesired social behaviors ("noise," "out of place," and "aggression," in particular) occur at frequencies that are greater than are desired by the child's smaller society. SERTs develop discrepancy charts for these behaviors through direct observation of the target child and a representative sample of his peers. The two sets of frequencies (one for the child and one for the peer sample) are then conventionally charted with "behavior frequency" on the ordinate, and calendar days on the abcissa. Discrepancies in social behavior can then be directly observed and interventions evaluated.

Resource teachers are encouraged to observe directly pupil performance within the curriculum areas of the mainstream. The assumption is that performance on mainstream tasks results in the child's being viewed as successful or not. Performance on mainstream curriculum tasks is criterion performance and the handicapped child's failure to function typically on these tasks lead to his being considered a problem.

Diagnosis within the context of the mainstream curriculum consists primarily of determining the child's current level of mastery of particular parts of the curriculum. In reading, for example, in what book, and on what pages can the child currently read at an acceptable level of correctness, with an acceptable level of comprehension? It is assumed that any individual program to be successful must begin by determining where the child is, and move him from that point as rapidly as possible. Diagnosis of this type has the considerable advantage of placing the child within an instructional materials sequence and, at the same time, of reducing the hiatus between diagnosis and remediation, which is so troublesome in special educational interventions. The process involved is a direct extension of the kind of "mastery learning" formulation articulated by Bloom (1971). The entire formulation fits neatly with the notion that the handicapped child's problem is not a condition residing solely within him; rather, the discrepancy is between his performance and the performance desired from him by his society.

A Relevant Aside. It is worth mentioning here that the kind of time series' monitoring of pupil performance that is used in the Seward-University Project is the same kind that is used by behavioral psychologists in evaluating the effects of interventions in the functional analysis of behavior. It is also the kind of recording that is used by highway departments to monitor accident rates, police departments to monitor crime rates, health organizations to monitor disease incidences, and physicians to monitor vital signs. The point is that the representation of performance in a time series is an analytic procedure that can be used whenever one is interested in changes in events occurring over time. Use of this technique does not *ipso facto* mean that the intervention is a behavior modification intervention. One problem encountered by resource teachers utilizing such analytic systems is that all the interventions they represent in such graphic form may be labeled "behavior modification techniques" and either embraced or rejected, depending upon the general disposition of the beholder toward behavior modification as an intervention technique. Unfortunately, we have not progressed to the point where persons easily distinguish between systematic analysis and theoretical or philosophical orientation.

Associate Problem C: How much is too much?

The development of an intervention system based on the discrepancy monitoring system just described assumes, at least implicitly, that any child whose behavior is discrepant may be eligible for special education service. Our experience, however, is that, depending upon the school population, the proportion of children who may be discrepant in their performance varies anywhere from 5% to 75%. (Some persons may have experience with higher percentages.) Two questions then ensue: "Are all children eligible for special educational service, regardless of the magnitude of the discrepancy between desired and actual performance?" "At what point does special-education-system responsibility begin?"

It turns out that serving all children is not feasible, given the limited amount of support that is available for special education. Furthermore, in real life, the basis of special education support does not rest simply on the degree of discrepancy found in individual children; the socio-politics of "handicap" dictate who gets served.

Two factors are involved in any selection decision: (a) How much of a discrepancy must exist before precious, limited quantities of special education service can be brought to bear to reduce the discrepancy, and (b) what predisposing handicap exists that justifies the expenditures of special education monies for the assistance of some youngsters and not others?

At the present time, we have not developed a satisfactory answer to the first question. Serious discrepancies are defined in terms of the rate of their development rather than as the absolute difference between desired and actual performance. A child who is falling behind at the rate of .5 grade levels per year is developing a cumulative deficit in performance that will eventually become more serious than that of the child who is a year behind but who happens to be in the fifth grade. We are presently attempting to develop selection-for-service criteria by using progress rates rather than absolute differences.

The answer to the second question, although initially confusing to us, seems clearer at present. Our resolution of the dilemma rests on the philosophy that society has stipulated certain performances that are desirable for its perpetuation and development. Most of the children in our society are able to acquire the level of performance stipulated by society under commonly prevailing conditions. Other children, for a variety of reasons, are less likely to gain the rewards because, under typical conditions, it is impossible for them to attain the level of performance society demands. We have chosen to view some of the reasons for children's performances as handicaps that predispose the children to failure. State and Federal legislation have been secured on the grounds that it is not fair to require these handicapped children to compete for society's rewards at the same level of dollar support that is available to the rest of the children. For that reason, extra dollars are appropriated to provide them with additional or special education assistance. These dollars are to be expended in those instances where handicaps can be identified, as defined in the socio-political laws that authorized the extra expenditure.

The foregoing philosophy leads to the inevitable conclusion that only in those instances where legally defined handicaps exist are we justified in spending special educational monies to reduce discrepancies. As far as we have been able to determine, this sanction is the only one that exists for spending special education funds. What we find outselves left with, as a result, is two children cumulating a discrepancy at the rate of .5 grade levels per year with one whom we can legally label as handicapped and another whom we can either not label or label as "disadvantaged." Although no sound basis in instructional planning exists for treating the two children differently, we feel legally compelled to find an appropriate legal classification (label) for the child before we can spend additional monies to serve him. In our program, we are left with the same problem that everyone else confronts: Labeling may be necessary for justifying fund expenditures but it is not necessary for the organization of special education programs. If labeling produces undesirable consequences, the solution lies in the realm of political action, not in the realm of instructional theory and technological development.

References

Bloom, B. S., Hastings, J. T., & Madus, G. F. *Handbook on formative and summative evaluation of student learning.* N.Y.: McGraw Hill, 1971.

Gallagher, J. J. The special education contract for mildly handicapped children. *Exceptional Children*, 1972, 38, 527-535.

More complete descriptions of the procedures described in this paper may be obtained directly from the first author.

Section III

Training Programs Accompanying Structural Change Efforts

In rare cases, staff inservice or preservice training programs have been integral to producing basic changes in service system organization and functioning. In the programs described in this section, personnel were trained according to the theory governing structural change.

In some cases, the management unit undergoing restructure was a single school building and in one, it was a whole school system. In the latter, the whole school system is part of a state-wide test of service delivery alternatives. In all of these cases, the workers anticipate that basic changes in the channeling of funding and the control of service quality may be necessary if their efforts are successful. The desire to expand system-wide approaches is widespread, however.

Rockford, Illinois Local Education Agency: The View from A Building Principal's Window

Achieving a "special" education for handicapped children by integrating them into regular education programs will not succeed without modifications in the system. Millions of handicapped children are now in regular classrooms and too frequently their fate is failure, frustration and social isolation. Most teachers share with most Americans the experience of having known or worked with few handicapped persons. Our societal mechanisms for excluding handicapped children from schools, from transportation, from public parks, playgrounds, and buildings, from jobs and from social contacts have worked all too well. This lack of familiarity and confidence in human relations with handicapped persons means that many teachers will need special assistance if they are to interact successfully to help handicapped children learn.*

Country wide, many regular teachers, through participation in EPDA Special Education programs, have acquired new understanding of the needs of children with learning problems and the skills for helping them. However, they have experienced demoralizing frustration when they tried to put the knowledge into practice in their regular classrooms. Although they had changed, the context in which they are required to function had not. They found they could go only so far in modifying their instructional methods before they came up against the organizational constraints and school policies that prevented full realization of their aspirations to be more accommodating to handicapped children in their regular classrooms.

Over the years since the EPDA Special Education program was initiated, there has been an increasing disposition among educators and parents to break away from rigid age-grade systems that require children to fit the system of organization (or beat it) to survive in it. Regular as well as special educators have tried various alternatives to achieve more effective individualization of instruction and more equivalent opportunity for each child to achieve his particular potential. Many workers suspect that special education services will be needed less, and that the regular-special education interface will improve only if the basic educational approach is modified to facilitate more personalized education for all children.

Regular teachers participating in an EPDA Special Education program at Northern Illinois University came from a number of different school districts and school buildings in northern Illinois. Some of them were fortunate enough to be working under building principals who were as committed as they to trying new ways to improve opportunities for all children. One of the buildings from which these trainees came was experimenting with the Westinghouse Project PLAN approach; others were testing the potentials of the Individually Guided Education approach (Uni-

---

* Martin, E. W. Individualism and behaviorism as future trends in educating handicapped children. *Exceptional Children*, 1972, 38, 517-525, p. 520.

versity of Wisconsin directed). Experiments with team teaching and "open classroom" delivery structures were also represented. This program provided opportunity to observe how readily learnings from the same training program could be applied within different regular education formats.

The critical importance of the building principal in setting the educational tone of a school program has long been recognized. Increasingly, regular administrators are being included in inservice training efforts that are dedicated to achieving more effective special education service delivery.

The development of materials and methods for training school administrators has been among the areas of concentration in EPDA Special Education programs at the Texas Region XIII Education Service Unit, Austin, at the University of Connecticut, and elsewhere. Appreciation of the critical impact of administrators raises serious questions about the role-definition and professional preparation of building principals, questions that are raised as strenuously by the principals themselves as by those who must depend on them to facilitate teachers' roles in the total educational process.

We asked for this report from the principal of a northern Illinois school. He has proceeded thoughtfully and energetically to capitalize on the possibilities provided by the participation of some of his regular teachers in the Northern Illinois EPDA program, and to provide vital leadership in the overall improvement of education offerings for all the children attending the school for which he is responsible.

A Building Administrator's Perspective of Individualized Instruction

Robert J. Lindsey

Principal, Garrison Elementary School, District No. 205
Rockford, Illinois

The concept of individualized instruction has arisen out of the awareness that every child has different needs. The popular acceptance of the idea has brought about the individual assessment of children in the classroom, not only educationally, but emotionally and socially as well. The old policy of the "shotgun" approach to education, aiming at the "average child" and hoping to hit a few on either side of the mean, is no longer sufficient or philosophically sound. Nor is it congruent with society's present emphasis on individual rights.

Countless educators urge the recognition of individual differences but few have been able to articulate where the responsibilities for designing relevant programs to provide the recognition should be placed. There are many reasons why so many educators have been hesitant about developing a working plan for individualizing education. The problems overshadow the efforts made by a courageous few. Space is too limited here to discuss the past disasters or question who has the responsibility of meeting the needs of children.

Administrative Role

If the preceeding observations are accepted as basic to modern education, then the question of where the responsibility lies for fulfilling the thoughtful objectives of education must be determined. This question is usually answered with another, "School administrator, what are you doing in your spare time?"

The role of the school administrator differs in every district. No school system can legislate leadership into its administrative positions. Although most job descriptions allude to leadership as a fundamental qualification of administrators, the definition of the leadership desired is often too ambiguous to be meaningful.

It has been said often that the principal holds the second oldest professional position in the school system. The position gradually evolved from that of head teacher to that of the key link between children and teachers, on the one hand, and among all school employees on the other, with another link connecting the school and the parents. The responsibilities and duties of the principal have multiplied to such an extent that he must now be a highly-trained, skilled, professional worker.

Although no self-respecting administrator or teacher would quarrel with the previous statements, the purpose here is not to discuss the role of the school principal. But some understanding of the principal as responsible administrator is necessary in considering the working program of individualized instruction for exceptional children that one principal developed and implemented.

Building Composition

Every elementary school has its peculiarities and idiosyncracies and Garrison School is no exception. It is a typical elementary school, located in the largest metropolitan area, outside of Chicago, in Illinois. The building is the oldest still in operation in the city of Rockford, although an addition of moderate proportions was recently completed. The new section houses a learning center and modern semi-open classrooms that are arranged around the materials center.

The school district borders the growing and expanding downtown business area. It is a section of old housing units that attract low-income families. In addition, the neighborhood has many families belonging to minority groups and integration is proceeding gradually. This composition of peoples results in a cosmopolitan effect in the classrooms of the school. This is not to imply that the condition is unhealthy but that it is an important educational consideration. However, as is often the case, children can be the best catalysts of neighborhood adjustment.

Pupil Description

If children are seen as problems they are often dealt with as problems and expected to respond as problems. But when teachers try to see children in positive ways, despite behavior that seems to be obstinate or rebellious, it becomes apparent that all American children are more alike than they are different. To see the positive is to see the dignity and worth of a child. The quality of response that can be expected from any individual depends on how he is approached. Since the child, problem though he may be to all of us, is likely to be trying his best to solve a problem of his own, he needs help rather than rebuke. So it is with the pupils at Garrison School. For the most part the neighborhood influence is positive and the parents support the school; as a result, children find comfort in their learning environment although they may have some unfulfilled needs at home.

Staff Description

The instructional staff of this building is just as unique as that in any other elementary school. One quality, however, predominates: the Garrison School staff seems to be obsessed with the idea of providing for individual needs. The attitude is apparent in the planning sessions that are held at the grade levels as well as in the universal building philosophy. The age factor probably has much to do with this general attitude. Most of the staff is under 30 years of age; the balance consists of recently recycled instructors who had either no or limited experience previously. Such a staff can disassociate itself from tradition, and what might have been considered mayhem in the past can be tolerated in the present as successful programs are developed.

As the teachers search for ways to improve instruction to match pupil needs, they look for support and help from the available sources. Thus the administrator can influence and bring direction to the program. Specific inservice training can play a big part in helping them also. In general, if the facilities for inservice training exist and serve their purposes well, almost any program has a high potential for success.

Learning Needs Assessment

In the typical enrollment in a school, and even in a single classroom, the pupils vary to a marked degree in abilities and aptitudes. Social concern for the welfare of the individual is reflected in the various arrangements that have been made to recognize and care for anyone who differs noticeably from the rest of the group. "Atypical" and "exceptional" are terms that denote some degree of extreme variation in one or more characteristics. For the sake of simplification, exceptional children can be divided into gifted and handicapped, and the latter group can be divided again into the mildly affected and the severely affected.

In most cases, the special-services department of the school system has identified and determined the placement of severely handicapped children. Thus, once they have been identified, they are no longer of immediate concern to the regular classroom teacher. The present resource-room concept still does not suffice for children such as the **trainable mentally handicapped and the emotionally disturbed** who need self-contained placement to function in the educational environment. However, they represent a fairly small percentage of the total number of handicapped children.

It goes without saying that the regular-classroom teacher is responsible for the learning needs of the remaining enrollment. In order that she might fulfill the responsibility, the Garrison School program of individualized instruction was organized and developed.

Learning Problems Identification

One of the crucial problems that had to be solved in the program was to define individualized instructional behavior more precisely. Another was how to evaluate all of the conditions that are present during instruction. Teachers needed to become familiar with studies that focussed on the observable responses that are important to basic-skill instruction. As the staff moved into this phase of development, the ability to identify individual needs began to present a glaring problem. When the staff became oriented to awareness, it was found that their skills in identification had not kept pace. Identification techniques needed to be learned as well as the ways of meeting individual needs following identification. It became apparent that the acquisition of additional training before building a program was essential.

When we examined the availability of personnel for inservice training, we found that the greatest number of staff with the least amount of training had been assigned at the primary level. Most of them were young, enthusiastic, and eager to acquire additional education. Since they displayed a "felt need," we capitalized on it. Our program called for the training of one staff member at each level from kindergarten through third grade who could share his expertise with the other staff members at the same grade level. With this kind of cooperation prevailing, a rosy future for children's learning could be predicted. But the problem at hand was to find the kind of inservice training that would facilitate the realization of our expectations.

The EPDA/Special Education program at Northern Illinois University provided the opportunity our staff needed. More importantly, administrators were permitted to join their staff members in the workshop to share ideas, information, and planning. The experiences proved to be invaluable for the development of our program; our staff acquired all the ingredients necessary to do the job. The next goal was putting our plans into action.

Program Development

In the true sense, the Garrison School program did not suddenly come into existence. It evolved bit by bit as staff acquired training and then tried out what they had learned. Each new lesson generated new ideas for experimentation. Many of the attempts failed because the designs lacked adequate planning. Eventually, it became apparent that if a solid program was to be established, the entire organization had to start from the same basis. The existing attempts were not eliminated, however; they continued as each level of pupils progressed through the building. But it was recognized that the logical group with which to start was the children not yet in school. Thus the plan for screening pre-kindergarten children developed.

Following the annual spring registration of prospective kindergarteners, each child and his mother were administered a composite of appropriate diagnostic instruments to determine the child's needs. After the results were evaluated by the special-service team, the pupils were placed in different class sections. Children who enrolled in the fall were also screened and placed in the same way. Each kindergarten section was made as heterogeneous a group as possible. The full range and scope of child ability and maturity were represented in each class, in contrast to the old method of placing the younger children in the morning sessions and the older children in the afternoon sessions. The intent was to allot to each section a mature group of children who could provide leadership within the class.

The administrator and the teacher, who had been trained in the EPDA program, designed a mini-center format with selected, purposeful, and designated activities. Each center was assigned a specific area of content. The eight stations included mathematics, art, science, language arts, music, social living, physical education, and visual motor activities. Within each center, the activities were planned to meet the individual needs of each pupil assigned to the center. As children gained competence during the year, the activities were changed in each center to allow for individual growth. The pupils learned to make their choices independently, using an eight-area color-coded selection board. Over an eight-day period, their selections were recorded and, with teacher guidance, the entire eight centers were attended. After an eight-day rotation, each area of instruction was supplied with new, appropriate activities.

Each kindergarten group was joined by a primary class who was following the same kind of programming. The centers were composed of kindergarten and primary pupils in groups of six. One of the features of this organization was the small-group approach.

The centers were staffed by regular teachers, volunteer parents, and intermediate pupils from the building. Special centers or activities were instructed from time to time by specialists from the community as, for example, a carpenter, a teacher of creative dramatics, and an expert in creative rhythms. To qualify as center staff, parents and pupil helpers attended special orientation sessions.

Similar needs at the second- and third-grade level were met through a central resource learning center. When kindergarten and primary pupils became competent in their mini-centers, they moved on to the next level of individualization and independence through a centralized program in the learning center. Since this program is focused at the primary level, emergency needs requiring attention arise at the intermediate level. The primary staff had the training, the intermediate did not. Therefore, it was only natural for intermediate children to be screened for special instruction by the primary staff members who suggested programs of remediation to the intermediate teacher.

As the years roll along, the primary program should discover and eradicate a majority of the learning disability problems. Until similar programs are universal, transient pupils will still need remediation and it is necessary, therefore, to provide a learning-disability resource teacher for such pupils. This procedure is followed at Garrison School.

General Observations

An evaluation of the program is inappropriate at this time because sufficient data are not yet available for any worthwhile conclusion. Too many programs have met their demise because of short-term evaluation of long-term objectives. However, for those who might be interested in trying similar programs, some general observations can be recorded. These observations may be of some help in determining the value of the program.

The most noticeable effect so far is in the attitudes of the children toward learning. The individualized lessons make it possible for each child to be successful in his own right, and children with high success experiences display a positive attitude in their general behavior. The behavior pattern creates an atmosphere of enthusiasm and poise throughout the school.

Although general testing has not indicated any significant academic gains, the general achievement is commensurate with ability levels. Children seem to progress within expected levels. Teachers are more aware of individual needs and, therefore, are able to provide for a more complete achievement. The expectation level of the pupil is raised when teachers have knowledge of the assessment level.

The staff must function as a team since children are dependent upon each other throughout the levels. The climate within the building is one of a large family: Each member has a role to play to produce successful learning experiences.

The provisions for individualization make all children individuals. Even the special education child becomes an individual with a need as opposed to one with a handicap. Teachers view each child with a positive frame of reference. In the final analysis, the real purpose and goal of the program is to encourage all children to practice and become responsible school citizens.

The Houston Plan

Much interest is expressed currently in the plan of organization of the Houston Independent School District which is based on the assumption that all children deserve a special education. Working from this conception, the service plan dissolves as much of the regular-special education separatism as current circumstances allow. The effort is facilitated by the fact that the Texas Education Agency had already set the stage for the reduction of traditional categorical barriers; the Agency authorized local districts to test the potentialities of a proposed Plan A system of special education service delivery and state aid support.

EPDA Special Education funded projects have been in operation at three Texas stations: the Region XIII Service Center at Austin, where Dr. Meisgeier was formerly a member of the staff; the Region XIX Service Center at El Paso; and the Houston project. All of these programs have provided opportunity for the testing of service delivery concepts and the development of personnel training techniques. The training materials for principals developed at the Austin Service Center may be of interest to many readers. (Information may be obtained from Mr. Donroy Hafner, Region XIII Educational Service Center, 6504 Tracor Lane, Austin, Texas.)

The eyes of the country are on the State of Texas as it moves to resolve some of the difficulties of realizing its innovative approaches to the educational service of handicapped children.

The Houston Plan: A Proactive Integrated Systems Plan for Education

Charles Meisgeier
*Coordinator,
Center for Human Resources Development
and Educational Renewal
Houston Independent School District*

The schools of this nation are not meeting the needs of its youth. Teachers and administrators alike recognize a deepening sense of crisis in education, especially in urban schools, and an urgent need for change. In response to this need, the Houston Independent School District (HISD), the sixth largest school system in the country, is instituting a dynamic system-wide change through the Houston Plan. In the Spring of 1972, 85 elementary schools were designated to participate in the Plan.

The long-range goal of the program is to transform schools into institutions that will foster the growth of competent individuals who can deal realistically and effectively with the rapid growth of new technology and knowledge. The Plan's immediate goals are as follows:

1. To make the entire educational process responsive to the strengths and weaknesses of every child.
2. To make the curriculum relevant and interesting to the child.
3. To humanize and personalize the environment in which the child learns.

The basic philosophy of the Houston Plan is that every child is special and brings a unique set of educational needs to school every day. Its essential aspects are the retraining of teachers and the total restructuring of the classroom which will lead, in the future, to the continuous search for the better delivery of services in the classroom to ensure continuous progress and growth for every child, including the exceptional.

Early in 1972, the HISD Special Education and Psychological Services reorganized as the Center for Human Resources Development and Educational Renewal in order to provide a more responsive and efficient delivery of services. The name reflects the new structure's

---

The Houston Plan could not have been conceptualized or operationalized without the cooperation, support, and help of many individuals, notably, Dr. George Garver, General Superintendent; Dr. J. Don Boney, Chief Instructional Officer; members of the Board of Education; and a number of other administrators. CHRD staff members, Jim Clark, Mike Evans, Henry Lindley, Barry Dollar, and other members of the management team contributed greatly to the development of the Plan and sections of this paper.

stress on human development rather than on a negatively oriented categorical problem approach, and its human resources emphasis in decision making. A significant departure from traditional patterns, the Center is organized according to a team management approach. Three major management teams, each covering a different program area, have been established: (a) *educational renewal* through teacher retraining; (b) *student services* through multidisciplinary consultative teams drawn from 60 MA-level persons in psychology, education, counseling, and speech; and (c) *program planning and development*, in which several new programs are in the process of development.

Because the Houston Plan involves a total change in the way education is defined and children are taught, and because change in any form must begin with people, another key element in the Plan is the Educational Renewal Project; it complements the new methods of working with children through an extensive program for the growth and enrichment of the teacher.

Center for Human Resources Development

The philosophy of the Center is that all education should be special education, each child is unique, and the goal of education is to find and meet the needs of the individual child. Special Education in the State of Texas now appears to be committed to the idea that education must be appropriate to the child. Traditional labels are no longer suitable because exceptional children are seen as more alike than different from other children. All children learn and adjust to life better in every way if they can participate in the flow of learning and life in the school. Thus, the total program for all children must become special and incorporate the following goals:

1. To integrate the special and regular education programs, recognizing that each child is unique in the way he learns and that each child has different educational needs.
2. To make available the technology of a Continuous Progress Learning curriculum to meet the individual needs and differences of the entire educational community through teacher retraining.
3. To provide the regular classroom teacher with additional teacher aides, teacher specialists, and instructional materials.
4. To provide specialists in diagnostic and treatment procedures to support the efforts of the classroom teacher. To individualize the instructional programs and, thus, to provide the opportunity for individualized learning.

The immediate objectives, under these goals, are as follows:

1. To develop an intervention strategy that stresses prevention in the formative years rather than treatment after the fact.

2. To develop a consultative model in the delivery of specialized assistance to the classroom teacher.
3. To provide a continuum of services from the classroom teacher to the most highly-skilled specialists in specific learning or behavior problems.

Schools must provide the setting in which diverse needs can be met and a wide range of growth experiences can take place. In its "Goals for the Seventies," the HISD committed itself to providing teachers, principals, and schools that will nurture in each child the following abilities:

1. To value and view himself as a worthy person.
2. To think realistically and communicate effectively with others in solving life's problems.
3. To develop marketable skills.
4. To experience joy in creative activities and to appreciate the many ways in which leisure time can be used.
5. To appreciate the complex and changing world and society and to take an active part in channeling that change in constructive ways.

Few persons find fault with this philosophy; most say it should have been applied years ago. Parents and educators both recognized the need for an educational system that would permit a personalized approach to each child to assure his social growth and academic success. Over the past 10 to 20 years, major advances have been made in methods of personalized instruction that take into account the individual differences in the way children learn. These new methods, techniques, and materials, however, have been very slow to find their way into the average classroom. It has been difficult in the past to implement the best philosophies of learning, classroom management, and organizational theories because the administrative processes needed to effect change have not existed. The steps necessary to take any new concept, break it down, and apply it creatively in the day-to-day activities of children have been impossible in the rigid, inflexible classroom designs which evolved in this country over the past 50 years.

In practical terms, the Houston Plan is a comprehensive action program that picks up where the philosophies of education leave off. It pulls together advances in educational technology into comprehensive programs that are flexible and responsive to individual needs, and to the limitations of less than ideal urban school buildings. It provides a concrete, realistic, workable set of steps to individualize instruction and learning in schools.

The Houston Plan is two-pronged: First, it provides a setting in which teachers and administrators are given vastly more freedom to work creatively with each child. Second, it aims to create within the entire system mechanisms for responsiveness to educational advances and to the changing world which will ensure the constant renewal of educational practices on all levels.

It is plain that the Houston Plan is the outgrowth of the schools' failure to cope with urban problems in its present structure, and of their inability to effect change and utilize new methods and materials to improve its programs.

Another major stimulus to the development of the Houston Plan was the new state program for special education known as "Plan A." Provisions for this new state plan for special education were spelled out by the amendment to Article 2922-13, Section 1, subsection (4)a (Vernon's Texas Civil Statutes) which was passed by the 61st Texas Legislature in 1969. Under these new laws, all school districts in Texas must operate under Plan A by 1976. Essentially, Plan A has two major features: (a) the provision of comprehensive services for exceptional children beyond those that have been provided in the past, and (b) the creation of a number of new alternatives to meet the needs of exceptional children (as opposed to the self-contained, special education classroom, the major option under the old system). Schools are given the opportunity to develop comprehensive services for exceptional children, including their integration into the mainstream of school life.

To provide these additional services, school districts are funded for teachers, supportive personnel, and materials according to the needs of the total student enrollment, rather than on the basis of identifying and labeling children before any services can be made available. The Houston Independent School District, however, opted to develop a comprehensive program that included the provisions and resources of Plan A but went far beyond it.

Rationale for the Houston Plan

Several observations are necessary at this point on the influence of the concepts of organization behavior, systems analysis, and applied behavior analysis on the evolution of the Houston Plan, and on their effects on the main educational system. In the past, organizations have developed sub- or parallel systems to deal with children and programs that did not fit into either the behavioral or programmatic regularities (Sarason, 1972, pp. 62-68) of the system. For example, one of the major effects of large-scale testing programs has been to identify behavioral irregularities, remove them from the main system, partially or totally, and place the burden of resolving the irregularities either upon the children, parents, or staff of the sub- or parallel system. Little or no adaptation or modification was made in the main system. In fact, the effect of these mechanisms was to reinforce the behavioral and programmatic regularities of the main system.

Contrary to this approach, the Houston Plan recognizes that the development of the sub- or parallel system is a strategy that has been unfruitful, has created its own set of problems, and is contrary to modern learning theory, instructional strategies, and organizational practices. The Houston Plan emphasizes the development of an adaptive system that is responsive and relevant to the needs of all children; the focus of change is the program regularities of the main system. The burden for adaptation, which, previously, had rested unproportionately upon the child, now shifts to the system. The child is responsible only as one aspect of the environment comprising that system.

This approach calls for an analysis of both the programmatic and behavioral regularities of the main system. When there is a disparity between a regularity and the stated goals, a change in either the goal or regularity must logically follow. Since there was little probability that HISD would change its stated goals, systematic change of the entire system was the necessary alternative.

The Houston Plan for education has been conceived as a concrete strategy for achieving an appropriate personalized instructional program for each individual child. Parents and educators alike know that each child, from the most gifted to the most handicapped, learns in his unique way and at his own rate. The materials, resources, and specialists made available through Plan A marked a step toward individualizing instruction for all children in Houston schools.

With knowledge of the techniques and methods of personalized continuous progress learning, funds from the new state plan for special education, and U.S. Office of Education funds for the retraining of teachers, principals, and others, the HISD committed itself to the concept of individualized instruction and learning in a concrete, observable way. Several new programs have been developed which, when put together, will culminate in a truly personalized curriculum for each child.

The programs can be summarized as follows:

1. The development of an academic curriculum based on the concepts of multisensory and continuous progress learning.
2. The development of new instructional and classroom-management skills through retraining programs sponsored by the District.
3. Increasing the number of highly-skilled supportive personnel available to the classroom teacher on an immediate need basis.
4. Focussing these new personnel, resources, and materials in Precision Learning Centers that will be established in each elementary school.
5. Local student services committees that will develop and periodically review individualized instructional plans for each child. These plans may be implemented in either the regular classroom, the Precision Learning Center, or a supplementary class, or in any combination thereof, depending solely on the needs of the individual student.

The Role of the Teacher

During the past one hundred years of grade school development, the role of the teacher and the method of teaching changed from what is best for the child to what is most convenient for the teacher. The activities of the classroom are often selected according to their effect on the teacher. Personalizing instruction, however, means returning the emphasis of learning to the child. The classroom can and should become a place of enrichment and growth, not boredom and restriction; of excitement and joy, not frustration and anger; of success and not failure.

In the past, classroom teachers have been seen typically as the dispensers of knowledge, and students have been viewed as passive, dependent listeners. With the tremendous amount of knowledge being generated today, it is increasingly apparent that one person can no longer pass on all this information to students. It is also evident that, in the future, all adults will need to be involved in a continuous process of learning and relearning if they are to keep up in society. For this reason, children must learn *how to learn* and how to take responsibility for learning on their own. In a personalized instructional program, the role of the teacher is not that of the director of the class but that of *facilitator* or advisor or specialist of the learning process.

This attitude toward learning frees the teacher first, from thinking of himself as the sole source of knowledge in the classroom, and second, from the confines of the lock-step curriculum that assumes that all the children in the class are interested in and able to learn exactly the same things at the same time. With the new freedom, the teacher can begin to look at how each child learns and, with the help of supportive personnel, he can plan programs that focus specifically on each child's strengths and weaknesses. With individualized planning, flexibility and adaptability become the keys to preventing chronic failure and early withdrawal from school.

As flexibility is introduced into the regular education classroom, a much higher tolerance of the child's individuality becomes possible. It is no longer necessary for children to be regimented—to behave exactly alike at all times.

Relation of the Houston Plan to the Precision Learning Center Concept

A Precision Learning Center (PLC) (Fig. 1) to provide a high-intensity support service for the teacher and the child is being developed in most elementary schools. This Center will house the most modern instructional equipment and materials available. It will serve as a resource center for all children and teachers in the school and will be staffed by teams of specialists who are skilled in precision and diagnostic teaching and in the uses of instructional materials. Significantly, the Precision Learning Center will be the cornerstone for the implementation of the Houston Plan.

Under the present organizational structure of the HISD, regular and special education have been parallel systems. The barrier separating the programs allowed children to move from regular to special programs but seldom allowed children to move the other way. With the implementation of the Houston Plan, the departments of regular and special education will more effectively share their collective resources in an integrated program which will meet the needs of every child in the District. The point of convergence of the two programs can be the PLC.

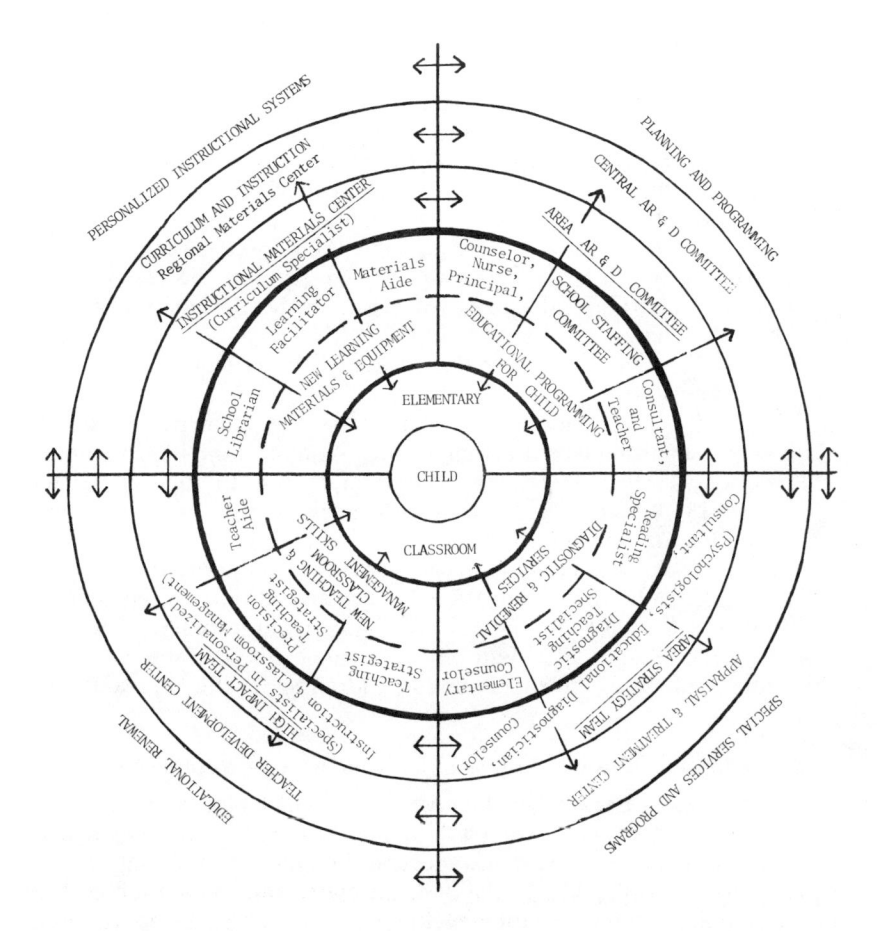

Figure 1. Components and Organization of a Precision Learning Center

Spatially, the PLC will be at least the size of two or three large classrooms (adjusted according to school size). Designed with architectural flexibility, it will be organized around multiple learning stations, media posts, individual study booths, and a variety of activity areas. An integrated system of advanced learning equipment, teaching methods, and materials of demonstrated effectiveness will also be included. Staffing and equipment will be designed to serve adequately the educational needs of a given school, and the children will move through the center as often as needed.

The PLC will be able to meet a broad spectrum of educational needs through the use of correlated learning resources that are tailored to each child's learning style. These needs might range from those presented by the child with learning difficulties to those characteristic of the very gifted child. Although special emphasis will be placed upon the 20 to 30 percent of the school population who encounter moderate to severe learning difficulties in the elementary grades, the center will be available for use by every child in the school.

Four major support segments of the PLC will be directed toward creating a high-intensity learning environment. These divisions, Educational Renewal, Special Services, Planning and Programming, and Personalized Instructional Systems, and their interrelationships, are diagrammed in Figure 1. Thus the PLC integrates the resources of previously separate and isolated programs. The design of the PLC enables the school to organize its supportive resources into a single integrated unit that serves as the educational heart or core for both children and staff.

The PLC represents a significant departure from traditional resource and learning center arrangements. As a unit, the PLC will have two complementary objectives: (a) to operate as a fully individualized learning environment for children with special needs, and (b) to serve as a model for behavioral management techniques, uses of instructional materials, and individualized curriculum planning. It will be the gateway through which educational renewal and curriculum innovations can be brought into the total educational environment of the elementary school. The PLC will represent one of the major avenues for the advancement of the education of children under the Houston Plan.

Educational Renewal Project: The Teacher Development Center

Educational Renewal is the program by which classroom teachers, principals, and administrators will be provided with continuing education in the use of the latest advances in the methods and materials of personalized instruction. In the past, the classroom teacher left college with training in the newest developments in research and teaching methods and then found little time to apply them because of the day-to-day concerns of teaching. Time and the technological explosion of the '60's isolated the teacher from the most recent developments in methods, techniques, and materials. The same problem in business and industry has forced many private corporations to establish instructional centers to bring a constant flow of new knowledge to their employees. Education has caught up with this trend and, in Houston, educational renewal is among the highest priorities.

The program is being conducted by the Teacher Development Center in the Center for Human Resources Development and Educational Renewal; it is the only known facility of its kind in the country today. Physically, the Teacher Development Center includes three elementary schools and one secondary school which were established as training sites. During the first school year, the program began the training of master teachers and the faculties of these schools.

In September 1972, a team of six teachers from each of the 85 schools participating in the Houston Plan started to cycle through the Teacher Development Center for approximately 120 hours of training in the latest methods of classroom management and personalized instruction. The long-range goal is to expand this program over the next several years to include all the teachers in the district. During the summer of 1972, the activities at the training sites were directed toward the training of (a) principals from the designated Houston Plan schools; (b) the precision, resource, and diagnostic teachers who will make up part of the staff of the Precision Learning Centers in those schools; and (c) members of the High Impact and support teams for the Precision Learning Centers.

The three Teachers Development Center campuses model the efficacy of programming for the handicapped child in the regular program through (a) the individualization of instruction and learning; (b) the use of TDC's differentiated staffing concepts for special education support personnel.

Regular-classroom teachers, special education teachers and leadership personnel are presented with the human, technical, and conceptual skills and strategies necessary for integrating and maintaining handicapped children in the regular classroom. The acquisition of these teaching skills and strategies will be facilitated by the opportunities to observe classroom models, rehearse teaching skills during simulation exercises, and receive immediate feedback concerning approximations to training objectives afforded by the TDC's modular curriculum.

During the next three years, teams from each of the 170 elementary and 70 secondary schools in the Houston Independent School District (HISD) will rotate through the training center for a total of five working days. After a follow-up period, the TDC staff provides home classroom consultation to the trainee for four working days. The trainee then returns to the TDC campus for three days for further observation of instructional materials and additional training content. By the end of the 1973-74 academic year, six regular classroom teachers in 85 schools and 240 special education teachers will be providing their school faculties with the instructional models necessary for the success of the handicapped child in the mainstream of Houston's education programs. In addition, more than 1500 regular classroom teachers will rotate through nine satellite centers for three days of training. These teachers will return to schools staffed with the 510 teachers trained during the 1972-73 academic year. Lastly, secondary TDC campuses will be completed for training of secondary personnel during 1973-74 year.

Special Services and Programs

A number of new supportive personnel in the local schools will be working with special education and regular children and teachers in the classrooms and in the Precision Learning Center in the school. Among these new roles will be that of the learning facilitator, the diagnostic teacher, and the precision-teaching strategist. In addition, the Center for Human Resources Development provides back-up through High Impact teams of skilled professionals, which consist of an Educational Diagnostician, Psychologist, Communication Specialist, Counselor, and Consultant. Each team will provide information, training, and support to the teaching specialists, the classroom teacher, parents, and other interested people in the community.

The new state plan for special education, by providing additional funding for new personnel, has made it possible to begin to fill the gap between the classroom teacher and appraisal and treatment services. Most of these new supportive personnel will work out of the Precision Learning Centers established in each school. The PLC will, thus, become the focal point in the school for consultation and interaction among the various support teams. Thus it becomes possible for the first time in the school district's history to pull together all the specialized programs, personnel, and materials, and to make them available immediately to any child experiencing difficulty in the classroom. These alternatives to the self-contained special class can be melded into an efficient delivery system that is aimed at meeting the educational needs of all children without removing them from the educational mainstream.

Educational Planning and Programming

Under the new program, a student services committee has been established at each local campus. With the help of the various support personnel, an individual educational plan is prepared for any child experiencing difficulty in the regular classroom. This plan may call for the introduction of new teaching methods and materials that are appropriate to the child's personal learning style and level of functioning. In addition, it will permit a child to divide his time, for example, among a self-contained special education classroom, a regular classroom, and the Precision Learning Center in the school, or any combination thereof. The amount of time spent in each learning environment will necessarily vary according to the needs of the particular child. If the problem is severe enough, the school planning committee may refer the child to the Area Services team from the Division of Human Resources Development and Educational Renewal so that the team of specialists may initiate whatever additional diagnostic or remedial services are needed.

Summary

The Houston Plan *is* a proactive plan designed to bring about major long term system-wide change.

The Houston Plan *is not* an attempt to develop more "special" programs.

The Houston Plan *is not* a plan designed only for educationally handicapped children.

The Houston Plan *is* an attempt to provide personalized instructional programs for all children through an integrated systems approach.

The Houston Plan *is* an attempt to provide flexible educational planning for any child experiencing difficulties in the classroom.

The Houston Plan *is not* going to move all children now in special education classes back into the regular classroom.

The Houston Plan *will* enable handicapped children to return to the regular classroom as long as they demonstrate that they are benefiting from that environment.

The Houston Plan *is* an attempt to utilize better all the resources of the District.

The Houston Plan *is* designed to provide quicker, more efficient student services.

The Houston Plan *will* provide teachers with new teaching skills.

The Houston Plan *will* create a Precision Learning Center in each school.

The Precision Learning Center *is* designed to provide assistance to every child from the most gifted to the most handicapped.

Reference

Sarason, S. B. *The culture of the school and the problem of change.* Boston: Allyn & Bacon, 1972.

Santa Monica School District Madison School Plan

In Exceptional Children in Regular Classrooms *(LTI/Special Education 1971), Frank Hewett called attention to the Santa Monica School System's "Madison School Plan for Exceptional Children." It is an attempt to foster the successful integration of handicapped children in regular classrooms and to serve them without grouping or teaching them according to categories. In pointing out some of the critical problems that had emerged when the program was instituted, Dr. Hewett warned that the effort to give every child who is able to benefit from regular-class participation the opportunity to do so requires administrative commitment from the top down to the local building level, and a policy that such an opportunity is a basic child right rather than a favor to be granted or withheld according to the convenience or disposition of individual teachers or administrators. All who have struggled to make this child right a reality for handicapped children would strongly agree.*

In the report that follows, Dr. Taylor has described the progress of the Madison School Plan since its beginnings in the "engineered classroom" which Hewett helped to develop. The program provides a way of accomplishing a service approach that has been long urged by Reynolds (in Exceptional Children in Regular Classrooms, *1971), that is, to label the service rendered but not the children served.*

The program's organization into placement settings that are graded according to individual child readiness to participate in regular-class activities constitutes a continuum that has some resemblance to the "Cascade of Services" model (Deno, Exceptional Children in Regular Classrooms, *1971). The Madison School continuum is based on assumptions of the levels of competence required to cope with regular-class expectancies. The continuum assumed in the "Cascade of Services" is described as the degree of specialized setting required to achieve adequate control of learning-related variables. In practice, the distinction between the two models is probably of little practical significance, especially if the conceptions of competency levels that are the bases for determining academic settings in the Madison School plan correlate highly with the degree of setting specialization that is required to control learning-related variables.*

The Madison School Plan: A Functional Model for Merging the Regular and Special Classrooms

Frank D. Taylor

and

Michael M. Soloway

Santa Monica Unified School District

Two issues have been of major concern to special education as it has struggled for a unique identity over the past several decades. The first is a re-orientation toward handicapped children based on educational and learning characteristics rather than on traditional medically based disability categories. The second is a definition of the role of special education in relation to regular education. Both issues were affected by the increased Federal funding of the '60's that reinforced the uniqueness of special education and brought about legislative reform, increased services, improved programs, better curricula, enlarged special education facilities, and a major emphasis on research.

As we enter the '70's we find that the issues are more clearly defined but still unresolved. With its new separate identity, special education is in a better position to assume more direct responsibilities for conceptualizing exceptionality in educational terms; nevertheless, specific examples of the assumption of these responsibilities are not widespread as yet. In addition, it is possible that the separation of special education from regular education is no longer a tenable position because of court decisions on the unconstitutionality of labeling and isolating children in special classes, and the continuing questioning of the efficacy of special-class placement.

The two issues were considered by the Santa Monica Unified School District in 1968 and 1969. Earlier, the District had developed an "engineered classroom" model to educate emotionally disturbed children; now it sought an alternative solution to the labeling issue, an operational model that would change the separate nature of the special classroom and, simultaneously, move the special classroom closer to the regular classroom. With support from Title VI-B (California State Department of Education) and Title III (United States Office of Education), the Madison School Plan evolved.

Readiness for Regular Classroom Functioning

The Madison School Plan began by adopting two points of view toward exceptional children:
1. All exceptional children are learners, first and foremost, and handicapped intellectually, emotionally, and physically, secondly.

2. Most exceptional children can profit from some time in the regular classroom provided steps are taken to schedule them appropriately and to offer necessary outside supportive help.

These two points of view reflect a shift of emphases away from the traditional special educational practice of relying primarily on medical labels as the basis for grouping handicapped children, and from the position that handicapped children require a separate educational experience. To organize these assumptions into a conceptual framework, the Madison School Plan discarded the traditional practice of viewing exceptional children in terms of IQ scores, sensory-motor ability, or socio-emotional functioning. Instead, a new standard —the dimension of readiness for regular classroom functioning (RRCF)—was established. Accordingly, all children, regardless of their disabilities, are viewed in terms of educationally salient variables: learning strengths and weaknesses. Thus, any child can be placed along this dimension, the inefficient learner at one end and the efficient learner at the other.

Traditionally, the inefficient learner has been the candidate for special educational programming. Because of the inflexibility of the special-classroom framework, however, children were placed full time into the special classroom or, when no such programs existed, they remained full time in the regular classroom; and there was nothing to bridge the gap between the two. The advent of the resource room provided some flexibility by providing supportive services for inefficient learners who remained in the regular classroom but, because of cost considerations, a dichotomous classroom arrangement was often dictated. Conceivably, one school could offer self-contained, special classes while another could offer resource-room service. Consequently, a model to provide both settings simultaneously was still needed.

Some handicapped children require full-time, special-class placement but others may need considerably less time in a special class. If such children are viewed according to the dimension of readiness for regular-class functioning, then those who need full-time, special-class placement fall at one end; those who can function full time in the regular classroom fall at the other end; and those who need both regular and special educational services are distributed in between. Thus, the dimension of readiness for regular classroom functioning is a continuum that ranges from inefficient learning and full-time, special-classroom placement to efficient learning and full-time, regular-classroom placement. All children, regular and special, fall somewhere along this dimension.

Because every regular classroom is different, any attempt to delineate the general characteristics of how a child should function is difficult. In Mrs. Jones' regular classroom, for example, functioning would be defined in terms of her particular teaching practices; in Miss

Smith's room, on the other hand, the definition of functioning would reflect her instructional techniques and organizational preferences. However, certain general levels of competence must be learned by all children if they are to function in any regular classroom. As a result, we specified the following four levels of competence along the dimension of readiness for regular-classroom functioning.

1. *Pre-Academic Competence.* This skill relates to the child's ability to function at the "readiness" or "process" level of learning. It includes the abilities of paying attention (A), starting an assignment immediately (S), working continuously without interruption (W), following task directions (F), doing what he is told (D), taking part verbally in discussions (T), and getting along with others (G). Pre-Academic skills also relate to adequacy in perceptual-motor functioning and proficiency in language.

2. *Academic Competence.* This level relates to the traditional core subjects that are basic to all school programs: reading, writing, spelling, and arithmetic. The abilities of being right (R) and neat, efficient, and well organized (N) are also included.

3. *Setting Competence.* This level relates to the student's ability to function and profit from instruction in the various settings found in all regular classrooms. Such settings include (a) instruction by the teacher standing in front of the entire classroom (T/LC), (b) the student working independently among the entire classroom (I/LG), (c) the teacher instructing a small group of students (I/SG), (d) the student working independently within the small group (I/SG), (e) the student working alone with the teacher (T/S), or (f) the student working independently with the teacher readily available for assistance (I/S).

4. *Reward Competence.* This level relates to the child's susceptibility to traditional classroom rewards. Does the child work for such incentives as the pure "joy of learning"? to acquire new knowledge and skills? for knowledge of results? or for social praise and recognition? Less traditional types of reinforcement include sensory and activity experiences, task completion, social attention, and tangibles.

The Madison School Plan was particularly concerned with organizing an administrative and instructional setting for educable mentally retarded (EMR) and educationally handicapped (EH) children. In California, the EH category refers to children who are traditionally called emotionally disturbed and learning disordered. However, every EMR and EH child falls along the dimension of readiness for regular-classroom functioning and within the four levels of competence. The parameters of the levels are stated in educational terms that can be translated directly into classroom practices. Indeed, the dimension of readiness for regular-classroom functioning offers the field of special education an alternative to viewing children in medically based terms.

In order to establish operational procedures under the dimension, the following four problems were considered first:

1. How to provide supportive settings for children not ready to function at the positive end of the dimension of readiness for regular classroom functioning, and what to emphasize in our setting?

2. How to assign staff to teach in these settings?

3. How to assess children in the four areas of competence: pre-academic, academic, instructional-setting functioning, and susceptibility to reinforcers?

4. How to coordinate the program with the entire school and assign responsibilities and total school staff?

Supportive Settings Along the Dimension of Readiness for Regular Classroom Functioning

At one end of the continuum are some EMR and EH children who are inefficient learners and unable to profit from any time in the regular classroom. Thus they need full-time, special-classroom placement. The problem was to provide them with a setting that would offer the least expectancy and the most support in terms of pre-academic, academic, instructional setting, and reward. The degrees of expectancy established for each level of competence for these children were as follows:

Pre-Academic: Major emphasis on "attending," "starting," "working," "following task directions," and "doing what he is told."

Academic: Minor emphasis on academic assignments, "being right," and "being neat."

Setting: The child works independently at a large desk or in a study booth in a one-to-one relationship with the teacher.

Reward: A checkmark system, by which the child's task and behavioral functioning are evaluated, is linked to tangible rewards and free-time activities. Other more traditional rewards are utilized when the children have demonstrated that they can profit from such incentives. Consideration is given to any type of incentive that will motivate the child to learn. Because of the strong emphasis on pre-academic skills, this supportive setting has been designated *Pre-Academic I.*

Not all handicapped children are inefficient learners requiring full-time, special-classroom placement, however. Some children are ready to function in non-academic activities, such as art, music, or physical education, away from the special classroom. Thus, a second setting is needed that offers more emphasis, and provides less support, in terms of our four parameters. The following expectations are needed for them:

Pre-Academic: Minor emphasis on the behavior stressed in Pre-Academic I and major emphasis on "taking part" verbally and "getting along" with others.

Academic: Major emphasis on the basic school subjects. Academic remediation is supplemented by special materials and resources.

Setting: In a teacher-small-group setting, the children work independently in shared desk space. Group interaction and cooperation are emphasized.

Reward: The checkmark card is still utilized but tangible reinforcement is eliminated. Children work for free-time exchange with greater emphasis on more traditional types of rewards, such as social approval.

Since some emphasis on Pre-Academic functioning has been retained but the setting is closer to a typical classroom, this supportive setting was designated *Pre-Academic II.*

Provisions were also made for those EMR and EH children who are able to spend increasing amounts of time in the regular classroom and need opportunities to demonstrate their learning skills in a simulated regular-classroom setting. The expectations for them are as follows:

Pre-Academic: Minor emphasis on these behaviors as the child is ready to master higher-order skills.

Academic: Major emphasis on school subjects with a shift from only remedial instruction to remedial and grade-level curriculum.

Setting: In order to simulate a regular-classroom situation, a large number of children are grouped together to receive instruction primarily from the teacher. Opportunities to function independently within the large group are also provided.

Reward: Since the child is moving closer to regular-classroom functioning, the checkmark system is replaced by a numerical grading system for effort, quality of work, and citizenship.

Since this setting emphasizes academic learning, it has been designated *Academic I.*

The next step is the other end of the dimension of readiness for regular-classroom functioning, the regular classroom for the efficient learner. For purposes of our conceptual framework, the regular classroom has been designated *Academic II.*

Staff and Space Utilization

Cost factors are an important consideration in any attempt to make a conceptual model operational. A program that offers an alternative service-delivery framework is not viable if it exceeds the cost effectiveness of more traditional, self-contained classrooms. Consequently, the Madison School Plan aimed at utilizing the materials and furniture that are commonly found in most school settings, and to avoid elaborate learning environments or expensive classroom materials. (This same approach was used in 1965 when the "engineered classroom" was implemented in the Santa Monica School District.)

Two adjacent special classrooms, one for the EMR and one for the EH, were combined by an inner, connecting door. The Pre-Academic I setting was assigned to one classroom and the Pre-Academic II and Academic I settings were assigned to the other. This arrangement is now referred to as the Learning Center, a name that replaces more traditional labels like "special classroom," "room for the retarded," or "room for the disturbed." In essence, two special classrooms became the foundation of an administrative/instructional framework in which handicapped children are grouped according to salient, educational variables.

The Learning Center, with its three transitional settings that lead back to the regular classroom, are staffed by the existing personnel who normally would teach separate EMR and EH classrooms. The EH teacher and teaching associate are responsible for the Pre-Academic I setting, and the EMR teacher and teaching associate maintain both the Pre-Academic II and Academic I setting. The teacher's primary responsibility is to teach either a small-group lesson in Pre-Academic II or a large-group lesson in Academic I. Simultaneously, the teaching associate assists children in the corresponding setting during the periods of independent work. The arrangements are quite flexible in terms of teacher and teacher-associate movement as they can be changed according to the instruction planned for the children. The needs of the students to be served and the composition of the groups must be considered before the rooms within the center are arbitrarily organized.

We learned that, although the Pre-Academic I, Pre-Academic II, and Academic I framework is generally used in the Learning Centers in Santa Monica, it must be flexible. Several other variations have been used when the particular needs of the students in a school required different instructional emphasis. When all the students need instructional emphasis in readiness skills, two Pre-Academic I settings can be established. When some students are beyond Pre-Academic I and can function in Pre-Academic II, but none can function in Academic I, than a Pre-Academic I and two Pre-Academic II settings may be organized. The educational needs of the exceptional children, that is, their readiness for regular classroom functioning (RRCF), dictates the nature of the instructional framework. The children are not just arbitrarily placed in an instructional setting that is unable to meet their educational needs.

In Pre-Academic I, the room is organized into pre-academic and academic work areas. The latter consists of 12 tables, each 2 x 4 feet, that permit each child to work independently and with sufficient room for the teacher to assist the child without overwhelming him physically. A teaching station provides additional instruction in a one-to-one setting. Several study booths are set up to supplement the work area.

The room also includes several areas that are designed to develop pre-academic skills. The order center teaches children to learn how to pay attention, work, and follow directions. The exploratory center emphasizes the teaching of environment through enriching science and art tasks. The communication center is designed to foster social relationships among the children. These centers are integral parts of the Pre-Academic I design; they are the bases of intervention strategies and the places where rewarding activities may be enjoyed when academic tasks have been completed. The teacher's desk, several storage cabinets, and some bookcases complete the physical set up of Pre-Academic I.

The major focus of Pre-Academic II is on the encouragement of group interaction and verbal participation. This instructional setting is achieved by moving three 2 x 4 desks into a horseshoe-type arrangement. The teacher sits in the middle with a blackboard directly behind her which she uses for written lessons. Several tables are arranged nearby so children can learn how to work independently while sharing desk space. This setting is situated near the connecting door to Pre-Academic I so that children may be moved back and forth with a minimum of disturbance. Pre-Academic II is separated from Pre-Academic I by a partition of storage cabinets, or perhaps a bookcase. The setting takes up approximately one-fourth of the classroom.

The other three-fourths of this second classroom is used for Academic I. Because this setting is a simulated regular classroom, the desks are arranged according to the existing regular classrooms in the school. Most of the lessons in this setting are taught by the teacher in front of the classroom. The students share desk space and are expected to function independently, as in a regular classroom.

Pre-Program Assessment

In order to assess the readiness of handicapped children for regular-classroom functioning, we need to find out how ready a child is to function in one of the instructional settings. Because the intent of the Madison School Plan is to shift emphasis away from the diagnostic-medical model for grouping purposes, we needed a pre-assessment instrument that was related to the four levels of competence for regular-classroom functioning. Through such an instrument, we could eliminate the problem of translating medical-diagnostic data, which are of limited usefulness in educational planning. In the Madison School Plan's philosophy, elaborate pre-program assessment is de-emphasized and more emphasis is placed on ongoing assessment. Once the child is placed in the special classroom, assessment procedures become critical to determine how long the child will require special educational programming.

To achieve the objective of relating pre-program assessment to educational planning, we developed the "Madison Plan Placement Inventory" (MPPI), which takes about 10 minutes to complete. The measure consists of 24 questions that relate to the four levels of competence on our RRCF dimension. Before assigning a child to the Learning Center, the inventory is filled out by the teacher, regular and/or special, who last taught the child. A tally sheet determines a weighted score that reflects "how ready" the child is to function in the PAI, PAII, AI, or AII settings.

We have labeled the setting but not the child. This difference is reflected in the way that children may function in several settings throughout the day. The MMPI reflects our point of view that, traditionally, too much emphasis has been given to pre-program evaluation while ongoing assessment after placement has been neglected. This situation resulted in a "locking-in effect" in which children were placed in special classrooms and often remained there for their entire school experience. The Madison School Plan has been designed to eliminate such self-containment by providing a systematic process for reintegration into the regular classroom.

Reintegration

To combat the influence of the self-fulfilling prophecy, the Santa Monica School District has maintained a policy of compulsory reintegration since 1966. All special-classroom rosters are destroyed at the completion of the school year, in June. The following Fall, most EMR and EH children are placed into regular-classroom rolls. Our data indicate that 33% of the EMR and EH children are not referred out for placement during the new semester. This phenomenon may possibly be attributed to maturation over the summer or to teacher variability. However, the policy of compulsory reintegration is one method of preventing locking in. It must also be mentioned that this policy is not applicable to the entire population of children. Those EMR and EH children who are unable to function in a regular classroom for even a limited amount of time are certainly not placed there. They begin school in the Fall in the Learning Center. Although the policy reintegrates one-third of the handicapped children in the mainstream, our Plan is designed to facilitate the transition back for the other two-thirds.

Compulsory reintegration establishes a link with the regular classroom that is maintained after the child is referred out for special-classroom placement. The regular teacher perceives the child as a member of her class, and retains a desk for him throughout the school year. Although the child may spend most or all of his time in the Learning Center, provisions for his eventual return are considered. This framework eliminates "shopping," the practice in which the special teacher hunts for a willing regular-classroom teacher to accept a handicapped child.

The link with the regular classroom is preserved through compulsory reintegration. All children who are assigned to the Pre-Academic II and Academic I settings spend some time in the regular classroom. Initially, participation in the regular classroom may be limited to opening exercises or to non-academic subject areas like music, art, or physical education. The PAI, PAII, AI settings are designed to facilitate the handicapped child's increased participation in the regular classroom; they culminate with his participation in academic subjects and, eventually, for the entire school day.

Flexible Grouping within the Learning Center

Of course, not all handicapped children are able to profit from regular-classroom participation. It is highly unrealistic, on the basis of the knowledge within the field of special education today, to consider that the self-contained classroom can be totally eliminated. For those children who are not ready to meet the demands of regular-classroom functioning, the need for a self-contained classroom remains. The Pre-Academic I instructional setting is designed to handle the EMR and/or EH child who needs the support of full-time placement in the special classroom. Because of the availability and close proximity of Pre-Academic II, the teacher has the option of moving the child between settings when his behavior is within range of handling the degree of expectancy in the new setting.

Flexible grouping is reflected by movement patterns within the Learning Center and between the special facility and the regular classroom. In 1971, 86% of the EMR and EH children spent time in more than one setting, that is, during the school year they moved from PAI to PAII, or PAI to AI, or PAII to AI. Of the population of handicapped children, 82% (90 EMR, 72 EH) spent at least one hour daily in the regular classroom. These statistics reflect the flexible nature of our functional model. It offers an administrative/instructional framework that facilitates movement within the special classrooms and between the regular and special classrooms. The static quality of the self-contained, special classroom is supplanted by a more dynamic grouping arrangement.

In addition to being more functional for the handicapped children, the grouping arrangement has several distinctive advantages for both the EMR and EH teacher. In the traditional EMR classroom, every year the teacher is faced with a heterogeneous population of "retardates." The children vary considerably in terms of academic and behavioral functioning and those who display behavioral disturbances often upset the learning climate for the entire classroom. It is unfortunate for the children and for the teacher, yet one is prevented from solving the predicament. The availability of a "special class" for the special class is highly improbable. In the Madison School Plan grouping arrangement, however, children with behavioral problems are placed in the Pre-Academic I setting, which is designed to handle the repertoire of conduct problems. By eliminating the several behavior problems from her classroom, the EMR teacher is able to instruct more children than she could customarily, because the consuming duties of discipline are minimized.

The EH teacher handles those children whose behavioral repertoires often fall outside the limits of regular-classroom parameters. Often, after utilizing special strategies and shaping these behavioral repertoires to acceptable regular-classroom limits, the EH teacher is rebuffed when she tries to find a regular-classroom teacher to accept the children. Thus, the practice of "shopping" is perpetuated. This phenomenon disappears in the Madison School Plan framework. When the EH child is ready to move from the self-contained placement, he is assigned to the Pre-Academic II setting. This assignment need not be a dichotomous decision in terms of time constraints. The teacher may decide to move the EH child, for one hour daily, only during reading, or full-time assignment. Thus, grouping flexibility is evidenced once more. If the child succeeds in PAII, he spends more time in that setting. If he is not able to handle the increased demands, reassignment to the PAI setting occurs with minimal disruption to all. These advantages make teaching in this framework highly desirable for the EMR and EH teacher.

Because of the integration process, the Learning Center also serves as a **resource-room** facility for **regular children who are experiencing academic and/or behavioral problems in the regular classroom.** Consequently, the Learning Center is a school resource that provides service delivery to 50 children, both regular and special, in lieu of the 27 that would be serviced under the traditional, self-contained special classroom.

The time will probably never come when a single program will provide a panacea for the myriad of complexities involved in the education of exceptional children. The time, however, has arrived when the nation's schools, teachers, and parents are seeking alternatives to solutions now available. New solutions are necessary to solve current problems that encumber programs for the exceptional child. Improvements will encompass the following considerations:
1. Present grouping by disability categories is no longer desirable.
2. The individual teacher has difficulty dealing with the wide range of learning problems within a single category.
3. Small school districts have difficulty providing a full range of services to meet the educational needs of all children.
4. Many children do not fit a single category of disability.

5. Educational models with well-defined objectives that lend themselves to empirical measurement are needed in the field of special education.
6. Lack of specific educational tasks, techniques, daily schedules, and program approaches have sometimes led to "cafeteria" or "intuitive" approaches.
7. The integration of handicapped students into the mainstream of the regular classroom is highly desirable.
8. Constantly increasing expenses necessitate the evaluation of special programs in terms of cost effectiveness.
9. The labeling of students with its possible changes in self-concept is the concern of everyone, not just the various minority groups.

All of the above factors were considered and incorporated in the original formulation of the Madison School Plan Model. The program has been tried out in the "real world" of a public-school setting for the past three years. The continued development of the model and its widespread use in public schools are dependent on the answering of three major questions: How does the handicapped child profit from being grouped in this framework in comparison to traditional grouping arrangements? How ready is the public school to implement a new administrative/instructional model that will facilitate integration of handicapped children into the regular classroom? Are the regular teachers equipped with the necessary knowledge and skills to educate the exceptional child? These questions must be dealt with in the future if the field of special education is to continue its growth as an independent discipline.

References

Hewett, F. M. *The emotionally disturbed child in the classroom.* Boston: Allyn & Bacon, 1968.

Hewett, F. M. Educating engineering with emotionally disturbed children. *Exceptional Children*, 33, 459-67, March 1967.

Hewett, F. M., Taylor, F. D., & Artuso, A. A. The Santa Monica Project. *Exceptional Children*, 34, 387, February 1968.

Hewett, F. M., Taylor, F. D., Artuso, A. A., & Stillwell, R. J. The Santa Monica Project: Phase two. Final Report (U.S. Office of Education, Bureau of Research, Project No. 7-1298), 1969.

Taylor, F. D., Artuso, A. A., Soloway, M. M., Hewett, F. M., Quay, H. C., & Stillwell, R. J. A learning center plan for special education. *Focus on Exceptional Children*, 4, May 1972.

Film: "The Madison School Plan"—21 minutes, color.
   Copies of the film may be obtained from:
   Mrs. Frances Layman
   Department of Special Services
   1723 4th Street
   Santa Monica, California 90401

The Fail-Save Model

Glen VanEtten and Gary Adamson began to develop their Fail-Save model while they were participating in the EPDA Special Education project at Olathe, Kansas. The training program developed at the Olathe Education Modulation Center has made a substantial contribution to the field through the training it has provided for educators and other persons from all over the country. Many individuals have attended the workshops, observed demonstrations, benefitted from staff consultation, and profited from the learning-task analysis of teaching materials and the materials retrieval systems developed at the Center. The concept of the M and M teacher (Materials and Methods specialist) was developed there. The final report* for the 1971-72 year describes the Olathe project activities in detail.

The Fail-Save Model is included here because it builds on the Olathe work to tackle the problem of how to keep a child with special needs from becoming permanently trapped in a service plan that is either ineffective or outgrown. Increasing attention must be directed to this problem because of the recent court decisions that have focussed on how educational placement and demission decisions are made, and whether the treatment opportunities, which are given as the reason for program assignment, actually are provided once placement is made.

---

* Welch, D. C. Prescriptive Materials Laboratory Development, EPDA Special Education Final Report, Olathe Unified School District, No. 233, Olathe, Kansas 66061.

The Fail-Save Program:
A Special Education Service Continuum

Glen VanEtten
Associate Professor, Special Education
University of New Mexico

and

Gary Adamson
Associate Professor, Special Education
University of New Mexico

The effective, efficient, and economical delivery of services to handicapped children has emerged as a major challenge to special educators today. Because the traditional self-contained classroom has been found to be inadequate (Dunn, 1968; Guskin & Spicker, 1968; and Hammond, 1972), a number of educators have proposed new models either to replace it or to extend its delivery of services.

Lilly (1971), for example, described a model that is a radical approach to classrooms. Based on the Regional Resource Center (RRC) concept, a new professional in special education has been proposed who would provide diagnostic and educational consultation for the classroom teacher. Earlier, Dr. Adamson had designed and implemented a role for a special education consultant which he termed a "Methods and Materials Consultant/Teacher." All three models, however, utilize a single mode of service delivery model. The large variance among children is recognized in them but not the necessity for varying the methods of delivering services to the children.

Reynolds (1962) and Deno (1970) called for the development of varied types of services; Reynolds, through a "hierarchy of special education programs" and Deno, through a "cascade of services." Essentially, both recognized the necessity of different levels of service for children depending upon the severity of a child's problem and the intensity of treatment he needs. Neither model, however, provides an operational basis for implementation; the decision data for placing a child in any given level are not given nor are the criteria provided for moving a child from one level to another.

What is needed, apparently, is an operational model that is based on both experience and data. Such a model, what we have termed the "Fail-Save Model," is described here. Without the encumbrance of labels, it has the capacity to provide children with a continuum of services that can meet their educational and psychological needs.

This educational continuum system draws heavily upon successful and unsuccessful experience of the past and avoids generalizing beyond the available data. It is based on the work of the Educational

Modulation Center (E.M.C.), a Public Law 89-10, Title III Project in U.S.D. No. 233, Olathe, Kansas, whose purpose was

> . . . to effect a procedural model whereby children with educa-. tional problems may be provided with an efficient educational program and remain in the regular classroom (Adamson, 1970, p. 1).

The purpose was accomplished by a model that provided aid to the teacher, parent, and child through a key person, the Methods and Materials Consultant/Teacher (M & M). The M & M's primary functions were as follows:

1. To assist in diagnosing and pinpointing the child's specific academic and behavioral problems.

2. To develop an instructional prescription utilizing the child's available responses, the scope and sequence of the curriculum, and the application of instructional materials and techniques to move the child forward through the scope and sequence of the curriculum.

3. To train parents and teachers to deal effectively with the child's learning and/or behavior problem.

4. To monitor the child's progress throughout the program.

E.M.C. data were completed on 308 children over three years. Of them, 70% improved their rate of achievement in reading after consultant intervention developed educational prescriptions for them (Adamson, 1970). The remaining 30% did not respond; their rates of achievement in reading either did not change or went down. However, the results in arithmetic achievement were slightly better. When the results of the intervention group were compared with those of a control group that received no intervention of any type, the first were significantly better.

In addition to the educational improvement, 85% of the children serviced at the E.M.C. improved significantly in measured self-concept scores, and over 90% significantly improved their classroom behaviors, according to teachers' ratings. Less than 10% of the control group improved in either self-concept or behavior.

The Fail-Save Continuum

Paralleling Gallagher's (1972) time-limit contract, in which special-service personnel are limited in the amount of time they have to attain stated goals, the Fail-Save model limits the time that a child can spend in any of its phases and, consequently, the amount of time available for the achievement of a program. If a child cannot be helped within 2 or 3 years, one can assume that continued input also will be ineffective. A time limit forces program accountability as a child is given every possible opportunity to show that he can succeed in the mainstream of education. If, during the time limit, a child makes no progress, it is apparent that either the system has been unable to adapt to him and meet his needs or it does not have the resources to deal with him in a normal way. If the Fail-Save system fails to help a child progress, a special environment is then created for him (Alternate Phase IV).

The Fail-Save continuum consists of the following five phases and an alternate placement provision:

Phase I. Consultation

Service must always begin in Phase I. It can be initiated only by the classroom teacher who refers a child. Before making the referral, however, she must confer with the child's parents and the building principal. Upon receipt of the referral, the Methods and Materials Consultant/Teacher (M & M) consults with the teacher and building principal, first, to gather additional data, and second, to arrange for a period of time in the classroom to observe the child's specific academic deficits and behavior problems. This observation period is part of the diagnostic process.

Diagnostic Procedures. The diagnostic process must accomplish the following four goals:

1. *Determine that all of the child's sensory systems are intact.* Vision screening, both near and far point, is essential. Hearing testing is also advisable as many children with mild learning problems often have mild hearing problems as well. Although audiograms may not always be medically significant, they may have educational significance. Special seating and planning is needed even for children with mild hearing or vision deficits.

2. *Determine the child's best mode of learning.* Some existing evidence suggests that some children learn better by one mode than by another. While the evidence is incomplete, the M & M must be alert to the fact that some children may learn better visually while others prefer auditory stimuli. It is the M & M's responsibility to determine the child's preferred and most efficient learning method.

3. *Identify a motivation system.* Part of the diagnostic function is to determine what turns the child on to learning. Each individual has different reinforcers; only when these are known to the teacher can she utilize them to increase the child's learning rate.

4. *Identify the child's specific academic and behavior problem.* Problem behaviors are a function of perspectives—the child's, the teacher's, and the parent's. The role of the M & M is to separate the child's problem from the teacher's and parent's interpretations of it. The Target Behavior Kit (Kroth, 1972), a game that utilizes a Q-sort technique in which parents, teachers, and students identify and agree upon a problem that can be approached systematically, has been used successfully as an aid to achieving this goal.

5. *Identify academic skills deficits.* The accurate and specific identification of academic deficiencies is critical if Phase I is to be successful. The function of academic diagnosis is to pinpoint critical curricular skill responses that are in the child's repertoire and critical responses that are lacking. Appropriate skills responses are determined by looking at the curriculum scope and sequence and asking what responses can he make that the curriculum demands of him. In the diagnostic process, the child's present level of achievement through the curricula is measured by a standardized achievement test, preferably one that is simple and brief and has a high level of reliability and validity. (The Wide Range Achievement Test (W.R.A.T.) has been used successfully for this purpose.) The test should be used only as one objective measure of change for purposes of evaluation.

Several instruments are now available for specific skills diagnosis. The most complete and comprehensive is the Basic Education Skills Inventory (B.E.S.I.) (Adamson, Shrago, & VanEtten, 1971). The Inventory is used to identify deficit academic skill responses. It is composed of four sections, two reading and two arithmetic. The items are designed to provide the M & M (or diagnostician) with an inventory of basic-skill responses that are demanded in most reading and arithmetic curriculum and that are mastered by most children in most curricula by the end of the third or fourth grade.

The B.E.S.I. is based upon the principle that the most important aspect of such diagnosis is the identification of responses needed in the child's curriculum and the determination of those responses that are lacking. It is not sufficient to know that a child has a reading problem or even that he has problems with work-attack skills. It is more helpful to know that he has a problem with phonic skills, although even this information is not sufficient. What is necessary, for example, is to know that the child has difficulty with initial consonant sounds, and to know exactly which sounds the child can and cannot make when he is presented with the visual stimuli of sounds.

Consultation Procedures. After the B.E.S.I. has been administered and all other diagnostic procedures have been completed, the results are shared by the M & M with the teacher, parent, and principal. The teacher is shown how the tests were given and instructed in the interpretation of the results.

During the first week after the referral, the M & M has been visiting and observing in the classroom often. The primary purpose of the observations is to understand the methods and materials the teacher is using with her children in order to be able to provide suggestions for change and to design programs that fit into the teacher's *modus operandi.* The M & M observes how the child interacts with his peers to be able to suggest possible ways of improving or utilizing such interactions. During the second and third weeks, the teacher and the

M & M develop an educational prescription for the child. In this process, the regular-class teacher is taught to use the Prescriptive Materials Retrieval System to identify rapidly and select appropriate instructional materials (VanEtten & Adamson, 1970; VanEtten, 1969; VanEtten & Adamson, 1969). The selection is made on the basis of characteristics that match the child's response deficits and learning style and the teacher's teaching style.

Only one specific task is selected for programming. When educational prescriptions are attempted for all deficits, the results are usually frustrating for the teacher and demoralizing for the student, as both fail to see the needed progress, and the child's inability to learn is reinforced. The adequacy of a prescription for one deficit, which can be measured continuously, will soon be revealed with precision-teaching techniques. Should progress not be evident, then a program change can be made easily. Since the regular-class teacher has been taught to use the PMRS and has been involved in the prescription-planning activities, she can often make the program changes unassisted. The teacher is also taught to use operant procedures to control social and educational aspects of the child's behavior.

The parents, all this time, have been attending and participating in a four-week (12 hours) training sequence in which the application of behavior principles to the control of their child's behavior is emphasized (McDowell, 1969). They are taught to identify (pinpoint) behavior that needs to be modified. These may be behaviors whose rate needs to be increased or decreased. To learn how to count, graph, and consequate behaviors, the parents are required to modify both an academic and a social behavior. The Target Behavior Kit (Kroth, 1972) has been a valuable aid in helping parents to pinpoint and select behaviors for modification.

During the next five to six weeks, the M & M maintains close contact with the child and his teacher. Continual on-the-job training of the regular-class teacher is accomplished by assisting her in the ongoing prescriptive process. As the child progresses and masters new skills, his program must be changed and new skills must be identified and programmed. If the child does not respond as anticipated it may be necessary for the M & M to tutor him temporarily in order to gather more relevant data. This one-to-one tutoring ratio should be of very brief duration because the M & M must never assume the responsibility for the child's education; that belongs to the regular-class teacher and she must be allowed and encouraged to maintain it.

At the conclusion of the 10-week period, the child's progress is checked. The achievement test is readministered to ascertain change in his rate of achievement. The rate of achievement is computed with achievement at the time he entered the program as the base. The simplest way of showing the rate of achievement is by graph, although it can be done statistically also.

Decision Point 1

If the child's rate of achievement during treatment is higher than before treatment, the direct service of the M & M to the teacher can be terminated and regular-class instruction can be continued. Prescriptive instruction should be continued by the regular-class teacher and the M & M should remain available on a call basis. The amount of change in learning rate necessary for the special services to be terminated varies from child to child. Any decision on termination must involve the parents, teacher, M & M, principal, and other important decision makers in the system.

In the event that the child has not changed his learning rate in a positive direction, or if the rate of change is not satisfactory to the decision makers, two subsequent actions can be taken: (a) the child can be recycled through Phase I (the Consultant Phase) of the system, or (b) he can be moved in to Phase II (the Resource Room).

Phase II.   The Resource Room/Regular Class

Diagnostic Procedures. In Phase II, diagnosis of a different dimension, which involves a greater array of professionals, is necessary. Because the strictly academic program of Phase I was not successful, the child's basic learning process must now be studied. Such diagnosis includes the testing of his intelligence, visual perceptual skills, motor learning skills, basic language skills, psycholinguistic skills, and auditory skills; a complete medical examination; and a study of his extra-school environment.

Implementation Procedures. Following the in-depth evaluation, a meeting is held with all the concerned persons and specific plans are made for the future education of the child. His educational program is determined and the role and responsibility of each concerned person are defined, particularly those of the parents, the resource room teacher, and the regular-class teacher. Considerable flexibility is possible as the resource room program is, by design, highly experimental.

The child spends most of his day in the regular class with short periods in the resource room. In this phase, placement is made for a maximum of 90 school days only and then a decision is made on the child's program. The results of the multidisciplinary diagnostic team's work provide the resource room teacher (RRT) with data for programming, and she provides supplemental instruction in the areas in which the child is experiencing the most difficulty. The RRT works with individuals or small groups, scheduling them for varying periods of time according to individual needs.

Scheduling is an important aspect of the resource room's success or failure. Children are not scheduled when it will preclude their participation in important activities in the regular class. For example, if a child has a major reading problem, he is not scheduled in the resource room during the period that reading instruction is given in his regular class. Instead, the RRT helps the regular-class teacher by giving supplemental instruction.

The RRT functions as an educational and remedial specialist. With the small-group load, she is able to use methods such as kinesthetic and multi-sensory approaches that require more time than the regular-class teacher is able to give. The RRT also works on specific communication and perceptual deficits, such as auditory process, visual motor deficits, and deficits in language development, which have been determined by the team evaluation.

The RRT provides valuable assistance to the regular-class teacher by continuing the consultation activities of the M & M. She is able to assist the regular-class teacher in diagnosis, program planning, and selection of appropriate materials in a continuous, close, working relationship which helps to assure success in this phase.

It should be noted here that the regular-class teacher is still responsible for the child's educational program; the M & M and RRT merely provide expertise to support her. The M & M maintains relationships with the child, parents, RRT, and regular-class teacher, and she helps to coordinate all services for the child. The parents continue to provide instructional assistance at home and they are continually involved with the programming of their child.

Decision Point 2

At the end of 90 school days, if the child's rate of achievement has increased satisfactorily, two program actions by the decision makers are possible: (a) the child is returned to the regular class and special services are terminated, or (b) the child is returned to Phase I. If the rate of achievement has not improved satisfactorily, two decisions are again possible: (a) the child is recycled through Phase II for another 90 days (he can be recycled only once in this phase) or (b) he is transferred to Phase III of the system.

Phase III

Phase III consists of placement in a special-classroom/resource room program that has several advantages over an abrupt placement in a self-contained special class. The effect on the child's self-concept is less deleterious as it allows him to maintain relationships with his peers. Although he spends the major part of the day in a special class, a small part is spent in the resource room. Placement in Phase III is limited to nine months; administratively, the function of the special classroom/resource room is similar to that of the resource room in Phase II. The special classroom has a small enrollment (10 to 12), which permits concentrated instruction in specific areas. Programming is intense in it and the goal is to return the child to his regular class.

The programming concentrates on academic progress as well as on the training of the basic perceptual processes that had been determined to need strengthening by the team diagnosis. The child is programmed according to his modality strengths, that is, auditory learners can be taught through the auditory channel while their visual perceptual functions are strengthened.

Phase III is the first time in the system that responsibility for the child's educational program is taken from the regular-class teacher; it is given to the special-class teacher, instead. The M & M and RRT support and provide her with their expertise.

At the end of Phase III, the child's rate of learning is re-evaluated. Decisions at this point are limited. The child has been in the program for nearly two or three years and the time-limit contract has expired.

Decision Point 3

If the child's academic behavior shows no progress, decisions are made on the basis of his social development. In the model being presented here, two decisions are possible: (a) the child can be returned to Phase II, resource room/regular class, or (b) the child can be referred to Phase IV, which is long-term placement in a special class. If the child is recycled through the resource room (Phase II) and the desired progress is still not achieved, Phase III may be repeated and then the child must be returned to the regular class or moved to Phase IV, the special class.

Placement in a Phase IV self-contained classroom can be made for a maximum period of 36 weeks. Such a placement strongly suggests either total failure by the system or recognition that the child's problems are unique and his presence is detrimental to the education of other children. Any child referred to Phase IV needs extensive support and assistance because he is either so physically handicapped that the facilities of the regular class are not adequate or his non-school environment has created a situation that is beyond the scope of the school to deal with it effectively. He may also be so low in adaptive and intellectual behavior that he is unable to function in any setting other than the special class. The decision to refer the child to Phase IV is made only with the approval of all concerned persons.

Phase IV.   The Special Classroom

The special-classroom phase functions entirely differently from the previous phases. It probably should utilize a well-developed and tested curriculum, such as the persistent life-problems approach (Bransford, 1969) or a social-learning curriculum (Goldstein, 1969), and it should include a heavy emphasis on vocational training.

Phase IV. Alternate

An option at the end of Phase IV is another component of the continuum, special residential or day school. In this referral, the child is placed at a maximum distance from the mainstream and re-entry is much more difficult. Such a referral is made only as a last resort and under unusual circumstances.

A child referred to a residential or day facility, or to long-term, special-class placement in the school, should be given an opportunity to re-enter the Fail-Save system at any point. Although the model allows a child to move toward the regular class during any number of phases, he cannot be moved away from the mainstream more than one phase at a time. Each move away requires an evaluation and a decision by the group of persons concerned with the child. Parents play a vital role in decision making and in instruction. The regular-class teacher is allowed to maintain her legal and moral duty to be responsible for the child's instructional program as long as he has any association with her class. The child is isolated from his peers only as a last resort, and then for a contracted period of time. Special education personnel are under pressure to produce change *now*—not later—as time is limited by the design of the program.

Careful and judicious use of the model allows special educators to protect the human and legal rights of children. The special educators also have the opportunity to serve the children without the dubious necessity of labeling them before the service is delivered. Children are protected from prejudicial labeling because of language, cultural, or environmental backgrounds. The model provides the opportunity to observe a child's learning behavior closely before he is "labeled." Above all, the child always has ready access to the mainstream.

One caveat should be noted, however. This model cannot work without trained personnel who are dedicated to children rather than to models. As in any other model, the key to success in this one is not in administrative design but in the training and dedication of the personnel. Undoubtedly, the major reason that the self-contained class has failed is related more to people than to all the other variables that have been isolated by researchers. Good pedagogy is not dependent upon a model. Poor teaching can hide behind any administrative design.

References

Adamson, G. *Final Report of the Educational Modulation Center.* Olathe, Kansas: Olathe Public Schools, 1970.

Adamson, G. W., Shrago, M., & VanEtten, G. *The basic education skills inventory.* Olathe, Kansas: Select-Ed, 1971.

Bransford, L. *A total assessment program for the mentally retarded.* The University of New Mexico Press, 1969.

Deno, E. Special education as developmental capital. *Exceptional Children,* 1970, 37, 229-240.

Dunn, L. M. Special education for the mildly retarded: Is much of it justifiable? *Exceptional Children,* 1968, 35(1), 5-22.

Gallagher, J. J. The special education contract for mildly handicapped children. *Exceptional Children,* 1972, 38, 527-536.

Goldstein, H. Constructions of a social learning curriculum. *Focus on Exceptional Children,* 1969, 1(3), 1-7.

Guskin, S. L. & Spicker, H. H. Educational research in mental retardation. In Norman Ellis (Ed.) *International Review of Research in Mental Retardation,* Vol. 3. New York: Academic Press, 1968, 217-278.

Hammond, G. W. Educating the mildly retarded: A review. *Exceptional Children,* 1972, 38, 565-574.

Kroth, R. *The target behavior kit.* Olathe, Kansas: Select-Ed, 1972.

Lilly, M. S. A training based model for special education. *Exceptional Children,* 1971, 37, 747-749.

McDowell, R. L. Parent counseling: An experiment in behavior modification. *Kansas Studies in Education* (University of Kansas), 1969, 19(3), 16-19.

Reynolds, M. A framework for considering some issues in special education. *Exceptional Children,* 1962, 28, 367-370.

VanEtten, C., & Adamson, G. W. *Analysis of instructional materials: a prescriptive materials laboratory.* Selected papers on Learning Disabilities, 6th Annual Conference of Association for Children with Learning Disabilities. Fort Worth, Texas, 1969, 69-74.

VanEtten, C., & Adamson, G. W. *Prescriptive materials retrieval system.* Olathe, Kansas: Select-Ed, 1970.

VanEtten, M. C. A handbook for the development of a prescriptive materials laboratory: Analysis and retrieval of instructional materials. Unpublished Master's Thesis, University of Kansas, 1969.

Section IV

Commentaries

Where Do We Go From Here?

Evelyn N. Deno

Reading through the papers in this monograph, one must be impressed with the energy, thought, and care that have gone into the development and execution of the programs described. The results achieved by those projects that have been in operation long enough to have established records are impressive. We can conclude that it really is possible to develop regular-classroom, operating conditions to meet effectively a wider range of individual child-learning needs than heretofore has been thought possible. If regular-class teachers express fears about accepting the responsibility of teaching certain handicapped children, their counterparts who participated in these programs can reply, "Don't be afraid to try. It can be done. We have done it."

Now that we have the demonstration of *what* can be done, our concern should shift to the problem of *how* promising findings can be exploited to improve educational opportunities for children on a broader scale. At the same time, the workers who are already involved in the search need the opportunity to build on what they have learned. They are important resources for education's further advance. None of the authors, fortunately, considers his goals to have been fully achieved as yet.

Many of the attempts to improve assistance services through research into and development of ideas have run into difficulties at the point where apparently productive practices have been moved from small-scale operation to widespread application. Sometimes the results are not disseminated widely enough to have much impact; sometimes field workers choose to ignore available information out of the parochial belief that nothing done anywhere else can possibly apply to their "unusual circumstances"; and, in some cases, essential conditions are not controlled adequately to yield the earlier gains. Instead of instituting studies to determine why the results obtained in the initial study cannot be replicated, many field workers throw out good ideas in the wash of reaction to failure. Thus, important opportunities to build on what has been invested and learned in research are lost, and time and resources are dissipated in continually rediscovering the same old wheels.

Little that is startlingly new was discovered about learning in the programs described in this monograph. In the main, the programs represent the successful application of propositions that have been articulated for some time. What stands out is the care that was taken to see that working assumptions were adequately tested and important factors were adequately controlled. In the large-scale application of these programs, a major problem is likely to be the inability to achieve adequate control of significant operating conditions.

We now need to consider these reports in terms of how any of their valuable insights can be put to use in educational programs elsewhere. It may be helpful, therefore, to look for the common threads that run through these ventures in the light of what other research and development programs have learned about the processes of dissemination and institutionalization.

Commonalities

In most of these programs, the central focus of inquiry and training has been on process. More emphasis was directed to how improvement can be brought about than to what the ultimate form of action ought to be. The investigators were more inclined to assume that a final answer cannot be found rather than that the answer awaited discovery.

This emphasis on process probably must be expected in programs with the primary goal of producing change. Workers did not assume that they knew for sure what form institutions should change into, but they knew what they wanted to get away from. Their driving force was the belief that the conventional approaches to the education of handicapped children were not sufficiently profitable to counterbalance the labeling and segregation constraints imposed on the children as an integral part of the conventional practices. The basic commitment of these workers has been to search; their basic devotion has been to the principle, "First do no harm."

The workers in these programs assumed the uncomfortable personal and institutional risks that are almost always entailed in attempts to change the status quo. In their program designs, they recognized that change and the effort to improve performance quality need continuous support because the pull of tradition is unrelenting and there is a strong tendency to fall back into familiar ways as soon as support for the change directions flags. Those programs were most successful in which technology and mechanisms were developed to sustain change and commitments were supported strongly at influential administrative levels.

The programs reflect a common view: If the goal is broader learning opportunities for handicapped children then it is not enough to tinker just with the special education system. Many social units govern what children have the opportunity to learn. These effective elements need to be brought into productive alignment if new growth and learning opportunities for the children are to be secured. This realization has called attention to the influences of parents and peers and to health, welfare, and correction system practices, as well as to the practices within the regular and special education systems.

Another commonality is the tendency to employ systems analysis techniques to tackle the problems of service improvement. A high proportion of the programs might be described as systems approaches to educational service delivery. Program operators considered the social psychology of institutions, as well as management theory, in designing and evaluating their strategies.

We see, in these programs, the increasing involvement of people who do not identify themselves primarily as special educators. School administrators, psychologists, physicians, and other professionals are aggressively and effectively joining the cause of providing better educational opportunities for handicapped children. Also, significant numbers of special educators are moving into broader roles to facilitate the process of expanding total system capability. Cross-fertilization and cross-infiltration are at work.

Finally, these programs demonstrate the acceptance, by the participants, of the responsibility to be accountable, ultimately, for the welfare of the individual child and to defend the use of public resources for him.

These common elements necessarily interact in practice to determine the range of problems with which a program is able to deal and the quality of those dealings.

The Action Arena

As special educators seek to expand the range of opportunities for children regarded as handicapped, they look upon the educational mainstream, other children, other helping service systems, and, especially, the home as learning-promotion resources. The movement to exploit and enhance all of these learning opportunities started years ago. On-the-job, vocational training of the handicapped; the training of pre-school, hearing-impaired children's parents to make them effective "first teachers"; provision of homebound and hospital services; formal collaboration of special education programs and residential treatment agencies to provide rehabilitation-oriented education programs in non-school stations; and special education's long-standing use of peers as "pushers" of wheel chairs, readers to the blind, and tutors to the less able are proof that special education has not been limited in its approaches by the assumption that education is something that can be carried on only in school buildings by certified teachers.

With this history, special education may have to be reoriented less than regular education if people begin to take seriously the recommendations of Coleman (1972), Bruner (1972), and others that the purpose of "schooling" should shift from its present concentration on acquiring knowledge outside of an action context to learning how to put information to work in personally and socially constructive action programs. However, we suspect that it may be many years before a large enough proportion of the tax-supporting public will sanction the use of schools in the ways that are recommended by Coleman and Bruner to effect the drastic change in the goals and substance of the school curriculum. In the meantime, special education can contribute to education in general its experience in the collaboration of schools and other community educational forces. Special education always has had to attend to the opinions of consumers and related workers; indeed, the growth and improvement of the field has been spurred by consumer demand.

Special education, like education in general, needs to expand its ability to help parents, physicians, and other agents to become more effective "teachers." Educators need to accept the counterpart of Miller's recommendation to psychologists in his 1969 APA Presidential Address. He advised his fellow psychologists to give away whatever they knew that might be useful in helping people to improve the quality of their lives. He proposed that knowledge of human behavior belongs to those who need the knowledge; it is not something to be harbored as a professional secret. Bruner (1972) suggested that because intermediate age peers seem to be more influential behavior models than adults, we should teach these peers to be more constructive, effective teachers of younger children. Parents are a child's first teachers; the thread runs on and on.

The implications of these points of view are that different relationships should be established among the persons who govern the child's experience, and that the packaging of educational services should differ from the interdisciplinary teams and school involvements that parents have accepted in the past. The impact of these concepts is reflected in the degree to which many of the training programs described here include a component for preparing trainees to teach other adults, in and out of the school walls, as well as children; the concepts are reflected also in the acceptance of consumers as partners to set intervention goals.

These programs reflect a common assumption: To make communication effective among people of different types and levels of educational background, enough knowledge must be held in common so that everyone can understand the conceptual framework in which he is expected to think; and language or symbols must be made available to each person to facilitate the communication. This belief is translated into practice in a number of ways in these programs, as, for example, in the development of performance criteria in terms of daily life tasks that everyone understands, the use of assessment procedures that relate directly to these criteria, and the general tendency to avoid professional jargon. Many of the programs are trying to develop assessment procedures that can be comprehended by all participants in the child's education and that can be used in whatever form is appropriate to the participants' levels of expertise and responsibility. The programs do not seem to be dedicated to the maintenance of a professional mystique or the preservation of institutional forms just because they are there. The energies of the program developers are invested in helping front line doers do better what they are going to be doing anyway.

Similar comments can be made about underlying theory. Explanatory concepts of the programs are directed mainly to the clarification of goals and procedures. There is little attempt to stretch any shreds of whatever theory may be employed to cover all of the unexplained facts of operation. We get more of a sense of the workers saying, "We don't know all that goes on when a child does or doesn't learn so we stay at the level of the functional analysis of the relation between what we do and what happens in child performance." The underlying approach is empirical and pragmatic: What works? For whom does it work? The question of why something works is left for theoreticians or tomorrow's analysis.

Systems Approaches

Once the assumption is made in a program that a stand-alone special education is not likely to meet all the needs of handicapped children, two problems immediately confront one. The first is to maintain adequate control of treatment quality when so many people are involved. The second is to order the activities of the various involved treatment vendors so that they do not get in each other's way. These problems become potentially serious as more and more specialists assume that they can reach more needs if they work indirectly (by consulting with front-line workers) than if they provide direct service to needy clients on a one-to-one or small-group basis. The educators represented here have turned to systems theory for what it may have to offer for the solution of such problems. They are using systems analysis to study their own operations and to develop alternatives for packaging problem-solving efforts.

Interesting questions have been probed in these programs through systems analysis but many need to be probed further. When we talk about service that needs to cross many administrative lines, who calls the meetings to determine how these systems should interface? How can we insure that the meeting will be called at all so that the professional and agency roles can respond to a new drum beat? How do we turn the energy now going into the rotation of problems from agent to agent, agency to agency, into improving the quality of the child's life? Who monitors whether agents are relating effectively once interface ground rules have been established? Who follows up to see whether a child is getting the treatment prescribed or whether he is falling into the cracks as the responsibility for him is transferred from hand to hand? Who decides when treatment should be stopped or changed? In order that operating principles may be consistently translated into action, who, or what process, mediates differences of opinion which are not resolved through amiable discussion among the participants? Who establishes program management policies and by what means? The list could go on indefinitely.

Some of these programs have been training what may be called treatment interface facilitators under such titles as "Consulting Teacher," "Diagnostic Prescriptive Teacher," "Stratistician," and so forth. Such a person cannot be fully effective without strong administrative support. Other programs have invested their resources in a single school building as the next level beyond the home in the hierarchy of sub-systems that represents society's institutional approaches to the socialization of its developmentally immature members. The Santa Monica program, the University of Minnesota-Minneapolis Public Schools projects, and the Rockford, Illinois, effort represent attempts to upgrade the effectiveness of the functions of a total building program so that better accommodation to the needs of the handicapped can be achieved without referring the child out of the learning community in which he would ordinarily participate.

The basic hypothesis being tested in these building-based approaches is that if a school building staff is properly equipped (with materials, suitably trained personnel, physical space, and administrative and community support), it can devise ways to deal effectively *within that building* with all but the most exceptional needs. Under these conditions, a building staff should need to refer only a small proportion of its catchment area population elsewhere. What that percentage may reasonably be is one of the points under investigation in these approaches.

The Houston program takes a total local education agency as its level of system concern. The community sanction for such an ambitious goal must be strong. The close, interactive relation between Vermont's Consulting Teacher program and the state education agency's program planning allows the development of a statewide system in accordance with the evidence of needs that are acquired through operations of the system. At one level, a system is an instrument for the continous improvement of the larger system of which it is a part.

In a BEH-funded project at the University of Missouri, Connally and Meyen have used a problem-solving approach to develop a performance-based prototype training model for the preparation of curriculum consultants who will develop and improve instructional offerings for exceptional children. Their work utilizes a systems analysis approach that is applicable to almost any kind of social action problem (Connally & Meyen, 1972).

Many of these programs use an applied behavior analysis approach in the teaching of exceptional children, parents, and teachers; the design of systems; and the evaluation of action outcomes. This approach is applied also to advancing the personal growth of the persons who work with children to make them better helping instruments. We even see the influence of the approach in those programs that are not identified as proceeding exclusively from this orientation. Apparently, the approach is compatible with humanistic goals.

This approach to instruction fits nicely with systems analysis approaches to delivery system design and evaluation. However, those who exploit its potentials most effectively do not restrict their attention to the limited aspects of operational technique. They exhibit broad concern for the many factors that need to be taken into account in setting action goals, designing treatment methods, and judging benefits.

Increasing Involvement of Non-Special Educators

With the increasing awareness that special education obligations cannot be met simply by referring misfit children to a separate, parallel system, and with the emergence of methods that make possible greater individualization of instruction for all children, more people are drawn into the action framework. When attention turns to the impact of the total system on who is regarded as handicapped and how a disabled child's instruction needs to be managed, it helps to have the problem tackled by people who are in positions to provide broad information input and to make basic changes in how the total system operates. Special education programs are being improved by a significant number of people who are not primarily special educators working through special education systems. Many of them may say that, in fact, they are special educators, although not necessarily so certified, because they are committed to achieving a special education for every child. We heartily endorse this definition when it is effectively operationalized! The implication may be that profound changes are needed in the administrative organization and in the training of school administrators, particularly building principals.

The increased involvement of people outside the special education system accompanies the admission that whatever the learning principles, most of the intervention strategies used by special educators apply to the handicapped and non-handicapped alike. Highly specialized techniques, such as braille, mobility training, special methods of language acquisition for the deaf, and so forth, are needed by only a small proportion of handicapped children. Mostly, special education is the design of strategies to accommodate the learning-relevant differences among handicapped children. Thus, any number of people may be helpful in achieving these accommodations.

Accountability

Projects operating under federal funding are always required to provide some kind of evaluation of their efforts. The programs described here go beyond minimum requirements in their acceptance of responsibility to show that the children they serve profit from their services.

Few of these projects are designed as efficacy studies in which comparisons are made between one approach or method and another. For instance, none of the programs that train interface mediators (Stratisticians, Consulting Teachers, Diagnostic Prescriptive Teachers, Resource Teachers, etc.) is designed to compare its particular approach with other such approaches, with the traditional pupil personnel or interdisciplinary team approach, or with other kinds of mediation mechanisms. Workers in these programs may even question whether there is any point to such comparisons as they are, at this stage, far more concerned with the identification of useful processes than with the form in which a process may ultimately be packaged. They have not yet even refined their present forms.

The independent design and conduct of these programs under differing conditions within a context of systematic evaluation provide some comparative data. At this point, most of these programs are concerned with the clarification of criteria and the development of adequate assessment procedures so that inferences can be drawn from their data with reasonable security. They are tackling problems at the level of who ought to be accountable for what, and by what methods accountability can be demonstrated. Once a firmer grasp of such instrumental technology is achieved, it may be possible to do more meaningful studies of the relative effectiveness of various ways of serving.

How Do We Move?

If asked, the directors of these programs would probably say that they would go about applying the ideas they have gained in these exploratory efforts with the same basic approach that most of them used in the explorations.

1. Their plan of movement would recognize that, if they are to succeed, new approaches cannot be imposed on the people who have to carry them out. The old planning platitude that change is most likely to be successful when it involves those who will be affected is trite but too painfully true to be ignored safely (e.g., Bennis, 1972). Projects with the least effect on their host institutions seem to be those

that were developed as relatively isolated "warts" on the hosts, that is, with little prior involvement of the staff or publics who might need to sanction the incorporation of innovations if the results warranted their adoption.

2. The directors would prepare the communities (parents, professional organizations, students, related agencies) for the changes that are proposed, the reasons for them, how the effects will be evaluated, and how individuals who may be "dislocated" will be helped to find new places in the scheme of things. People do not like to be surprised.

3. The directors would relate realistically to the responsibilities of all social systems. Public obligations are imposed on colleges, health care systems, and state and local education agencies. These obligations necessarily govern priorities in the use of the resources which are made available to execute specific charges. Program workers would probably recommend that educators open up to public determination the decision of how public education resources, such as transportation facilities, buildings, and so forth, should be deployed. They would anticipate that significant changes may occur in who controls the resources from time to time.

4. The directors would use the scientific method of problem-solving, which is employed in almost all of these programs, to assess change needs, develop hypotheses regarding strategies, and continually test the results of action decisions. They would accept subjective judgment and conventional wisdom as guides only when no more objective evidence was obtainable. They would be prepared to show data when practices were challenged.

5. The directors would not try to transfer intact a model developed in one context without going through the basic process of assessing whether it best meets the needs of another setting. Nevertheless, they would point out that they have found important commonalities in the functions a system needs to cover and in the substance that all "teachers" and professionals need to know.

Barriers

There are hurdles to be gotten over or around to accomplish some of the changes in practice that appear to be reasonable on the basis of the results obtained in the programs described here. Some of these hurdles are technological and some are political, in the broad sense of the term. It would be foolhardy to venture an opinion on which type of impediment may constitute the greater hazard in the long run. Because of the reciprocal, dynamic characteristics of the interaction between the two, what happens in one realm can generate dramatic changes in the other.

We invent techniques to realize goals set in the political arena (including the courts and legislative halls), but expectations generated in the political sphere are colored by evidence of what is technologically possible. Many of education's present concerns might disappear overnight if a pill that improved learning ability significantly came on the market. On the other hand, political forces now support the struggle to assess learning needs and carry out treatment in ways that stigmatize children less and are less socially rejecting of differences among children. The need for these measures was recognized by special educators long before the courts mandated attention to the IQ testing problem. However, it was treated mainly as a professional problem to be tackled at the usual slow pace of academic research until outside political forces made it a political issue that demanded *action now*. We can safely assume that this kind of interactive relation will always need to be dealt with.

Teacher attitudes

A common reaction to recommendations that more handicapped children be served within the educational mainstream is the contention that the attitudes of regular teachers toward the handicapped and their teaching responsibilities will need changing before these different children can find a satisfactory educational home in a regular-class setting. The EPDA/Special Education experience seems to support the propositions that (a) the degree of anxiety felt by regular teachers is closely tied to the degree of confidence they feel in their ability to manage a situation, and (b) feeling flows from action as much as action flows from feeling (e.g., William James' proposition that we do not run because we are scared; we are scared because we run).

The evidence obtained does not seem to support the idea that change of practice should wait until we have been able to promote attitudes fully receptive to the change proposed. The wait could be long and civil rights have already been too long abridged. The hypothesis that strong public and administrative support for changes in practice, accompanied by simultaneous educative interpretation and competency building, is sufficiently validated by the programs described here to warrant the continuation of the push to change practices *now*.

Public Attitudes

It is difficult to predict how far the general public is willing to go to support the change of either basic or particular school practices. Too much has already been written to justify a lengthy discussion of the question here. However, it may be appropriate to consider some aspects of it because whatever the schools do must be sanctioned by a sufficiently large or politically strong enough constituency for change to be possible.

Maintaining handicapped children in regular classrooms is part of the broad trend toward maintaining handicapped persons of all ages in as "normal" life conditions as is effectively possible. The thrust for integration in school is cut from the same bolt of cloth as the development, for the retarded, of community living centers—small homelike residences—which allow them to receive training and to work in community stations. Segregated institutional living is dehumanizing too often for both those who experience it and those who permit it.

As such living units begin to be built on sites that have been selected with due regard for ease of transportation to school and work, community recreational possibilities, or other rational considerations, we find that nearby residents mobilize to resist such "intrusion" on the same grounds that they usually advance to resist the building of low-cost housing: They fear that "undesirables" will be brought into their midst and property values will depreciate, the peace of the neighborhood will be disturbed, their children will be raped, crime will increase, and so on. At a recent public hearing on whether a city council should grant a permit for building a living center in a suburban community, a protester remarked that speaking out publicly on concerns truly felt was difficult; it was like "talking against motherhood" to speak against something deemed beneficial for the retarded. If the protestor is reading public sentiment correctly, much progress has been made in the public awareness of the rights of the retarded and in the public willingness to view the matter as a moral issue.

The values of integration reside not just in the right of the individual child to participate as fully as possible in society's satisfactions, but in the opportunity for broad public education that is provided when children at an early age participate in a learning community in which human differences are accepted as a fact of life to be cherished and respected, not something to be feared.

Administrative Rigidities

It seems obvious that changes are necessary in the ground rules which govern practice before full release from traditional constraints can be achieved. Some of the limiting bureaucratic regulations are, of course, rooted in law. Nevertheless, we see in these reports evidence of the degree to which important advances can be made within the confines of present categorically based laws and administrative regulations. Furthermore, the state and Federal agencies seem to be willing to take a hard look at the effect of their rules on practice and to try to do as much about it as they can—and it appears they can do a lot to relieve the constraints.

Technological Limitations

One of the primary problems confronting us now is our need to devise means for insuring the protection of individual, handicapped child-rights to good growth conditions while, at the same time, we do what we can to insure that right for all children. The problem, of course, leads to the question of what proportion of its resources the public is willing to invest in maximizing the growth opportunities for all of its children. In turn, this question is entangled in the fundamental economic question of how society believes its resources should be distributed.

Within this whole context of social-political-economic issues, there are questions of whether we can devise techniques to allocate our resources in ways that allow us to determine whether the investment is worthwhile in terms of its basic, social purposes. The task is enormous in magnitude and it needs to be addressed strenuously and with strong resources. Some embryonic solutions can be seen in some of the projects presented here, but the development of adequate assessment technology remains a priority need if the social goals which fired the movement toward more opportunity for the handicapped to participate in a wider learning community are to be achieved. If evidence of value cannot be presented after the effort is made on moral grounds, there is danger that adverse reaction will set in and isolate even more than now the children who are different.

We maintain our faith that public opinion responds to sound evidence. We continue to believe that the various communities that need to support less alienating treatment (consumers, taxpaying corporations, individuals, professional groups, etc.) have a right to ask for proof that the moral goal we advocate is better approximated by the means we advocate than by some other way. We have a heavy responsibility to get on with our tasks of technical development.

References

Bennis, W. The sociology of institutions or, who sank the yellow submarine? *Psychology Today*, 1972, 6, 112-120.
Bruner, J. Nature and uses of immaturity. *American Psychologist*, 1972, 27, 687-708.
Coleman, J. The children have outgrown the schools. *Psychology Today*, 1972, 5, 72-75, 82.
Connelly, A., & Meyen, E. Training program for the preparation of curriculum specialists for exceptional children. In L. Schwartz et al. (Eds.), *Proceedings of the Special Study Institute: Innovative non-categorical interrelated projects in the education of the handicapped.* Florida State University, Tallahassee, 1972, 18-19.

Reflections on a Set of Innovations

Maynard C. Reynolds
*Professor, Special Education and
Director, Leadership Training
Institute/Special Education
University of Minnesota*

Like other observers of special education, I believe that the field is facing some critical problems in this decade of the '70's. We find old patterns of special education services eroding everywhere, especially in the cities, and serious challenges to some procedures being voiced by the courts. As a start in making necessary changes, we need to draw up new cognitive maps to chart our terrain and direction and we need to revise administrative and instructional arrangements to provide new and better services. This monograph is the second publication of the LTI/Special Education devoted to those goals.

Most of the programs described here are concerned primarily with those children who are most likely to be accepted in the mainstream of education—the mildly and moderately handicapped. The models focus on providing new arrangements for such children at the critical point of interface between regular and special education. Because the interchange across the boundaries is certain to be very active over the next decade, the approaches to education taken by the project investigators deserve serious study and consideration. As a relatively close observer of a number of the projects, I believe that they represent some of the promising ways of meeting this active and challenging aspect of special education, but I also believe that each faces a number of problems that must be recognized and solved.

A program that focusses on mildly and moderately handicapped children and stresses the necessary interchanges between regular and special education can easily be misinterpreted as neglecting children with more serious handicaps and the highly specialized resources they require. It is quite likely that too much of an emphasis on the "mainstreaming" of handicapped children will provoke counter-movements in defense of special education in its more distinctive forms. Hopefully, it will not be necessary to expend our energies on giant swings of the ideological pendulum between mainstreaming and whatever its opposite pole may be.

Clearly, our commitment should be to education for *all* children. It can be argued that only as services to mildly handicapped children are reasonably successful can the case for more and better education for seriously handicapped children—all of them—be made credibly. Evelyn Deno, the editor of this monograph, and I and many others have advocated a "cascade" concept of special education administrative arrangements, an idea that embraces many kinds and levels of instruction and services to meet the needs of all children. It is notable to me that although the concept is not mentioned by name, its principle is evident in some of the programs described here.

The Context for Change

The assumption is incorrect that the delivery of special education services can be transformed directly and easily from, for example, a special-class model to a resource room or consulting teacher model, simply by training and inserting new personnel in unchanged schools and systems. To make the transformation, fundamental changes are required, changes that involve educational personnel, parents, universities, and state departments of education. Some of the ways in which such persons and institutions are involved are as follows:

1. Changes in special education must be understood and supported by school principals and other administrators.
2. Special educators themselves—at least a sizable proportion of them—must be convinced of the need for change and they must be vigorous and flexible enough to make the changes.
3. State departments of education may be required to change certification standards for teachers and to revise regulations on such matters as program standards and special financial aids.
4. Changes in programs may necessitate the difficult re-designing of training programs in nearby colleges and universities.
5. Individual parents and organized parent groups may be deeply apprehensive of "decategorization" or of other issues.
6. The pupil personnel workers in the schools and in the community may not be attuned to the changes.
7. Negotiations to change patterns of collaboration may need to be undertaken with school systems' curriculum specialists in various areas.
8. Teacher organizations, in scrutinizing some of the plans, may offer resistance to various parts of them.

These facets of change in the delivery system are only a partial listing of the total number that must be considered.

Time and resources are necessary to plan for change in the context of schools. Unfortunately, many school systems do not have the capacity to deal with all the problems of change. Somehow, special resources must be made available for the support of school leaders who undertake the difficult problem of redesigning special education programs.

A specific decision that must be made in communities wishing to change the special education program is whether to institute the changes gradually or massively and rapidly. The Houston plan illustrates an attempt at massive change in a short period of time; the Minneapolis program of establishing resource centers represents a less rapidly paced program; and, between them, is the Vermont plan which, from the beginning, was explicitly oriented to instituting change by stages in the whole state. There are good reasons for being pessimistic about the use of gradualism in the reform of schools; the strategy of starting with an exemplary program in a limited situation and then depending on the ripple effects to permeate and change the system has not often succeeded. Thus, it might be argued, that changes in a school district may, from the beginning, just as well be sought on the broadest possible front.

On the other hand, attempts for massive and rapid change run the risk of colossal failure while more gradual programs, such as those in Minneapolis and Vermont, appear to be progressing solidly through their respective systems. Perhaps success is possible through either the gradualist or revolutionary mode but, since massive, rapid changes require resources, commitment, support, and energy that few school systems are likely to possess, most systems will probably do well to take the longer course.

An equally important consideration is to allow time for the systemic installation of innovative programs and the development of understanding and support in the concerned segments of the community. Changes, in their early stages, are likely to be superficial and fragile. Sometimes their surface aspects, such as the rearrangement of the school's internal architecture, the scheduling of frequent teachers' meetings to discuss new topics, and the display of new kinds of data on bulletin boards may persuade observers that major changes have been accomplished. Yet, the basic regularities may not have been altered. Fundamental changes of the kind discussed in this monograph require several years of continuing and intensive work to penetrate such dimensions as curriculum, child study, administration, and teacher preparation.

Hopefully, it is also apparent that not all innovations succeed at uniform rates and, consequently, evaluation should be specific and situational. Even with new arrangements some children will continue to have difficult problems in education. New practices, therefore, must be continually sought for the children who are poorly served by the delivery system in use, however innovative it may be, and the personnel working with the children must be ready to revise the programs or to introduce new ones.

Notable Features of Innovative Programs

The training and service models outlined in earlier chapters of this monograph share several features that help to solve major problems in special education. Four of these features are discussed here.

Enhanced Child Study Resources in Individual Schools

In many school programs of the recent past, children considered for special education services were referred outside their home schools for diagnosis and for recommendations on programs and placements. The child study procedures used in this mode were time consuming and, consequently, the referral lists literally became waiting lists. The tendency of the psychologists, social workers, and other experts who examined the children was to consider them with little reference to their school environments. As a result, the reports were considered to be dull and useless by most teachers.

This whole process has been changed in many programs now being developed. Instead of referring the child to an external child study facility, the programs enhance the diagnostic capacity within his home school. The diagnosis, thus, relates the child's problems and the school situation. Referrals to specialized diagnostic teams are reserved for children with the most complex problems.

It must be counted as a major "plus" that more children are being studied in their environments and without referrals or waiting lists. When studies of children are made by personnel who remain with the children in their schools and maintain the responsibility to follow through with programs, the probability of more useful service to the child is heightened.

New Roles

One of the ways to achieve an increase in in-school strength in child study is by creating new roles for teaching and consulting personnel. Psychologists, social workers, and counselors may no longer be assigned to every school building; instead, there may emerge a "consulting teacher," "resource teacher," or "diagnostic team" of teachers who have been upgraded by training to perform the functions formerly handled by highly specialized personnel.

In the process of making such a change, psychologists, social workers, and counselors sometimes assume a training role, that is, they become trainers of the persons who perform the more general roles in the individual schools. This trend presents one very promising alternative to the use of strict specialists who keep children waiting in long lines at the clinic doors.

Field-Based University Training

Many of the training programs presented in this monograph have been conducted cooperatively by institutions of higher education and local schools. At a time when some writers are doubting the future role of colleges and universities in the professional training of school personnel, a view that appears to emerge from discouragement over past performances, the reported collaborations are indeed significant.

In a number of the instances, the joining of resources by colleges and schools to do a job that neither could do alone is very encouraging.

Perhaps the most remarkable single instance of this collaboration is the Vermont project wherein consulting teachers are trained cooperatively by the University of Vermont and the public schools of the state. A feature of the program is that the consultants are authorized to become continuing agents of the University and to serve as instructors of approved courses in their field stations. One can be greatly encouraged by this aspect of University-school collaboration; perhaps the universities can train teachers after all, despite the claim to the contrary of a recent volume entitled, *The University Can't Train Teachers*.*

An aspect of the IHE-LEA collaboration is the emphasis on basing major parts of the training program in field situations. Training programs are widely favored today when they emphasize the procedural rather than the propositional aspects of knowledge and when they stress a performance rather than a strictly cognitive test to determine competencies and credentialing. It is clear that the programs described in this volume either fit these trends or, at least, are developing in that general direction.

Some Problems and Concerns

Careful observations have suggested that the process of change, as described in these innovative programs, has not been entirely free of problems. Several concerns and problems that need attention are in the following areas:

Retraining Pupil Personnel Workers

In many school situations, pupil personnel workers are finding their work greatly devalued, at least in those aspects that relate to special education. Much of the traditional testing and classification done by school psychologists, for example, has been discredited by the courts and candidly dismissed as useless by many educators. The decentralization of administrative arrangements in many large cities has thrown pupil personnel workers into new neighborhood groupings at the very time that testing and specialists of all kinds are being attacked. As a result, many of the workers are self-conscious about their roles and more than a little frustrated.

Problems are heightened in situations when the persons employed have had only marginal training and insufficient capacity to move out to new frontiers. For example, psychologists who have been trained

---

* James Bowman, Larry Freeman, Paul A. Olson, & Jan Pieper (Eds.). *The University Can't Train Teachers.* Lincoln, Nebraska: The University of Nebraska Curriculum Development Center, June 1972.

primarily as psychometricians and have had only introductory training in remedial instruction, mental health, and special education find themselves in little demand for their accustomed services and in poor position to deliver services from the broader domain of psychology.

A special challenge exists in the several settings where new modes of special education service are led by vigorous advocates of applied behavioral analysis and contingency management. There, pupil personnel workers of other persuasions or those who lack backgrounds in Skinnerian procedure are sometimes badly frustrated. Retraining programs, however, probably will be of help to some of them. It would be useful, perhaps, to all the persons involved in such situations to develop dialogues at several levels to make explicit the alternatives that are available in such areas as measurement, diagnosis, and consultation.

The Gifted

In the restructuring of special education that is underway, one must hope that attention will go to all children with special learning problems or needs, including those who have the ability to learn more rapidly and to perform the most complex of tasks. So far, there appears to be less focus on such gifted or talented children than might be desired. When consulting teachers, resource teachers, or other support personnel are employed in the schools, we must hope that they will give equal attention to children whose rates of performance are already very high and who need to be challenged intellectually by the materials and instruction available. One of the conditions that may need to be changed is the financial provision for them. Federal and state officials should make it possible to join programs relating to the handicapped and the gifted so that special education personnel can service the full spectrum of exceptional children without constraints by governmental regulations.

Adequacy of Diagnosis

A fundamental concern of special education programs is that too often changes may be no more than a rejuggling of administrative arrangements within the same doubtful provisions of the delivery system. It is appropriate, therefore, to look with great care at the basic adequacy of the diagnostic and treatment procedures that are emerging.

At least two major ideas are apparent in recent programs. The first is the development of consulting procedures that maximize the utilization of resources already available within the staff complex of the school. The consulting teacher or stratistician, for example, appears to work most often, not as a "specialist" in diagnosis and treatment, but as a colleague who can elicit from and encourage teachers to use more fully and openly all of their talents, skills, and insights. His/her mode of operation sometimes explicitly rejects the notion of the "expert" and assumes that schools have virtually all the personnel resources they need to solve the majority of learning problems if the personnel but care deeply enough and try hard enough.

A second common paradigm in emerging programs is that of the applied behavior analysts with their techniques for task analysis, precision teaching, charting, and contingency management. Undoubtedly, these procedures are enormously useful. Sometimes, however, programs oriented to these principles are weak on the stimulus side. Occasionally, one sees instructional programs in which consequences are managed with much ingenuity but stimulus materials are neglected. More interaction among behavior analysts and curriculum specialists is needed.

Much of the diagnostic work that goes on in some centers at the level of modality preferences is, in this viewer's opinion, mostly a doubtful enterprise. If this is the wine that is being vended in new bottles, it should be recognized as pallid fare. Hopefully, more attention will be given to details of diagnostic and instructional procedures over the next few years and the best of emerging practices will be implemented on a broad front.

Work with Parents

Many of the emerging programs involve new conceptions of handicaps that should be carefully interpreted to individual parents and organized parent groups. It is a fact, apparently, that some parents can derive comfort when their handicapped children are diagnosed as having a specific problem such as dyslexia, perceptual impairment, brain-injury, Strauss syndrome, mental retardation, or learning disability. When school programs are organized to bypass such classifications, the problems of interpretation that are entailed can run the gamut from new slants on the individual child all the way up to parent-group labels and the language used in Federal legislation.

In this context, the desirability of dealing with children individually and with very little dependence upon single categorization systems for diagnosis and treatment can be assumed. Parents, school policy makers, and legislators will surely find it encouraging to see professionals in the field of special education move to early interventions and to refined diagnostic/treatment procedures that are different from those of the past. But that the new approaches do not come as a surprise to parents anywhere requires that efforts be made to educate them and the community.

Conclusions

Special education is in the process of major changes. Some of the models for new approaches to training teachers and serving mildly and moderately handicapped children—and, hopefully, gifted children, if programs are extended in ways that seem quite feasible—are outlined in this monograph. Perhaps the most remarkable feature of the emerging models is the interchange between special and regular education that is developed by each.

Boundary lines between separate "regular" and "special" systems are less and less discernible than in the past. Thus, it is evident, wherever special education has vitality, conviction, and reasonable quality it can be a major force for the redesigning of all of education—to the end that all children will have truly equal educational opportunities.

Contributors to the Monograph

Adamson, Gary
   Assistant Chairman of Guidance and Special Education
   (Director of Special Education)
   University of New Mexico
   Albuquerque, New Mexico 87106

Dr. Adamson is also Director of the Prescriptive Materials Laboratory, the Comprehensive Special Services Cooperative (10 school districts), and the EPDA Training Grant, "Prescriptive Process." He received the EdD (special education) from the University of Kansas. His previous experience includes public school teaching, college lecturing, admininstrative positions, and the directorship of the Education Modulation Center, Olathe, Kansas. He is the author of a number of publications.

Buffmire, Judy Ann
   Director,
   Rocky Mountain Regional Resource Center
   2363 Foothill Drive, Suite G
   Salt Lake City, Utah 84109

Assistant Professor, Department of Special Education, University of Utah. Dr. Buffmire was educated at the University of Utah (MS in special education; PhD in educational psychology and special education) and has had experience as a teacher for trainable mentally retarded children; itinerant work with emotionally disturbed children; school psychologist; college teacher; curriculum and psychological consultant for Indian Headstart program; counselor for alcoholics, Veterans' Hospital; and leader in group dynamics.

She has been state president of the Council for Exceptional Children; president of the Salt Lake County Association for Retarded Children; and a member of the Governor's Manpower Subcommittee and of the Utah State Advisory Committee for Handicapped Children. Currently, she is a member of the National Board of Governors, Council for Exceptional Children, and of the Utah Title III Advisory Committee; Membership chairman, Region IV, American Association on Mental Deficiency; and on the program committee of the 1973 National Convention, National Association for Retarded Children.

Dr. Buffmire's interests are creativity in the retarded; the affective area (values, attitudes, and interpersonal communication skills); and cooking, camping, river running, and hiking.

Deno, Evelyn N.
   Professor in Educational Psychology
   School of Education
   University of Minnesota
   Minneapolis, Minn. 55455

Associate Director, Special Education Leadership Training Institute, NCIES program of the National Center for the Improvement of Educational Systems, U. S. Office of Education.

Born and raised in Wisconsin. All academic degrees from the University of Minnesota. Undergraduate work in preschool and elementary education, graduate focus in child development, clinical psychology, and sociology. Teaching experience at preschool, elementary, and college levels. Administrative experience as Director of Special Education and Rehabilitation, Minneapolis Schools (9 years), Director, Psycho-Educational Center of the University of Minnesota (3 years).

ABEPP diplomate in school psychology. President, Minnesota Psychological Association (3 years), Chairman, National Legislative Committee (3 years), and member of the Board of Governors of CEC. Chairman, Minnesota Statutory Advisory Board on Handicapped, Gifted, and Exceptional Children (5 years), a member (10 years). Member, Board of Directors of various organizations concerned with the handicapped.

Published in *Exceptional Children, Focus on Exceptional Children, American Psychologist, Child Development, Special Child Publications Learning Disorders Series Vol. II,* American Personnel and Guidance Publications, and the monograph, *Exceptional Children in Regular Classrooms.*

Particularly interested in development of more humane and effective helping service systems.

Deno, Stanley L.
>Associate Professor,
>School of Education
>University of Minnesota
>Minneapolis, Minn. 55455

In addition to directing the development of the Seward-University project and teaching at the University, Dr. Deno is coordinating the development of the Special Education Resource Teacher (SERT) training program. It is to be a cross-categorical, competency-based program with a strong orientation to field-based retraining of inservice special-class teachers and learning-disability tutors. Dr. Deno's special concern is how to ensure high quality of instruction regardless of organizational arrangement.

He holds the BA from St. Olaf College in biology and the PhD in educational psychology from the University of Minnesota. He has been a biology teacher and has taught at the University of Delaware.

Egner, Ann Nevin
>Instructor
>Special Education Program
>College of Education
>University of Vermont
>Burlington, Vermont 05401

With a BA (mathematics, *magna cum laude*) from Westminster College (New Wilmington, Pa.) and an MEd (special education) from the University of Vermont, Ms Egner has participated in the development and implementation of individualized instruction programs for eligible students at the elementary, junior high, and secondary levels, and individualized teaching training programs for inservice and summer coursework. She is the author (with Burdett and Fox) of *Observing and Measuring Classroom Behaviors.*

Her special interests include the dissemination of successful teaching/learning programs through the *Journal of Behavioral Education* (of which she is currently editor) and the "Annual Convention for Behavioral Educators," a forum for Vermont's teachers, principals, and parents who serve the eligible child.

Fox, Wayne L.
>Director, Special Education Summer Program
>Special Education Program
>University of Vermont
>2 Colchester Ave.
>Burlington, Vermont 05401

Dr. Fox is also an Associate Professor of Special Education at the University of Vermont. He was educated at San Jose State College (BA, psychology) and the University of Arizona (PhD, experimental/physiological psychology) and has had past experience as a statistician and a research scientist with the Human Resources Research Office (HumRRO) in Monterey, Calif. While with HumRRO, he was engaged in research and development of vocational training programs for disadvantaged adults brought into the U.S. Army under a special manpower project sponsored by the Department of Defense (Project 100,000).

He is the author of two recent books, *A Teacher's Guide to Writing Instructional Objectives* (with A. Wheeler) and *Observing and Measuring Classroom Behaviors* (with A. Egner & C. Burdett), and journal articles.

Dr. Fox's special interests include the development of minimum reading objectives for elementary children (K-4), the development of precise measurement techniques for use by classroom teachers, and the application of principles derived from the experimental analysis of behavior to classroom problems.

Garvin, Jean S.
State Director of Special Educational and Pupil Personnel Services
Vermont State Department of Education
Montpelier, Vermont 05602

Ms Garvin has been instrumental in developing a statewide system of special educational services for Vermont's handicapped children, including the adoption of the Consulting Teacher Program for handicapped children in regular classrooms in Vermont.

She holds the MA degree from the University of Iowa and has had prior experience as a psychologist in the Department of Education, teacher of nursery school, and fourth-grade teacher, in Iowa; and as an instructor at Johnson State College.

Gross, Jerry C.
Assistant Director for Program Services
Department of Program Services,
Division of Special Education
Minneapolis Public Schools
807 N. E. Broadway
Minneapolis, Minn. 55413

Dr. Gross's department is currently in the process of reorganizing service delivery systems to make them compatible with an educational vs. a medical model of special education programming. The department's leadership structure is also being reorganized to complement these intercategorical delivery systems.

Dr. Gross is active at the state level in the development of comprehensive legislation for the handicapped.

Grismer, Rita M.
Coordinator, University Training Programs,
Minneapolis Public Schools
Department of Special Education
109 Pattee Hall
University of Minnesota
Minneapolis, Minn. 55454

The first years of my professional career were devoted to classroom teaching in mainstream education. In that role I became increasingly concerned with those few children whose various educational deficits interfered with their classroom functioning. Any attempts to accommodate to their needs usually resulted in responsiveness and achievements that I found most rewarding as a teacher. These experiences led me to graduate study in special education at the University of Minnesota, with emphasis on the areas of emotional disturbances and mental retardation.

With the opportunity to act as a special education teacher and to administer special education programs, I became concerned with the need for change in administrative structures, instructional methodology, and the accommodative skills of mainstream education for handicapped children. At present, I am serving in the dual role of teacher trainer and public school administrator with the opportunity to pursue needed changes with preservice and inservice teachers in both regular and special education.

Haring, Norris G.
>Director, Experimental Education Unit
>Child Development and Mental Retardation Center
>University of Washington
>Seattle, Wash. 98195

Dr. Haring is also a Professor of Education and the Adjunct Professor of Pediatrics in the School of Medicine. He was educated at Kearney State, University of Nebraska, Merrill-Palmer Institute, and Syracuse University (EdD, special education).

His past experience includes director of special education in a public school system; professor of education and special education in universities; and educational director of the Children's Rehabilitation Unit and Chair in Child Development in the Medical Center of the University of Kansas. He was chairman of Task Force 11 (USOE and USPHS) and member of other national and state committees concerned with handicapped children and special education; associate editor of *Exceptional Children*; field adviser in special projects, Division of Training Programs, USOE; and consultant to the State of Washington.

Dr. Haring's recent publications include *Analysis and Modification of Classroom Behavior* (with E. Lakin Phillips) and *The Improvement of Instruction* (with Alice H. Hayden); he has written other books, many chapters in collected volumes, and journal articles.

His present professional interests include learning disabilities, emotionally disturbed children, behavior modification, and precision teaching.

Johnson, Richard A.
>Director, Special Education
>Minneapolis Public Schools
>807 N. E. Broadway
>Minneapolis, Minn. 55413

Dr. Johnson's major interests are the application of change theory to organizational change. His particular emphasis is on adapting special education leadership structures and systems to meet contemporary requirements and on relating those special leadership structures to general school administrators. Currently, Dr. Johnson is managing an extensive reorganization of the Minneapolis Special Education program. He has served in a leadership capacity for other local and state educational agencies also.

Interested in creating awareness among leadership personnel of major needs, trends, and issues critical to quality leadership systems, Dr. Johnson has co-directed the first and second National Leadership Conferences on Leadership in Special Education. Currently, he is planning the third of these national conferences.

Lindsey, Robert J.
>Principal, Garrison Elementary School
>1105 W. Court
>Rockford, Ill. 61103

A principal for 15 years at the Garrison Elementary School, Mr. Lindsey holds the BS and MS degrees from Illinois State University. He is one of the authors of the Rockford Public School Social Studies Curriculum which emphasizes pupil independence and instructional diversity. The developer of The Manipulative Mathematics Resource Center for gifted pupils, which is used extensively throughout the school district, he is the leading proponent of the Illinois State Program for Gifted Children and directs the oldest continuous program for such children in Rockford. In addition, he is a promoter of educational television through writing, performing, and the demonstration of classroom techniques.

Mr. Lindsey is a member of Phi Delta Kappa, an officer in the local administrators organization, and a member of the national and state associations. His avocational interests include dramatics, music, and sports.

Mann, Philip H.
>Coordinator of Special Education
>University of Miami
>Coral Gables, Fla. 33124

My parents were immigrants to whom the most important thing in life was to provide the best for their children. To accomplish this goal, they felt that it was essential to become "Americanized" but, at the same time, to maintain the essence and customs of their native culture.

After earning the BA and MA degrees from the University of Miami and the PhD from the University of Virginia, I taught for seven years. In terms of personal growth, the most important years have been the last five. They led me to the development of a philosophy of teaching and learning that enables me to believe that there is hope for children who fail, labeled or unlabeled, in our educational systems. And I am learning how to cope with my frustrations when I interact with school people who sometimes perceive education with the same distortions with which I saw the world, as a youngster, through the warped, wavy window glass of the old trolley cars.

When I want to relax or when things get a little tight, I can always go fishing, dabble with my oils, or just take a long walk with my wife and children—if they have the time to go along.

McClung, Rose Marie
>Associate Director,
>Programs in Learning Disabilities
>University of Miami
>Coral Gables, Fla. 33124

With a B.A. in Elementary Education from Rollins College, I taught fourth grade in a self-contained classroom and then fifth grade as a team teacher, for 10 years. The more successful I became, the more "problem" children seemed to be placed in my classroom. I soon found that experience, motivation, skill, and interest were not enough to help me meet the needs of the learning-handicapped pupils. Subsequent training in learning disabilities, which led to the Master of Education degree from the University of Miami, broadened the scope of my skills to include teaching those children who do not learn through traditional formulae. These last two years as an instructor in the area of the learning-disabilities curriculum at the University of Miami has permitted me to share with teachers the skills that were not built into their undergraduate and/or graduate programs.

In my "spare time," I enjoy traveling, shopping, reading, sleeping, and talking with young children.

McGarry, Florence N.
>Instructor
>Diagnostic Prescriptive Teaching Program
>The George Washington University
>Washington, D. C. 2006

I hold a BA from Trinity College Washington, D.C.) and an MA from The George Washington University. Currently, I am a doctoral candidate at the latter institution.

Creating a more humanistic classroom environment, an environment that both teachers and students find exhilarating and exciting, and where both can begin to reach their potential is to me important, challenging, and more and more possible. During the four years I have been with the Diagnostic Prescriptive Teaching Program, I have become more convinced that humanizing education goes beyond adapting methods and materials to meeting each child's needs in subjects such as reading. Humanizing education involves adapting exercises and activities designed to foster personal growth, the understanding of self and others in classroom settings. I find getting humanistic practices and activities "out of the books" and into the repertoire of teachers not always easy but always productive of heartening results.

McKenzie, Hugh S.
    Director, Special Education
    University of Vermont
    2 Colchester Ave.
    Burlington, Vermont 05401

Dr. McKenzie is also Associate Professor and Chairman of Special Education at the University of Vermont. He received the BA and PhD in psychology from the University of Arizona and spent a postdoctoral year in research on special education for learning-disabled and emotionally disturbed children at the University of Kansas under the direction of Montrose M. Wolf. He joined the University of Vermont in 1967 as Assistant Professor of Education.

Dr. McKenzie originated and developed the consulting teacher approach to special education and established the University's Special Education Program. He is the author of numerous articles on applied behavior analysis and special education.

His current special interest is in developing precise learning goals for education that lead to accountable, effective, and humane special education and that are established by educational professionals with the extensive involvement of a school's community.

Meisgeier, Charles
    Coordinator
    Center for Human Resources Development and Educational Renewal
    Houston Independent School District
    3830 Richmond Ave.
    Houston, Texas 77027

Dr. Meisgeier is also adjunct professor of the graduate school, The University of Houston. He began his career as a special education teacher, served as a principal, was the chief executive officer of one of the largest state organizations for the handicapped in the nation, has been an associate professor of educational administration and special education at a number of universities, and has been a consultant to educational institutions and systems. Currently a member of the National Advisory Council-LTI/Special Education, Dr. Meisgeier has served on several national advisory panels and is an expert-advisor to the U.S. Office of Education; he held the position of coordinator of the mental retardation program at the USOE and has directed a number of special projects supported by that agency.

He is the co-author of the textbook, *The Process of Special Education Administration* and the author of *The Doubly Disadvantaged.*

Miller, Donald F.
    Program Analyst, Experimental Education Unit
    Child Development and Mental Retardation Center
    University of Washington
    Seattle, Wash. 98195

Having received the MEd (with emphasis in educational technology) from the University of Washington, Mr. Miller is currently working for the PhD in special education. He has had experience in the past as a junior-high-school teacher and audiovisual coordinator; an instrumentation specialist for the Experimental Education Unit; computer aided instruction project coordinator for the Washington Alaska Regional Medical Program; and director of educational systems, Synergistics, Inc.

His present professional interests include data analysis, decision making, and the prescribing for individual differences along with program evaluation procedures.

Mr. Miller is the recipient of the 1968 J. P. Kennedy Award.

Paolucci, Phyllis W.
>Instructor, Special Education Program
>College of Education
>University of Vermont
>Burlington, Vermont 05401

Educated at Castleton State College in Vermont (BS, elementary education) and the University of Vermont (MEd, special education), Ms Paolucci had five years of experience as an elementary-school teacher before becoming a consulting teacher in the Chittenden Central School District and then assuming her present position. She was nominated for the "Outstanding Young Educator Award" in 1969 and the "Outstanding Young Women of America Program" in 1972.

Her special interests include aiding Vermont school districts in defining and achieving minimum objectives.

Perelman, Phyllis F.
>Consulting Teacher and Instructor
>Special Education Program
>College of Education
>University of Vermont
>Burlington, Vermont 05401

With a BA (romance languages and education) and MEd (guidance and special education) from the University of Vermont, Ms Perelman received her elementary professional standard certification which was validated for learning and behavior disorders in 1969 and for consulting teachers in 1970. She participated in the development and implementation of a paraprofessional training program (with Hanley) as well as supervising consulting teachers in training.

Her special interests include the implementation of the child advocate role of the special educator.

Prouty, Robert W.
>Assistant Professor, Department of Special Education
>The George Washington University
>2201 G Street NW
>Washington, D. C. 2006

Mr. Prouty is also the Director of the Diagnostic/Prescriptive Teacher Project, Department of Special Education, The George Washington University.

He earned the BS in elementary and special education from SUNY at Geneseo, N.Y. and the MS in special education from Syracuse University where he did his doctoral work in special education, educational psychology, and educational foundations. His experience includes public-school teaching, clinic director, private practice as psycho-educational consultant, university teaching and research, project consultant to Headstart, C.A.P., and Migrant Education Programs, as well as O.E., S.E.A., and L.E.A. consultant work.

Married and the father of 3 children, Dr. Prouty's primary interests are family, sailing, pro football, political history, and educational innovation.

Reynolds, Maynard C.
Director,
Leadership Training Institute, Special Education, NCIES
110 Pattee Hall
University of Minnesota
Minneapolis, Minn. 55455

Professor in (and formerly Chairman of) the Department of Special Education at the University of Minnesota, Dr. Reynolds is currently on a sabbatical leave from his academic duties. He is Chairman of the CEC Policies Commission and Co-Director of the CEC Project on Professional Standards and Guidelines. Dr. Reynolds's main interests are the redesigning of special education programs and individual differences in schools.

Shaw, Stan
Assistant Professor of Educational Psychology
School of Education
The University of Connecticut
Storrs, Conn. 06268

Dr. Shaw is also director of the undergraduate training program in special education. He was educated at Queens College (City University of New York), the University of Northern Colorado, and the University of Oregon (EdD in special education). His previous professional activities include experience as a teacher of retarded and learning disabled children at the elementary and secondary level; college instructor in learning disabilities; and consultant to school districts, state departments of education, and university special-education programs.

Major interests include the special education-general education relation, inservice education, and training classroom teachers to teach mildly handicapped children in their classrooms.

Shaw, Wilma
Learning Disabilities Consultant
Lyme Consolidated School
Lyme, Conn.

Ms Shaw was educated at the City University of New York (BA in English literature and classical languages) and the University of Northern Colorado (MA in special education). She has completed further graduate study in secondary English education.

Her previous professional activities include experience as a learning-disabilities resource teacher, developmental and remedial reading teacher at both elementary and secondary levels, teacher-programmer for the Regional Resource Center at the University of Oregon, and learning-disabilities consultant. She has also presented workshops for the University of Hartford, University of Connecticut, and the Connecticut State Department of Education.

Particular interests include precision teaching, early reading education, and inservice teacher training.

Soloway, Michael M.
Coordinator, Santa Monica Madison School Plan
Santa Monica Unified School District
1723 Fourth Street
Santa Monica, Calif. 90401

Holding the BA in psychology and MA in special education from UCLA, Mr. Soloway is currently working for the EdD in special education at that institution. His past experience includes a research assistantship with Dr. Ivan Lovaas (Neuro Psychiatric Institute, UCLA) in the program of operant conditioning with autistic schizophrenic children; elementary school teaching; curriculum assistant to Dr. Frank Hewett; and coordinator of the Madison School Plan for Dr. Frank Taylor. He is a consultant to the states of California, Florida, Iowa, and Washington.

Mr. Soloway's recent publications have appeared in *Instructor Magazine* and *Focus on Education.*

Taylor, Frank D.
Assistant Superintendent,
Special Services for the Santa Monica Unified School District
1723 Fourth Street
Santa Monica, Calif. 90401

The father of 5 sons and 2 daughters, Dr. Taylor enjoys water skiing, surfing, swimming, photography and the 1923 Model T Roadster hot-rod, which he owns with several of his boys, that is capable of speeds in the 160 to 180 mph range. He camps frequently with the 5 boys (who are all Scouts) and other members of his family.

The Taylors have recently given up motorcycle riding and racing after several accidents and they have 5 motorcycles and one trailer for sale. They are now building a four-wheel drive, off-the-road vehicle to enter in the Baja 1000.

Dr. Taylor received the EdD from the University of Southern California, has taught all grades from kindergarten through college, and has authored numerous articles and books.

VanEtten, Glen
Associate Professor of Special Education
Coordinator, Training in Learning Disabilities
University of New Mexico
Albuquerque, New Mexico 87106

Dr. VanEtten was awarded the EdD (special education and human development) by the University of Kansas and has held a variety of posts in the area of special education. He was Coordinator of Research in the Educational Modulation Center, Olathe (Kansas) Public Schools, and later served as Project Evaluation Consultant of the Education Professions Development Act Project, in the same system. Before moving to New Mexico, he was Director of The Experimental School, John F. Kennedy Center for Research on Education and Human Development at Peabody College.

Dr. VanEtten's current research interests are in the testing of service delivery systems to learning disability children as well as cognitive development of learning disability children.